The Structural Trauma of Western Culture

Yochai Ataria

The Structural Trauma of Western Culture

Toward the End of Humanity

Yochai Ataria
Tel-Hai Academic College
and Open University of Israel
Upper Galilee, Northern, Israel

Translated by Donna Bossin

ISBN 978-3-319-53227-1   ISBN 978-3-319-53228-8 (eBook)
DOI 10.1007/978-3-319-53228-8

Library of Congress Control Number: 2017935478

Cover image: "Wild" © Yiftach Belsky

Printed on acid-free paper

This Palgrave Macmillan imprint is published by Springer Nature
The registered company is Springer International Publishing AG
The registered company address is: Gewerbestrasse 11, 6330 Cham, Switzerland

This book is dedicated with love, admiration, and awe to my grandfather and my father

ACKNOWLEDGMENTS

First, I want to thank Yemima Ben-Menachem. We have been working together for more than half a decade, and during this time Yemima has always allowed me to develop in directions that interested me and has supported me unconditionally. She is one of a kind, the type of advisor every student dreams of. It is an honor and a pleasure to be in her presence. I also extend my thanks to Yuval Neria, who has been advising me since I completed my master's degree and who is always there to provide help, support, and encouragement. Yuval is clearly a role model for me.

Thanks to Prof. Haviva Pedaya, who made me believe that my ideas are interesting and worthwhile and that I have something new to say. I also want to thank Amos Goldberg for his valuable suggestions and for providing answers to all my questions. Thank you to Mooli Lahad, a rare individual on the Israeli scene, a friend and partner and the object of my boundless admiration and love. I also would like to thank Dennis Sobolev, Koji Yamashiro, Michael Keren, David Gurevitz, and Ory Bartal for supporting me throughout this journey.

Amos Arieli, my advisor during my postdoctoral studies at the Weizmann Institute, is an outstanding individual and my guiding star, and I am grateful for every moment I spent in his presence. My heartfelt thanks go to Haim Nagid, editor at Safra Publishers, who was the first to believe in me and in my book.

I wrote the first version of one of the chapters in this book during my undergraduate studies at the University of Haifa. I would also like to thank the Ofakim Honors Program at the University of Haifa for their support and for giving me the opportunity to be my own person. I am grateful to Yossi Ziegler, who accepted me onto the program and was always there to put in a good word. I again want to acknowledge Dennis Sobolev's important contribution to my personal development. He exposed me to the world of Kafka, for which I will be eternally grateful.

I wrote most of the chapters of this book while I was studying for my doctorate at the Hebrew University. During that period, I received financial support from a number of foundations, and I extend my thanks to the university and to the Rotenstreich scholarship. Two additional chapters were written during my postdoctoral studies at the Weizmann Institute, and I am grateful to that institution for its support. I completed the final editing of the book after being hired to work at Tel-Hai College, and I want to thank the college for providing financial support for the final editing.

Thank you to Donna Bossin for translating the book into English and to Gadi Bossin for editing and polishing the translation. It took me a long time to find a translator I could depend upon, and Donna did not disappoint me. She always was able to find the right word and the proper phrase to express my ideas clearly and coherently. Without her, this book could not have been published.

Finally, I extend my heartfelt thanks to Rachel Krause Daniel, Senior Commissioning Editor for Scholarly and Reference Books at Palgrave Macmillan, for believing in me and in my work. Her support was of crucial importance in getting the book published. I would like also to thank Kyra Saniewski.

Last but not least, a big thank you goes to David Shimonovich, who did the initial editing of all the articles in the book. David has been giving me his loyal, patient, and precise support for more than a decade, and I thank him from the bottom of my heart.

Contents

About the Author

Yochai Ataria completed his doctorate at the Hebrew University of Jerusalem and his post doctorate at the weizmann institute of science. Ataria is currently a senior lecturer at Tel-Hai College and a researcher at the Open University of Israel. He has published over 30 theoretical, empirical, and philosophical papers. Together with others, Ataria has also edited the following books: *Kafka: New Perspectives* (Safra, 2013), the *Interdisciplinary Handbook of Trauma and Culture* (Springer, 2016), and *The Post-Humanistic Age* (Pardes, 2016).

LIST OF FIGURES

INTRODUCTION

This book suggests that the very notion of culture emerges from trauma. More specifically, traumatic events define a heterogeneous and diverse collection of individuals as a consolidated group. Without trauma there can be no collective, since trauma is a constituent factor in forming a community and preventing that community from falling apart. Trauma is thus the fuel that keeps a community alive and functioning. Hence, to be part of a community is in fact to accept, embrace, and internalize the iconic trauma that shapes that particular community. Nonetheless, it is not necessary for all the members of a certain group to undergo the constitutive traumatic event (Tal 1996). Indeed, one of the most important questions when attempting to link between trauma and culture is how members of the community who did not undergo the traumatic event itself can absorb the trauma. In a sense, the answer begs the question: The creation of culture allows a particular group to create symbols, which in turn enable, and sometimes even force, a particular individual to become part of a wider community. Tal (1996) defines this process as "cultural codification of the trauma" (p. 6). There is a closed loop between trauma and culture, so that trauma and culture are two sides of the same coin. Hence, the study of culture leads us to the iconic and constitutive trauma, and the study of this iconic trauma is, in fact, the study of the structure of culture. To study the one is to study the other.

The notion underlying this book is that it is impossible to understand trauma without understanding its cultural context and that the structure of culture today cannot be understood without understanding the trauma that shaped it. Furthermore, only by understanding the traumatic structure of contemporary culture can we understand how this culture generates new traumas by means of repetition compulsion (e.g., a situation in which the survivor repeats the traumatic event over and again without any control).

Seltzer (1997) argues that not merely does "a collective gathering around shock, trauma, and the wound" (p. 3) occur. Rather, he further suggests that trauma generates a pathological public sphere. "The pathological public sphere is everywhere crossed by the vague and shifting lines between the singularity or privacy of the subject, on the one side, and collective forms of representation, exhibition, and witnessing, on the other" (p. 4). Moreover, Seltzer (1997) has suggested that trauma is a kind of Archimedean point at which the private and public meet: "Trauma has thus come to function as a switch point between individual and collective, private and public orders of things" (p. 5). It would not be an exaggeration to say that traumatic identity exists at the core of cultures, for instance as a national collective memory. Accordingly, trauma is a nonexistent point in space and time that unites the individual and the collective. Indeed, trauma is the point where individual and collective meet and it is trauma that allows us to shift from I to WE.

Yet herein lies the problem. By its very nature, a traumatic event undermines the most basic concepts of our life. Indeed, concepts such as knowledge, memory, time, and truth all collapse in times of trauma. In fact, many studies (Herman 1992; Lifton 1967; Wilson 2006) have demonstrated that in the wake of trauma, the very notion of identity is fundamentally damaged. Furthermore, language itself collapses, rendering us virtually unable to represent, and consequently unable to process, the traumatic experience. The traumatic event resembles a black hole. It is absolute nothingness (Grotstein 1990a, 1990b; Pitman and Orr 1990; Van der Kolk and McFarlane 1996), as Perlman (1988) describes in the context of Hiroshima: "Hiroshima is the place of no place, revealing a deep lacuna, a placelessness, at the heart of postindustrial culture" (p. 91). Hence, if we accept that cultures are rooted in traumatic events, we are obliged to acknowledge the lacuna at the heart of any culture—an excess that rejects any kind of representation within the structure. If trauma is a physical or metaphorical point in space and time that unites the individual with the collective, we cannot escape the notion that the individual unites with the collective at a moment that does not really exist, either in space or in time. Indeed, trauma completely twists the dimensions of both time and space. Thus, it is clear that the powers pulling at different kinds of individuals and transforming them into a community are negative in nature. We are united by void and nothingness. There is a black hole at the heart of society.

This book asks the reader to consider the radical notion that the inherent connection between trauma and culture is not merely theoretical. Instead, this connection is tangible in our daily lives, for trauma stands at the very core of Western culture. Many researchers have suggested (Farrell 1998; Leys 2000; Luckhurst 2008) that the concept of mental trauma developed in conjunction with railway accidents. If we accept this premise, we cannot examine trauma without examining modernity, for transportation is one of the most important characteristics of the modern age (Thacker 2003). Thus, it becomes clear why Seltzer (1997) suggests that "the modern subject has become inseparable from categories of shock and trauma" (p. 18). If railways are indeed the icon of modernity, mental trauma is not merely a byproduct of the industrial era but rather stands at its very heart as a constitutive force that has shaped the structure of its cultural discourse. Hence, it should not come as a surprise that the Great War (World War I) is frequently depicted as an industrial battlefield, a factory of death producing mental trauma. Indeed, not for nothing were the shell-shocked soldiers of World War I known as "the iconic trauma victims of the twentieth century" (Luckhurst 2008, p. 50). Yet if modernity is defined as an industrial era generating ongoing mass mental trauma, World War II was clearly the climax of this process: The same trains that had been used to transport goods also transported humans to slaughter in the gas chambers.

If trauma is indeed at the very heart of Western culture, we may all be victims, or as Tal (1996) puts it, a "community of survivors" (p. 3). We have all experienced trauma. Therefore, we are all survivors.[1] In a society of survivors, it should come as no surprise that the traumatic figure becomes a hero and even a saint. "The victim becomes a site of identification" (Luckhurst 2008, p. 64), for every group needs an iconic figure to identify with. As we listen to traumatic stories, we bond with these figures and feel part of something bigger. Their stories enable us to shift from I to WE.

It is striking that Camus (1962a) altered Descartes' (1637/1996) famous sentence, "I think, therefore I am" (or better put, "I am thinking, therefore I exist") to "*I* rebel; therefore *I* exist." He then went a step further by formulating this notion as "*I* rebel—therefore *we* exist." In the posttraumatic age, we can reformulate this sentence once again as "*I* have been traumatized—therefore *we* exist" or even as "*they* have been traumatized—therefore *we* exist." Indeed, it seems that a traumatic event and the emergence of a group of survivors constitute a precondition for the formation of a community. The collective identity is rooted within the traumatic event, and the structure of this collective identity is based upon the survivors' stories.

This book seeks to examine the complex links between trauma and culture. It attempts (a) to identify the iconic trauma at the very core of Western culture and (b) to recognize the cultural mechanisms that create and preserve trauma. To that end, it analyzes some of the canonical texts of Western culture.[2]

The book's ten chapters examine different aspects of Western culture in order to expose and understand its traumatic foundations. One of the major insights emerging from this book is that Abraham, Sarah, and Isaac, in their relations with God and in their relations with each other, created an uncontrollable mechanism of trauma that has been passed on obsessively from generation to generation in the form of sacrifice and silence.

Through a new interpretation of canonical texts, this book examines whether and to what extent the story of Western culture is a "traumatic story," and whether from the monotheistic-Western perspective it is possible to say that the holy and the traumatic are two sides of the same coin. Particular focus is placed on the dual image of the male character in Western culture throughout history—the binder and the one who is bound, the one who makes the sacrifice and the one who is sacrificed. As such, this character is transformed into the preserver of the ancient trauma that makes its presence known repeatedly, violently, and uncontrollably in the public sphere.

***

The book begins with a rereading of the story of the Binding of Isaac, the *Akeda*, which exposes God as a murderous-automatic-sick mechanism lusting for blood. According to this new interpretation, Abraham is the first to understand that the divine mechanism is nothing more than the inner world of men. Sarah is depicted as someone who laughed and then was struck dumb, made to disappear, and almost turned into a bereaved mother. Finally, Isaac, who was bound yet remained alive, was transformed from an innocent into a traumatic being.

The story of the *Akeda* exposes the primordial trauma that has shaped Western culture. This constitutive event enables us to understand Western culture as posttraumatic culture. Yet in order to understand the origins of the trauma underlying Western culture, we must introduce some additional models. The first, Nietzsche's doctrine of eternal return, yields two distinct processes. Firstly: (a) When the eternal return model is driven by the obsession to reenact the traumatic moment, the posttraumatic dimension is intensified by means of acting out—a process of uncontrollable and unconscious repetition on the part of the posttraumatic survivor, who is relentlessly oppressed by the past even to the point of being captivated and confined within it. Acting out is expressed through compulsive repetition of recurring traumatic scenes. In this condition, the dimension of time collapses and the individual feels as if he is returning to the past and reliving the traumatic scene over and over again. Secondly: (b) In contrast, when the eternal return succeeds in destroying the obsessive need to reenact the traumatic moment (as described in Chapter 8), the process is one of working through the trauma—in this process the traumatic event is to a certain extent controlled and contained, and is even represented, if only partially. This process is likely to somewhat limit acting out and compulsive repetition, for it leads to creating a distinction and separation between the current moment and the traumatic event. Thus, the traumatic subject is capable of returning to the traumatic moment without uncontrollably sinking into that moment itself. That is, the subject recalls the trauma but at the same time continues to be present in the here and now.

The other model is the ever-present sense of Kafkaian guilt. This model intensifies and reinforces the repetition compulsion that leads to recurring reenactment of the traumatic moment and its reification in the public sphere. Through an understanding of these models, we can begin to describe the traumatic origins of Western culture and to understand how the primal trauma (the *Akeda*) continues to recur and reenact itself in the present.

In the second chapter, I examine three writers: Thomas Mann, Albert Camus, and Michel Houellebecq. In Mann's novel *The Magic Mountain* (1929) we encounter the character Hans, who I contend symbolizes the individual at the actual time of trauma, during trench warfare. The *magic mountain* represents the frozenness of consciousness during trauma. Thus, Hans represents the traumatic figure immediately before the moment of pleasurable death. From there I go on to Camus and to Meursault, hero of *The Stranger* (1962b), who signifies humanity's shift from the traumatic age to the posttraumatic age after World War II. Clamence, (anti)hero of Camus' novel *The Fall* (1984), represents the post-traumatic individual trapped in passivity and an obsessive self-consciousness that lead to infinite regression. Through an analysis of works by Houellebecq (2000; 2006; 2012), I show that today we have reached the end of the human era and are on the brink of the post-human era.

In the third chapter, I show how Clamence and Meursault develop into characters that are more complex. Through an analysis of movies by the Coen brothers, I examine whether our infatuation with authentic characters such as Meursault is problematic, for Meursault can metamorphose into characters like Chigurh in the film *No Country for Old Men* (Coen and Coen 2007).

The chapter focuses on Larry, the protagonist of the movie *A Serious Man* (Coen and Coen 2009). Larry moves along two main axes. One is his professional life, and specifically his application for tenure in the academic world of science. The other is his private life, and particularly his son Danny's bar mitzvah. We also see Larry's duality in the characters of Sy Ableman and Larry's brother Arthur. The tension in the film is between the world of religion and the world of science, that is, between the attempt to be a "serious and rational individual" and the dybbuk at the base of Western culture as a whole. On this journey, Larry discovers that no rabbi can give him an answer, simply because there are no explanations. On this journey, we as observers must confront our most basic beliefs: God punishes us through natural disasters. The antithesis of Larry, captive and imprisoned, is Chigurh, a man who represents total freedom, a truly free man. An examination of Chigurh's character shows there is nothing more frightening than an individual who is truly free, for he understands that there is no divine accounting ledger and no reason not to commit murder. Chigurh turns the existentialist approach into a travesty. The most important line in *No Country for Old Men* is when Ellis, the sheriff's uncle, explains: "This country's hard on people, you can't stop what's coming, it ain't all waiting on you. That's vanity." It is sheer arrogance to think that things happen to you and/or for you. There is no order. There is no reason. There is just a country that is "hard on people" and this is what Larry, the scientist, refuses to understand. To understand Chigurh, however, we must first understand his origins and posttraumatic roots—the white man who collapsed and then was reconstituted during the Vietnam War. This is the topic of the next chapter.

In the fourth chapter, I explore male characters during and after the Vietnam War through an examination of post-Vietnam movies such as *The Deer Hunter* (Cimino 1978), *Taxi Driver* (Schrader 1976), and *Apocalypse Now* (Coppola 1979) in an attempt to characterize the total collapse of manhood. The discussion focuses on the polarization of the posttraumatic figure, which leads to the ultimate understanding that humanity after trauma is dual and dissociated by its very nature. Accordingly, the only way to escape trauma in a world that has gone mad is to kill oneself. Among other things, in this chapter I consider whether it is possible to think about home after the jungle. I discuss this against the backdrop of the *Akeda* of Isaac, which has now become a form of social sacrifice in which fathers happily send their sons to die in the name of "just" objectives.

The fifth chapter introduces the new leader of anarchy—Tyler Durden, protagonist of the movie *Fight Club* (Linson et al. 1999). Tyler is the direct outcome of the posttraumatic structure of Western capitalist monotheistic culture, and particularly of characters like Camus' Meursault and Kurtz from the movie *Apocalypse Now*. In this chapter, I discuss the character of the posttraumatic leader after he has murdered the father figure. The conclusion is that this leader is much more dangerous than a leader imprisoned in the obsessively recurring *Akeda*, for the acts of this imprisoned leader are at least somewhat predictable. The central motif in *Fight Club* is disgust for the human body, the focus of the next chapter.

I based the sixth chapter on research I conducted among returned prisoners of war who had been held captive in Egypt, Syria, and Lebanon (Ataria 2010). The main insight of this chapter is that postmodern individuals are primarily posttraumatic individuals who as prisoners have lived their lives with uncertainty, fear of death, and the dissolution of sense of self. In the chapter, I return to Kafka and Nietzsche. I also refer to the character Leny from the book *Gruppenbild mit Dame (Group Portrait with Lady)* by Heinrich Böll (1976) and to Margarita from *The Master and Margarita* by Mikhail Bulgakov (1997). The primary insight of this chapter is that human beings in the postmodern age spurn the human body and turn the ideal of beauty into something that by its very essence rejects that body, so that the only solution is life in a virtual body. In this age, we have relinquished humanity. One of the consequences of post-traumatic culture is hatred for the body, for example, as depicted in *Fight Club*. This hatred leads to an unbearable split in the posttraumatic figure, as examined in the next chapter.

In the seventh chapter, I return to Kafka and his last major novel, *The Castle* (2009). I contend that the relationship between K. and Klamm represents the split in the posttraumatic individual in the postmodern age. This is a condition in which the self is split and human beings find themselves in an impossible inner struggle toward a single goal—destruction of the self, because they are unable to tolerate their own presence in the world.

In the eighth chapter, I consider the relationship between silence and trauma and discuss the possibility of expressing trauma through silence. This chapter proposes an alternative for the posttraumatic subject—to choose silence. Indeed, in a world in which human beings are sent to die for "justifiable reasons," the very use of words constitutes a form of cooperating with the hangman. In this chapter, I seek to show that often the only way to enable silence to speak is through physical appearance. In a world of silence, working through the body can break the cycle of obsessive reenactment. This is the topic of the next chapter.

In the ninth chapter, I examine a new character, Lola from the movie *Run Lola Run* (Arndt 1998)—a character that moves to the beat of techno, the language of trauma, and, by so doing, manages to revive the human heart and save her man. She does this not by disregarding the virtual world in which we live, but rather by crossing, and thus eliminating, the lines between "true" reality and virtual reality. Lola understands that it is necessary to undergo healing in the virtual world in order to revitalize the human body. The way to return to the body is through music linked to the pre-reflexive primordial physical experience. This is the body prior to the illness known as Western culture.

In the book's final chapter, I take a step back. Throughout the book, I emphasize the connection between the concepts of the posttraumatic individual on the one hand and the posttraumatic culture on the other hand, even though the shift from individual to society is not at all clear in this context. In this chapter, then, I examine how trauma can shift from the individual to society. I bring up what I believe to be a necessary reservation when describing trauma in terms of society.

NOTES

1. If, however, we all experience trauma and there is no real difference between being raped or merely seeing a rape occur on television, what happens to those who underwent the actual trauma? Does this lack of differentiation once again lead to ignoring and repressing the real posttraumatic survivor?
2. The choice of texts is subjective and therefore biased by definition. In fact, different texts might have led to a very different analysis. Because such an argument cannot be categorically disregarded, this book should be read with the necessary caution. Nevertheless, while I believe that other canonical texts, such as the story of the crucifixion of Christ, Moses shattering the tablets on Mount Sinai, *The Brothers Karamazov* by Dostoyevsky and others as well, would have enriched the analysis, none of the major insights would have fundamentally changed but rather would have been adapted and sharpened.

CHAPTER 1

The Sources of Western Trauma: From the *Akeda* of Isaac to Kafka

THE *AKEDA* OF ISAAC: TO PLAY OBSESSIVELY

Opening Game

The *Akeda* or Binding of Isaac as described in the *Vayera* Torah portion (Gen. 18:1–22:24) is no doubt one of the most significant and compelling stories in Western culture. In the modern age, a sense of entrapment and confinement has supplanted the sense of being at ease and at home. In this age of imprisonment, salvation is a problematic concept grounded in destruction and loss, and the way in which Abraham chooses to play with God is the key to salvation. In the book of Genesis, God is a violent and vengeful Being that acts in a technical and mechanical manner, without feelings. Indeed, God destroys and punishes anyone who deviates from His laws, even though these laws have no clear, unambiguous definition. Sometimes God even derives pleasure from considering whether to destroy all of humanity. In that sense God is the role model of the totalitarian leader. Abraham is the first human creature to stand up to God in order to restrain Him, in order to bargain and negotiate with Him about human life. Abraham carries on a dialogue with God and addresses God's obsession with killing, destroying, laughing and sanctifying.

The name "Isaac" (יצחק) is derived from the Hebrew root meaning "to laugh" (צ.ח.ק.). In the *Vayera* Torah portion, the Hebrew root "to laugh" is often repeated. "And Sarah laughed within herself" (Gen. 19:12) upon hearing the three angels promise that she would give birth when she was

© The Author(s) 2017
Y. Ataria, *The Structural Trauma of Western Culture*,
DOI 10.1007/978-3-319-53228-8_1

ninety years old and Abraham was 100 years old. Was Sarah chuckling to herself about the possibility that she would give birth and would become a mother at age ninety? Or was she perhaps laughing with joy? Maybe Sarah was laughing from the grotesque irony of this situation. After all, she is a worn-out old woman. God is also anxious to know the reason for her laughter: "And the LORD said unto Abraham, Wherefore did Sarah laugh?" (Gen. 18:13). "Then Sarah denied, saying, I laughed not: for she was afraid. And He said, Nay, but thou diddest laugh" (Gen. 18:15). When God does not understand, He activates the machine described by Kafka in his short story "In the Penal Colony" (2007), a machine that was first used to carve the mark of censure and disgrace upon Cain's forehead. The name of the newborn child, Isaac (literally meaning "he laughs"), defines God's attitude toward humanity: ironic and even painful laughter, the irony of fate. From the Lacanian perspective, Isaac is the signifier that touches upon the signified, the signifier that is in direct contact with what is real. Giving Isaac this name also released the dybbuk, and psychosis took over humanity.

God is aware of the destructive mechanism within Him. The name "Isaac" enables God to map out a method for working simultaneously against and with this mechanism. Indeed, perhaps this is God's expression of His attitude toward the entire human saga. This is a form of black humor stemming from an automated and mechanical mechanism. Abraham understands this all too well. He has internalized the automatic command at the base of the Divine Being and is aware of the hidden messages God is sending him. Abraham immediately understands that Sarah's laughter is the opening whistle in a fateful game against God. God's initial and innocent response is nothing more than the first link in an inevitable chain of responses showing that God operates out of the dybbuk. God is Kafka's punishing machine, that is, a cruel mechanism that cannot be controlled. At this point the only way to cope with God is to join in with His laughter, to play according to His cruel and twisted rules and to attempt to buy some time, because it is clear that in God's heart (though He has no heart) the thought is forming that "he who laughs last, laughs best."

This being the case, what we already know from the story of the Flood is sharpened and corroborated in *Vayera*—the story of Sodom and Gomorrah. In the middle of the Torah portion, God again reminds humanity "who's boss," and significantly, that the boss is violent and sick and operates out of neurosis. Indeed, according to Freud (1939), religion has been reduced "to the status of a neurosis of mankind" (p. 91), for "the original character of the god" (p. 55) is of a "bloodthirsty demon who walks by night and shuns the light of day" (p. 56). This also accounts for the name of the Torah portion, *Vayera* ("and He appeared"). Abraham, who from many perspectives can be considered the first human being, learns to fear God and to know God's true nature—that of a machine whose essence is automatic and mechanical. Thus, when Lot's sons-in-law laugh at him—"But he seemed as one that mocked unto his sons-in-law" (Gen. 19:14)— God wastes no time and squares accounts with them.

God does not like to be laughed at. Indeed, Abraham understands that even Sarah's laughter will not pass unnoticed without some sort of characteristic response from God. Thus, the name "Isaac" leaves no room for doubt: "And Abraham was an hundred years old, when his son Isaac was born unto him. And Sarah said, God hath made me to laugh, so that all that hear will laugh with me" (Gen. 21:5–6). Sarah has good reason to laugh. The female image, missing from the male post-traumatic discourse, expresses precisely what she feels. When God inter-venes, He does so through an ironic game that creates a reality that even God cannot control: the one who laughs is punished. Ishmael, the son of Abraham and Hagar, laughs at the feast Abraham makes in honor of the birth of his beloved son Isaac: "And Sarah saw the son of Hagar the Egyptian, which she had born unto Abraham, mocking" (Gen. 21:9). Even though Ishmael is Abraham's son, he is punished. In spite of Abraham's opposition, Ishmael is banished because that is what Sarah demands and "in all that Sarah hath said unto thee, hearken unto her voice" (Gen. 21:12). This is indeed one of the most important lessons of this story: obey your woman, even if she is cruel and mean. From this sentence we understand that if Sarah had so chosen she could have prevented the *Akeda*, for as we saw Abraham was commanded to obey her even if against his own will (as in the case of his eldest son Ishmael, who was born of Abraham's marriage to Sarah's handmaiden Hagar). Perhaps this would have changed the course of history and the very structure of Western civilization. But Sarah was not there, not then and not now, not in words and not in deed. Instead, the line "Mama's gonna make all of your nightmares come true" (Pink Floyd, *The Wall*, "Mother") is the most accurate description of Sarah's silence.

Hence, despite Kierkegaard's attempt to depict Abraham as "the hero of faith" (Kierkegaard 1985), it is nevertheless possible to interpret the *Akeda* quite differently: Abraham is the hero of humanity. God toys with people and laughs at them, yet this laughter can very easily and without any warning turn into pure brutalism. Thus, the moment God loses His restraint, He returns to His chaotic origins and destroys humanity like a child who destroys his playthings in a moment of anger. Abraham is no fool. He understands exactly who he must deal with. In this sense, Abraham is truly "the first man" (Camus 1995) for he understands that the only way to survive in the chaotic-automatic-cruel reality of God is to play along with God, not to oppose or resist. Abraham redefines the gray area about which Primo Levi (1959, 1993) and others (Agamben 1998) have spoken so much. Abraham is always in control of the situation and demonstrates what it means to be human under impossible circumstances— and to be mistaken. The situation is always impossible. Being human always exacts dreadful prices.

Abraham does not overcome or give up his humanity, as Nietzsche requires of his Übermensch (1999). Rather, he enhances his humanity by passing through the Kafkaesque gate, into the desert of the no-law. In an impossible reality, Abraham does not lose his wits and is not tempted by the dark instincts that exist in every individual. Abraham does not participate in genocide but rather attempts to save what can be saved, no matter how minor that may be.[1] In confronting God, one cannot avoid the path of destruction, but one can bargain. The game Abraham plays in his campaign against God is the story of Sodom (Gen. 18; King James Version).[2] This is a game that constantly repeats itself—a game between fathers and sons, between friends, between lovers, between posttraumatic victims. Neither Adam and Eve nor Noah nor anyone else before Abraham understood how to play this unbearable and cruel game with God. Abraham was the first who truly understood God and exposed Him in His nakedness: mocking, covet- ous, vengeful, hateful, furious, angry, and irritated, but no less than this, confused, perplexing, conflicted, and embroiled within Himself (Benyamini 2016). In the end game, Abraham exposes God. The narrative is the reenact- ment. Narrative is the dybbuk for the posttraumatic individual—the obsessive retelling. The major question, then, is how to survive the divine mechanism known also by the name "divine justice." How can this game be won? How can this game finally end without it being fatal? Abraham's main insight is that negotiating about the price and the products is a worthwhile and effective strategy (i.e., a ram instead of Isaac). Abraham, it seems, had a good under- standing of market economics. God works according to a simple "yes or no" equation. Abraham brought the gray area into play, and the resultant game played against and with God then became workable from the human perspec- tive and worthwhile (that is, interesting) from God's perspective.

God, then, must have His taste for blood satisfied. In circumcising himself and Ishmael, Abraham purchased a kind of life insurance policy, at least temporarily. For as we all know, at the most critical moment the insurance companies are never there to assist and meet their obligations. The circumcision of Isaac is an investment in the future, the opening gambit for future negotiations: "And ye shall circumcise the flesh of your foreskin; and it shall be a token of the covenant betwixt me and you" (Gen. 17:11). Furthermore, we must keep in mind that the technical description suggests that God may be Isaac's father: "And the LORD visited Sarah as he had said, and the LORD did unto Sarah as he had spoken" (Gen. 21:1). If this is the case, God's love of the game is even crueler, for He is willing to sacrifice his own son for the sake of a little fun: "His treatment was often stupid and always cruel—but this was the nature of power, this was how it showed itself" (Solzhenitsyn 1968, p. 455). No less important, if this is indeed the case, then Sarah's laughter is a life-altering event between Him and her, a joke at Abraham's expense, at her own expense, laughter based upon an absolute understanding of how things are: this is the way things are, nobody is going to help you, not now, not ever.

It thus seems that in describing the Island of W, Perec (2003) has enabled us to grasp the very essence of our existence. On the Island of W four villages compete against each other. It soon becomes clear that these competitions are in fact "selections" (p. 73) that apparently take place each and every day. The precise and accurate screening of the athletes "reduces checking procedures to a minimum" (p. 83). The selection does the work for the authorities. In order to understand the nature of these competitions on W it is enough to describe the Atlantiads' competitions "that are placed under the sign of total liberty" (p. 130). The purpose of these competitions is to reach women, who for this event have been removed from the closed areas where they live and afterwards must run for their lives because "as a rule it is right in front of the podium, either on the cinder track or on the grass, that they get raped" (p. 125). In this competition, the competitors, "like the women they pursue, should be entirely naked" (p. 127). Due to the nature of the competition it seems that at least one-third of the competitors are usually "knocked out and are lying unconscious on the ground" (p. 130) either while in the battle arena or before: "Pitched battles break out at night in the dormitories. Athletes are drowned in sinks and lavatory pans" (p. 133).

The further we read, the clearer it becomes that W is not an island where people are engaged in sport but rather a death camp where "the survival of the fittest is the law of this land" (p. 89). As expected, the so-called athletic performances are poor, the contests are bogus, and "the pentathlon and decathlon contestants enter the stadium dressed as clowns, wearing outrageous make-up, and each event is used as a pretext for mockery" (p. 85). The losers are unlikely to remain alive, for the result may be "the death of the man who came last" (p. 110). If the contest does not end in death, the loser must pay the usual price: "He will probably save his skin and undergo only the same punishment as the other losers,... like them, he will have to strip naked and run the gauntlet of Judges armed with sticks and crops; like them, he will be put in the stocks, then paraded around the villages with a heavy, nail-studded, wooden yoke on his neck" (p. 111).

The "winners" are of course rewarded with an additional meal. This is part of the "dietary system of W" (p. 91), which results in "the vast majority of Athletes...therefore be[ing] chronically undernourished" (p. 91). In turn, when the losers return, "exhausted, ashen-faced Athletes tottering under the weight of oaken yokes" (p. 139), they begin "tearing each other to pieces for a scrap of salami, a drop of water, a puff at a cigarette" (p. 139).

Until the age of fourteen, children are kept in separate areas, and then they are brought to one of the four villages and referred to as novices. "Novices have no names" (p. 99), just as "practicing Athletes have no names" (p. 99). During the first few months, the novices are held in detention. Their hands and feet are tied, their mouths muzzled, and at night they are chained to their beds. Indeed, life on the Island of W is a terrifying sight. The most important thing for novices to learn in order to survive, however, is that "the Law is implacable, but the Law is unpredictable. The law must be known by all, but the Law cannot be known" (p. 117). Thus in practice, in order to survive, the novice must understand that "what he is seeing is not anything horrific, not a nightmare, not something he will suddenly wake from, something he can rid his mind of." Yet, "[h]ow can you explain that this is life, real life, this is what there'll be every day, this is what there is, and nothing else." Indeed on W "[y]ou have to fight to live. There is no alternative... it is not possible to say no. There's no recourse, no mercy, no salvation to be had from anyone. There's not even any hope that time will sort things out" so that essentially "that is the only thing that will turn out to be true" (pp. 139–140). Not surprisingly, then, after six months, when the novices are freed from their chains, there is only one way for them to survive and that is to become a servant of one of the champions and to provide him with commercial and, of course, sexual services. This is the abridged format of the social structure on the Island of W—the relationship of dominator to dominated in which there is no access to the masters while the slaves tear each other apart. In sum, life on W is as follows:

Submerged in a world unchecked, with no knowledge of the Laws that crush him, a torturer or a victim of his co-villagers, under the scornful and sarcastic eyes of the Judges, the W Athlete does not know where his real enemies are, does not know that he could beat them or that such a win would be the only true Victory he could score, the only one which would liberate him. But his own life and death seem to him ineluctable, inscribed once and for all in an unspeakable fate. (pp. 159–160)

The End of the Game

The preparations have been completed and the game can now begin. God is ready and so is Abraham: "And it came to pass after these things, that God did tempt Abraham, and said unto him, Abraham: and he said, Behold, here I am" (Gen. 22:1). The word "tempt" is not just cruel, for it also indicates God's dependent nature. God needs Abraham more than Abraham needs God. Without Abraham, God, in His obsessive fixation with His believers, has no meaning. Without attention from Abraham, God remains locked away, completely isolated. The one who is in control of the situation is not God but rather Abraham. This is a virtual form of control seen in Abraham's confident response, like the response given to a fearful child: Here I am. I am here. I am not going anywhere. Don't worry, I'm not running away, I am all yours. This is how Abraham calms God down, for God is not convinced of Abraham's love and continues to test him with repeated tests and cruel games. But Abraham stands firm. He is going to finish this game. He will do what is required of him in order to free himself of the burden and to free God from His fear of abandonment, His fears and anxieties about being alone. Abraham also knows that there will be a heavy price to pay, almost without limit. The price is our daily reality, as we just saw in Perec's description of the Island of W.

God tells Abraham to take his son and again uses the motivating expression "get thee unto": "And He said, Take now thy son, thine only son Isaac, whom thou lovest, and get thee unto the land of Moriah; and offer him there for a burnt offering upon one of the mountains which I will tell thee of" (Gen. 22:2).[3] The next morning, Abraham calmly takes Isaac, his donkey, and two young men, together with the equipment necessary for making a burnt offering—fire and wood—and sets out for Mount Moriah. Abraham indicates to God that he is going to see this through to the end. On the literal level we assume that Abraham is an authentic individual who tells the truth, and thus tells my interpretation of the following verse: "And Abraham said unto his young men, Abide ye here with the ass; and I and the lad will go yonder and worship, and come again to you" (Gen 22:5). Abraham is calm. He knows that he is presenting himself before God, that matters will be resolved, and that God will know, or perhaps learn, His place, for it is not only man who "is always a prey to his truths" (Camus 1975, p. 30). Abraham does not get excited and does not try to outsmart God. He does not consider replacing Isaac with one of the young men, and he tells them explicitly that he will be right back. Abraham's total serenity is a tool in his long and difficult negotiations with God, a step along the way. When Isaac asks his father Abraham where they are going, Abraham answers God through Isaac as part of his overall bargaining with God: "And Abraham said, My son, God will provide Himself a lamb for a burnt offering: so they went both of them together" (Gen. 22:8). Abraham is not nervous. For his entire life, he has been waiting for the final confrontation. And the game goes on.

Abraham binds Isaac on the altar he built. Isaac does not object; perhaps he desires to die, is fed up with this life. From this point on, game or no game, objection or no objection, Isaac carries with him the greatest trauma that one can imagine: the price of being human in the presence of the divine/human/paternal passion to destroy, and no less the desire of the son to be bound on an altar and sacrificed. This, then, is what the game will cost Isaac. The alternative is God's ceaseless abuse of human beings. Abraham, the savvy, sophisticated trader, understands that this time there's a heavy price to pay, that "one has to pay something" (Camus 1975, p. 30)—in this case, Isaac's soul and also that of Abraham. "And they came to the place which God had told him of; and Abraham built an altar there, and laid the wood in order, and bound Isaac his son, and laid him on the altar upon the wood. And Abraham stretched forth his hand, and took the knife to slay his son" (Gen. 22:9–10). Now, at the height of the tension, at the point when the trauma has in effect already taken place in the form of the decision and the willingness to follow up on it, God backs down and gives in: "And the angel of the LORD called unto him out of heaven, and said, Abraham, Abraham" (Gen. 22:11). Abraham again presents himself: "Here I am" (Gen. 22:11). Abraham throws the ball into God's court and wins: "And he said, Lay not thine hand upon the lad, neither do thou anything unto him: for now I know that thou fearest God, seeing thou hast not withheld thy son, thine only son from Me" (Gen. 22:12). The game is over. Abraham has defeated God. He has exposed Him by playing the game out to the very end. The price of being human, then, is the collective trauma and the inevitable post-trauma that follows. Thus, this story becomes the constitutive story of Western culture. It is an integral part of monotheistic culture, and for this reason trauma lies at the very core of Western civilization.

In the poem "Parable of the Old Man and the Young," Wilfred Owen[4] describes this game from the point of view of the son (Fig. 1.1).

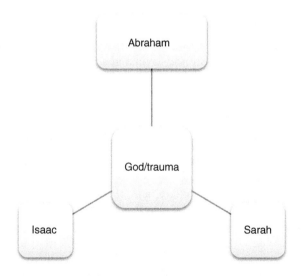

Fig. 1.1   According to the first model, at the center of the Abraham-Sarah-Isaac triangle is God, the essential trauma. The trauma that is God constitutes the black hole that shapes the family, tribal, and social structure. Trauma is at the core of the cultural structure in the form of this black hole. Hence, it is impossible to understand the cultural structure without understanding the trauma, which is in fact God

Isaac the first-born spake and said, My Father,
Behold the preparations, fire and iron,
But where the lamb for this burnt-offering?
Then Abram bound the youth with belts and straps [...]
But the old man would not so, but slew his son,
And half the seed of Europe, one by one.

Wilfred Owen

"HUMAN, ALL TOO HUMAN" (*MENSCHLICHES, ALLZ. MENSCHLICHES*)

According to Nietzsche, Christianity, like a snake coiling around and strangling its victim, creates a sense of impossible heaviness, a sense of guilt and sin. Nietzsche discovers in Christianity that which prevents humans from living. Christianity denounces life. With Christianity, "the worst and most insidious illness was introduced, one from which mankind has not yet recovered; man's sickness of man, of himself" (Nietzsche 1994, p. 57). Nietzsche admires Dionysus, who suffers no less than the Christ figure, but instead of being paralyzed by suffering, he lives with it. Dionysus is the suffering hero. His suffering is the suffering that death cannot put an end to, for Dionysus is resurrected again and again in order to suffer once more and return to death without salvation. From Nietzsche's perspective, Christian salvation rejects life. The Judeo-Christian God writes a writ of accusation against life itself:

> The Church's love of innovation had for centuries manifested itself in putting to the question the living idea, wherever she found it; throttling it, quenching it in smoke at the stake; to-day she announces through her emissaries that she rejoices in revolution, that her goal is the uprooting of freedom, culture, and democracy, which she intends to replace by barbarism and the dictatorship of the mob. (Mann 1929, p. 740)

Furthermore, according to Freud (1939) "such violent methods of suppression are by no means alien to the Catholic Church; she feels it rather as an intrusion into her privileges when other people resort to the same means" (p. 91). Hence, suffering and torment are an inseparable part of life, and there is no room to think about redemption, comfort, or total Messianic change. In Nietzsche's view, suffering and torment are conditions for personal and human development. Most importantly, it is possible to suffer without being guilty. That is, suffering and guilt are not dependent upon one another. This is the central motif of *The Birth of Tragedy from the Spirit of Music* (Nietzsche 1956). The Christian approach that adopted the notion of original sin turned guilt and suffering into something absolute. Guilt is affixed to the human race. Every human being is individually guilty and also guilty as part of the human race. Clearly, in an approach adopting the concept of absolute guilt, punishment quickly follows, so that every disaster is directly related to sin, and there is no chance for absolution. Moreover, guilt is never explained or clarified and disasters become more and more overwhelming.

In the world of ancient Greece, blunders were not considered to be sins and disasters were not seen as punishment. According to the Greek approach, suffering cannot and should not be ignored, but it is not turned into a metaphysical and moralistic form of suffering that cannot be coped with. As a result of the dissolution of the link between sin and suffering, the notion of redemption at the end of days loses its destructive power. According to Nietzsche, in the Christian eschatological model the only option available to humanity is total extinction. Christianity waits for the end of days as if that is the climactic event, the necessary and unavoidable shuddering Christian orgasm. Christianity requires an infinite sense of guilt and sin among its believers. The fuel of the Church is the blood of the believers, the intensification of their distress. Self-abuse and self-destruction constitute its loftiest goals. Ultimately, Christianity sends human beings off to kill themselves. The believing Christian, "full of emptiness and torn apart with homesickness for the desert, has had to create from within himself an adventure, a torture-chamber, an unsafe and hazardous wilderness" (Nietzsche 1994, p. 57). Put more simply, "religion had nothing to do with reason and morality" (Mann 1929, p. 584).

As far as Nietzsche is concerned, the Judeo-Christian model should be rejected altogether, for the Christian God "is still what He always was, a Jew." Moreover,

...this god of the "great majority," this democrat among gods, has not become a proud heathen god: on the contrary, he remains a Jew, he remains a god in a corner, a god of all the dark nooks and crevices, of all the noisesome quarters of the world!... His earthly kingdom, now as always, is a kingdom of the underworld, a souterrain kingdom, a ghetto kingdom...And he Himself is so pale, so weak, so decadent. (Nietzsche 1999, § The Gospel of Unbelief)

From here, Nietzsche rejects the sense of sin, of punishment, and of total guilt:

Although the shrewdest judges of the witches and even the witches themselves were convinced of the guilt of witchcraft, the guilt nevertheless did not exist. So it is with all guilt. (Nietzsche 2001, p. 149, chapter 250)

Guilt and the sense of sin clearly play an essential role in the victim's posttraumatic condition (Herman 1992). As we will see, particularly in Chapter 3, the sense of guilt pursues the posttraumatic hero.

Yet Nietzsche does not stop with rejecting the sense of sin, of punishment, and of total guilt. He continues toward the concepts of "noontide" and the "superman." The desire to be free of the fetters and stranglehold of Christianity brings us to Zarathustra, who heralds the news that we, human beings, have murdered God. Zarathustra asks that we go beyond human nature. He defines human beings as a bridge between the animals and the superman. He calls on humans to overcome the animal within them by an act of choice and be reborn as supermen:

And it is the great noontide, when man is in the middle of his course between animal and Superman, and celebrateth his advance to the evening as his highest hope: for it is the advance to a new morning. At such time will the down-goer bless himself, that he should be an over-goer; and the sun of his knowledge will be at noontide. (Nietzsche 1999, pp. 80, § The Bestowing Virtue)

At noontide there are no shadows and our vision is clear, sober, and cruel, like the vision of a crazy man, a genius, the posttraumatic individual, like the vision of Kurtz (Marlon Brando) in the movie *Apocalypse Now* (Coppola 1979). At noontide the beginning and the end are perceived as one, with the same degree of clarity. The dazzling noontide is the moment of clear understanding of the condition of Western/Christian humanity, and without a doubt this condition is sick.

At noontide it is clear that "dead are all the gods" (Nietzsche 1999, p. 80, § The Bestowing Virtue). The Day of Judgment will not come. This is the moment when humanity sees the twilight and the huge sunset, the moment humans commit themselves to life, commit themselves to live. At this moment, they understand that death is part of the cycle of life. At this moment they understand that in order to be free they must free themselves from the ailing, enfeebled God, remain loyal to the Earth (i.e., to the land, to the Earth Mother) and not to the Heavens, and they must do this without any guarantees that humanity and compassion are part of that "land."

Posttraumatic survivors are always in a state of mind that puts them at noontide and they cannot avert their eyes from the blazing sun. From their dybbuk, they return obsessively, over and over again, to the moment of trauma. Herein lies the great significance of the alternative proffered by Nietzsche—the eternal return to the way things were:

> What, if some day or night a demon were to steal after you into your loneliest loneliness and say to you: "This life as you now live it and have lived it, you will have to live once more and innumerable times more; and there will be nothing new in it, but every pain and every joy and every thought and sigh and everything unutterably small or great in your life will have to return to you, all in the same succession and sequence— even this spider and this moonlight between the trees, and even this moment and I myself. The eternal hourglass of existence is turned upside down again and again, and you with it, speck of dust!" (Nietzsche 2001, p. 194 § 341)

Instead of the Christian time line that ends in the apocalypse, Nietzsche proposes for human beings an infinite cyclical return to the same point. Human suffering is purposeless and meaningless and is nothing more than the human experience, as in *The Myth of Sisyphus* by Camus. For posttraumatic humans, the choice of life is the height of absurdity. In order for posttraumatic humans to achieve recovery, they must shift from the Christian eschatological model to the Dionysian model in which suffering is part of life but is not related to guilt or sin, and does not include the burning anticipation of the Day of Judgment. The transition is subterranean, via the fantastical and outlandish, taking things to their extremes. Just like Abraham, the individual must reach out beyond the self and keep moving all the time, exactly like Don Quixote, learning to live from within the absurd and learning to live the absurd itself. Perhaps the individual must simply learn how to wait, that is, to replace the model of expectations with the model of waiting.

Humanity's hour of grace, its hour of sobriety, is at noontide, the time of the first human being. Each one in turn can be a superman through release from the trauma, both of the victim and of the hangman. Humans must cling to life itself, or in other words, must learn how to forget. They must cease to see the discomfort of the past, stop seeing it as an open accounting ledger. In the dazzling, blinding light of noontide, humans must learn to see anew, to see the abyss—for in the posttraumatic condition the abyss always exists. Humans should not look for salvation, should not hope but rather live the absurd to the very end. In this sense, trauma contains the potential for a mighty liberation. Indeed, trauma can give birth to the superman. Yet this is a different kind of superman since it is the most human one that can be imagined.

As opposed to Nietzsche, who suggests the alternative of letting go, of releasing oneself from all restraints, Kafka appears to describe the reality of the posttraumatic experience more accurately: The posttraumatic subject is trapped in an impossible world of unattributable guilt with no way to find release, indeed with no way to do anything at all about it.

KAFKAESQUE GUILT AS THE REALITY OF THE POSTTRAUMATIC SUBJECT

Josef K., a bank clerk, is on trial. He does not know what he is accused of and what he is being tried for. When two delegates come to summon him to court, he hears that the "proceedings are underway and you'll learn about everything all in good time" (Kafka 2006, p. 2). Josef K. never sees his judges even though "there are court offices in almost every attic, why should this building be any different?" (p. 195). And of course it is clear he will never be informed what the trial is about: "[Y] ou don't know anything more about the case and won't be told anything of what's happening" (p. 146). Furthermore, no concrete fault exists and therefore it should be understood that "he must not entertain any idea of guilt" (p. 150). Moreover, according to the painter, Josef K. will never be found innocent:

> ... but only apparently free or, to put it a better way, temporarily free, as the most junior judges, the ones I know, they don't have the right to give the final acquittal. Only the highest judge can do that, in the court that's quite out of reach for you, for me and for all of us. We don't know how things look there and, incidentally, we don't want to know. (p. 188)

The courts are located in foul-smelling places, all kinds of attics. The lowest-ranking court officials are the corrupt clerks, the skirt-chasers, who are irresponsible and do not seek justice. Indeed the opposite is the case. Justice is depicted as an inhuman mechanism, just like God in Genesis, something that it is impossible to extricate oneself from. "The second acquittal is followed by the third arrest, the third acquittal by the fourth arrest and so on. That's what is meant by the term apparent acquittal" (p. 190).

Yet despite being aware of this, Josef K. refuses to reconcile himself to his condition and therefore he is guilty. Josef K. never stops fighting, even though he knows that everything he does to get himself acquitted brings him closer to the expected fate that he cannot flee from, cannot escape. "The only right thing to do is to learn how to deal with the situation as it is" (p. 143).

It is important to understand that in the Kafkaesque reality even the fact that the accused does not have a possibility of knowing what he has been accused of does not revoke his guilt. In effect, at no point is the guilt a matter of doubt and thus the individual is obliged to cope alone with accusations that will never be known to him. "They want, as far as possible, to prevent any kind of defence, everything should be made the responsibility of the accused" (p. 138). Only in this way can the individual "be weighed along with your [his/her] sins" (p. 229). The accused has no real possibility of defending himself in a court that will never change its opinion: "It's impossible to make it [court] think otherwise" (p. 178). Guilt, then, is fatalistic by nature.

Thus, under these circumstances in which the individual is guilty without knowing what he is guilty of, and without any possibility of acquittal, it is clear that "this punishment is both just and unavoidable" (p. 100). The fatalistic system leaves no room for doubt in the rightness of its ways and in practice we will never be innocent of guilt, nor acquitted under the law, not even when we die. "'Like a dog!' he said, it was as if the shame of it should outlive him" (p. 271).

I believe this reality accurately and sharply describes the sense of guilt of the trauma victim. More precisely, the Kafkaesque world describes the inner world of the posttraumatic survivor, who always feels infinite guilt—a guilt that cannot be formulated and hence nothing can be done to be liberated from it. Under these conditions, the posttraumatic survivor is dragged into a terrible fatalistic reality whose end is always destruction. In this sense, Nietzsche's model can perhaps serve as a potential solution. Yet this model is practically inaccessible for the posttraumatic victim, who is constantly pursued by a sense of guilt while being uncontrollably bound and unbound (Fig. 1.2).

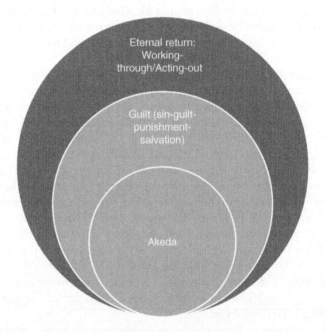

Fig. 1.2 Nietszche's model attempts to dismantle the model of sin and guilt. For this to succeed requires a process of working through the trauma rather than repetition compulsion. While this is a possibility, for the posttraumatic individual the sense of impossible guilt transforms Nietszche's process of eternal repetition into one of obsessive and uncontrolled repetition of the traumatic moment and thus does not allow for any working-through and healing processes. At the core of this sense of guilt is the *Akeda*—God who Himself is the black hole of the trauma

SUMMARY: THREE CIRCLES OF TRAUMA

In this chapter I have presented three circles of trauma. In the first circle is Abraham, who binds his son out of an inner insanity, an impossible dialogue with an automatic, obsessive, and cruel God. The son is bound to the altar with fervor, while the mother remains silent and thus in effect cooperates with the binding of her son and its apparently unavoidable end. In this setting the nuclear family itself generates trauma originating with the dialogue between a man and his inner insanity, which is identified with a cruel and bloodthirsty God.

In the second circle, the traumatic experience represents a possibility for release. Trauma opens the eyes of the victim, who discerns that the system is binding him out of a thirst for blood and that the "just causes" have nothing to do with justice and undergo frequent changes. This sobering of the victim allows him to be released from the restrictive symbolic dimension and to turn into a superman, a process that obligates him to be able to totally reject the model in which sin, punishment, guilt, and salvation are connected one to the other. He must understand that suffering is not a form of "payment" or of punishment and that he must stop looking for "signs of what is real."

Nietzsche's notion of eternal return, also known as eternal recurrence, is at the core of the second model. Nevertheless, to consider this model merely as a model of coping (i.e., as one that allows for a process of working-through the trauma) is not accurate. Indeed, the eternal return model can take the form of working through. In this process, the traumatic event is controlled and contained to a certain extent, and is even represented, if only partially. This process is likely to limit acting out and compulsive repetition somewhat, for it leads to creating a distinction and separation between the current moment and the traumatic event. Thus, the traumatic subject is capable of returning to the traumatic moment without uncontrollably sinking into that moment itself. That is, the subject recalls the trauma but at the same time continues to be present in the here and now.

Nevertheless, the eternal return model can also take the form of repetition compulsion. Acting out is a process of uncontrollable and unconscious repetition on the part of the posttraumatic survivor, who is relentlessly oppressed by the past even to the point of being captivated and confined within it. This finds expression in the compulsive repetition of recurring traumatic scenes. In this condition, the dimension of time collapses and the individual feels as if he is returning to the past and reliving the traumatic scene again and again.

The first case, working through, is indeed a process of healing and recovery. In contrast, the second case, acting out, represents the opposite process. The trauma becomes permanent and controls the life of the posttraumatic individual. Thus, eternal recurrence can be either the road to recovery or the road to compulsive repetition. Hence, Nietzsche's model does not ensure the possibility of breaking out of the cycle of trauma. Indeed, in a sense this explains how this model fuels itself, at least in the case of the posttraumatic individual.

In the third circle, the trauma victim develops an impossible sense of guilt as described by Kafka—guilt that cannot be formulated and therefore cannot be eliminated. This sense of guilt turns into a state of mind for the posttraumatic subject. Guilt governs him and turns him into a fatalistic entity, one that pushes and is pushed by volcanic inner forces toward the inevitable apocalyptic end.

It is important to stress that these three circles exist side by side and are to some extent congruent with each other. The posttraumatic individual moves through them and often is at the point of overlap—the boiling point that leads the posttraumatic subject to violent acts in the individual and public spheres. For example, when Nietzsche's eternal return model overlaps the circle of the *Akeda,* a character like Kurtz (*Apocalypse Now*) emerges. On the other hand, the character of Michael (*The Deer Hunter*), for instance, is a result of combining the *Akeda* model with the Kafkaesque model of an endless and impossible sense of guilt.

In the next chapters we will see how male figures move through these circles and will examine how each of these circles affects the nature of the posttraumatic human being. Each circle pulls the posttraumatic subject in its direction, and the more the circles overlap, the more the posttraumatic subject becomes embroiled, violent, dangerous, automatic, and thirsty for blood.

NOTES

1. In this context, see the actions and later the trial of Rudolf Israel Kastner, known as the Kastner trial (Barri 1997; Bilsky 2001; Kranzler 2000), and the verdict written by Judge Benjamin Halevi.

2. He "sold his soul to the devil": 17 And the LORD said, Shall I hide from Abraham that thing which I do; 18 Seeing that Abraham shall surely become a great and mighty nation, and all the nations of the earth shall be blessed in him? 19 For I know him, that he will command his children and his household after him, and they shall keep the way of the LORD, to do justice and

judgment; that the LORD may bring upon Abraham that which he hath spoken of him. 20 And the LORD said, Because the cry of Sodom and Gomorrah is great, and because their sin is very grievous; 21 I will go down now, and see whether they have done altogether according to the cry of it, which is come unto me; and if not, I will know. 22 And the men turned their faces from thence, and went toward Sodom: but Abraham stood yet before the LORD. 23 And Abraham drew near, and said, Wilt thou also destroy the righteous with the wicked? 24 Peradventure there be fifty righteous within the city: wilt thou also destroy and not spare the place for the fifty righteous that are therein? 25 That be far from thee to do after this manner, to slay the righteous with the wicked: and that the righteous should be as the wicked, that be far from thee: Shall not the Judge of all the earth do right? 26 And the LORD said, If I find in Sodom fifty righteous within the city, then I will spare all the place for their sakes. 27 And Abraham answered and said, Behold now, I have taken upon me to speak unto the Lord, which am but dust and ashes: 28 Peradventure there shall lack five of the fifty righteous: wilt thou destroy all the city for lack of five? And he said, If I find there forty and five, I will not destroy it. 29 And he spake unto him yet again, and said, Peradventure there shall be forty found there. And he said, I will not do it for forty's sake. 30 And he said unto him, Oh let not the Lord be angry, and I will speak: Peradventure there shall thirty be found there. And he said, I will not do it, if I find thirty there (Gen. 18; King James Version).

3. Note that there is a distortion here, for there is nothing to indicate that Abraham loves Isaac more than he loves his eldest son Ishmael, the son of Hagar.

4. Wilfred Owen (1893–1918), one of the leading poets of the First World War.

CHAPTER 2

Toward Post-Humanity: A Literary Consideration

Hans: The Traumatic Condition

When Hans arrives at the sanatorium in Thomas Mann's novel *The Magic Mountain* (1929), he protests vigorously that he is perfectly healthy, yet Krokowski, one of the doctors, says to him: "I, for one, have never in my life come across a perfectly healthy human being" (p. 19). Hans, who in any case is not endowed with a particularly warm nature and is even "afraid of showing too much feeling" (p. 6), goes up (or as we later see, down—it is not particularly clear) to the Magic Mountain sanatorium. There, as his cousin Joachim Ziemssen explains to him, "they keep us pretty cool" (p. 14). At the Magic Mountain Hans is cut off from his former life. The dimension of time collapses to the point where "you can't call it time" (p. 18), and Hans ultimately loses his sanity, collapses, falls apart at that Magic Mountain situated in a "dimensionless present" (p. 236). The Magic Mountain is a place where life ceases to exist: "you can't call it time—and you can't call it living either!" (p. 17). Indeed, already at the end of the first day Hans understandably says: "Good Lord, is it still only the first day? It seems to me I've been up here a long time—ages" (p. 106). Cut off from the world, Hans reaches a state in which he stops trusting his own body: "I can no longer trust my five senses" (p. 110). This is precisely the Cartesian conclusion in light of that deceptive demon.

On the micro level, Hans should be regarded as a character representative of humanity in pre-World War I Europe. On the macro level, the

© The Author(s) 2017
Y. Ataria, *The Structural Trauma of Western Culture*,
DOI 10.1007/978-3-319-53228-8_2

sanatorium provides a detailed description of the disease of Europe, making the situation quite clear: "the fact that all these people were inwardly attacked by well-nigh resistless decay, and that most of them were feverish" (p. 144).

As time goes by, Hans learns to acknowledge his illness and even to fall in love with it, for at a certain stage in life humans always choose to attach themselves to such pleasurable pathology. Hans becomes obsessive about his body temperature and about the chances and possibilities of actually becoming ill, for he is incapable of acknowledging his mental illness, or perhaps he does not want to admit to it. It becomes clear that the illness had:

> something solemn and ennobling about it—yet after all, you couldn't deny that illness was an accentuation of the physical, it did throw man back, so to speak, upon the flesh and to that extent was detrimental to human dignity. It dragged man down to the level of his body. Thus it might be argued that disease was un-human. (p. 587)

The Christian approach ties disease to its physical source:

> Thus far pathology, the theory of disease, the accentuation of the physical through pain; yet, in so far as it was the accentuation of the physical, at the same time accentuation through desire. Disease was a perverse, a dissolute form of life. (p. 362)

Disease is in effect the dependence of the spiritual element on the material-physical element. Material cannot be derived from the spirit. This is a Cartesian fantasy.

Western culture reinforces the gap between body and mind, between object and subject, between dream and reality. Indeed this is the well-known disease of Christianity: "Did you know that the great Plotinus is said to have made the remark that he was ashamed to have a body?" (p. 317). This disease operates on two levels. The first and superficial level is that of the physical injury. Yet on the second and more profound level, the disease is not a result of injury but rather of emotional harm radiated into the body. On an even deeper level, the disease is the result of a Cartesian/theological/Platonic attempt to separate the mind from the body. That is to say, we are the body, and from the perspective of our spiritual essence that is precisely the disease. When we refuse to acknowledge this and attempt to eliminate and disregard the body, the disease reaches epidemic proportions, becoming a deadly virus that incites murder and suicide. Its objective is to destroy the source of wretchedness in our lives—the body. This is how it will be unless we discover how to close the gap between human beings and the world, the gap between mind and body.

In Western culture, which differentiates between the spiritual and the material, human beings are divided and torn apart: "Man's being is dual" (p. 505). The spirit is above, while the body is below. The Magic Mountain is above, while the world is below. Physical reality is always cruel: "The air down there is cruel, ruthless" (p. 254). The spiritual dimension, in contrast, is linked to the sublime. Nevertheless, it is unclear whether the Magic Mountain indeed represents the sublime element, as can be seen in this seminal sentence: "So you come up quite of your own free will to us sunken ones" (p. 76). Similarly, it is also unclear that the body is linked to disease and sin. Ultimately the mountain is revealed not as a mountain of magic but rather a mountain laden with and soaked in sin. Indeed, at a certain point we already understand that the disease is not physical but rather mental. His soul was "full of troubled, involved, dubious, not quite ingenuous thought" (p. 236), that same emotional insanity that is projected through the body into the world. This being the case, the Magic Mountain is a hospital for those suffering from mental disease and not a sanatorium for those with physical illnesses. And if in fact there are physical illnesses, they are the manifestations of mental injury. This is exactly how trauma symptoms find expression in a variety of aches and pains, for trauma is a wound that at the same time is invisible and also bleeding.

Nevertheless, disease is not only something negative. It has positive aspects as well: "Illness gives you your freedom" (p. 750), the freedom to rethink our basic beliefs, the freedom to reexamine reality as we perceive it. As noted, Hans achieves this freedom. For him the Magic Mountain is nothing more than an altered state of consciousness,[1] one in which we are exposed to a new world of knowledge and under-standing, where "one's ideas get changed" (p. 8). It is my contention that this altered and mystic state of consciousness is the direct result of the traumatic experience and the posttraumatic experience, which lead to the collapse of major concepts and ideas such as "science," "mor-ality," "justice," and "progress." Therefore, it is also clear why Hans "even despaired of science and progress!" (p. 129). As the story continues it becomes clear that the illness represents the gist of the existence of enlightened, advanced, moral European humanity. The system of beliefs and perceptions of human beings raised in the lap of Christianity is sick, for they were educated to despise their bodies and to despise life.

Thus, Hans represents the crisis that preceded World War I and the collapse of two (ostensibly) competitive paradigms: religion and science. Religion cancels out the body, and science annuls humanity. Scientists have never helped make the world into a better place. Human beings are in a hopeless situation: On the one hand, humans murdered God, while on the other hand the world of science has rendered the subject null and void and has reduced the soul into pure matter: "Consciousness, then, was simply a function of matter" (p. 274). Hans has this insight before he sets out to die in the frozen fields of Europe.

World War I, the war of the trenches, transformed trauma so that it became a dominant theme in European life, perhaps even the only theme that remains today: the paradigm of being alone in a world devoid of possibilities. In trench warfare, men discovered the trauma women have known for thousands of years in its cruelest sense, for lack of movement, stagnation, and trauma go hand in hand. This type of examination makes it clear why World War II is a direct continuation of World War I. The posttraumatic individual always returns to play (see, e.g., the movie *The Deer Hunter*), to recreate the traumatic moment. In this sense, World War II is nothing more than the obsession to replay the game of horror to the point of total destruction of the object in space. World War II is also one of the games Abraham had already played in his encounter with God, the game between God and Sarah, between Sarah and Abraham, and between Abraham and Isaac.

During trauma the individual is frozen, time stands still, space is distorted, and the self is cut off from the body. Hans represents humanity at the onset of World War I. He is the representative of the Romantic Age, of the collapse of religion, and of disappointment with the world of science. At the same time he can also be viewed as the soldier crawling through the trenches. This is how the moment of being cut off from the real world looks for the traumatic subject: a shift to a world without a body, indeed the absolute denial of the body. That is, going up to the Magic Mountain is the only way to flee the traumatic situation. The different characters, who represent inner characters in his life, take on an important role during the trauma. The insights are those of someone who sees beyond lies and customary perceptions during trauma. The sunglasses have been removed and what remains is the "desert of the real" (Žižek 2006; 2002). The sobering of Hans does not lead to war but rather to the sobering of an individual sinking into the swamps, the trenches, the jungles, the fighting, the traumatic experience itself, the traumatic existence, within the insanity. This individual understands that the trauma is now impossible to stop because it is a dybbuk whose ultimate end is destruction.

The Magic Mountain represents the absolute rift during times of trauma. The Magic Mountain is a place that generates consciousness during the traumatic experience as a means of fleeing the impossible corporeal reality. The coldness of the Magic Mountain is the coldness of death. Time on the Magic Mountain is frozen, exactly as it is frozen at times of trauma. The inner world disintegrates, as it does during a traumatic experience. The body can no longer be depended upon, as is the case during a traumatic experience.

On the Magic Mountain the truth is revealed. For subjects that are aware of themselves, trauma is a fixed and absolute state of mind. If the subject survives the trauma, the bifurcation between life below (the body) and life on the Magic Mountain is intolerable, and this gap ultimately leads to the posttraumatic condition in which various symptoms such as flashbacks and avoidance take control over us. These are the same physical symptoms that Hans consistently develops, for he declines mental therapy. In this new condition, that of trauma as a fixed state of mind, the only way to maintain any contact whatsoever with the body is by projecting the disease of the mind onto the body in various and sundry ways—trauma as a state of mind is reflected in the body.

Interestingly, however, in this condition disease is the final option for remaining in contact with the body. In turn, this connection, regardless of how unstable and problematic it may be, is preferable to losing all contact with the body. It is preferable to a state of depersonalization (a cutting-off from the self), in which the main experience is a life of emotional death, a sense of being a robot in the world that observes life rather than living it, a sense of the self totally cut off from the body, a sense of the death of the heart (Simeon and Abugel 2006).

The Magic Mountain is a world created by posttraumatic individuals caught up in an impossible reality in which the physical-bodily dimension is lacking, a condition in which one can look at "life below" from a point of absolute sobriety. Moreover, the Magic Mountain represents the condition of the absolutely reflective individual, one who cannot be part of the world and thus totally wipes away the objective dimension and ceases to be part of that world. On the Magic Mountain, all previous perceptions collapse.

The most important insight of *The Magic Mountain* is that there is no idea or belief worthy of living or dying for. Yet despite this, one must bind and sacrifice oneself in the name of total helplessness. Death becomes the only way to encounter what is real for those who have cut themselves off from the world. To die is tantamount to returning to nature, and for this reason the posttraumatic individual yearns for death, for this is the only way to live, if only for a moment, and to be an integral part of the natural environment.

After harsh and ongoing trauma, the survivor can no longer continue in a state of "business as usual," for the only way to fight on is in the condition described as "Catch-22" (Heller 1961). Only someone who is not willing to go to war is qualified to go to war. In order to survive in the horror, the consciousness attempts to create a parallel world in which there is no time and no space, in which there is no body (Ataria and Neria 2013). Yet by its very nature, consciousness is rooted in the body,[2] and therefore the condition of consciousness will always find its way into the body and into the world. The traumatic state of consciousness affixes the subject within the framework of an apocalyptic-fatalistic system of causality. This is a state in which any kind of choice (and a decision not to choose is also a choice) necessarily leads to destruction, a state in which reality can no longer be differentiated from dreams, a state in which the world is seen through X-ray machines and there are no human beings but only skeletons.

In conclusion, Hans appears to be the posttraumatic figure following the *Akeda*. He represents the son who yearns to be bound, out of his obsession with reconstructing the history of his life. In the first chapter of this book, we saw that the model of binding/being bound has shaped Western culture. Hans is a classic example of a figure that has allowed himself to be bound out of a desire and belief that reliving the *Akeda* will release him. The *Akeda* is a form of redemption. Yet in practice, the compulsive repetition of the *Akeda* does not lead to release and redemption, but rather to imprisonment in the posttraumatic reality. Ultimately, there is no redemption. The road does not lead to recovery. Rather, it merely enlarges the cycle of trauma and preserves the model of binding/being bound. Even if in the end the father does not bind and sacrifice his son, the son develops an obsession with completing the mission. Perhaps it is even an attempt on the part of the sons to atone for the historical sin that Freud (1939) referred to as the murder of Moses by his followers.

MEURSAULT: FROM TRAUMA TO POSTTRAUMA

In the novel *The Stranger* by Albert Camus, we meet the character of Meursault, a man whose life is controlled by the sun. He is totally focused on the present, with no thoughts about past or future. His time line is limited to the present moment only. Meursault is completely honest with himself and those around him. Just as, in the first part of the book, he does not judge himself, neither does he judge those around him. He does not pretend. He does only what seems right to him under the circumstances. He has no regrets about committing murder or about any of his other actions. Meursault refuses to behave hypocritically regarding the death of his mother and he is not willing to tell Marie that he loves her. He does not want to ask anything any more. Thus he has given up the very notion of questioning and does not want to answer: "I'd rather lost the habit of noting my feelings, and hardly knew what to answer" (Camus 1962b, p. 41). Meursault is the natural human who takes the simple and direct path. The accusations made against Meursault at the trial, that he lacks a soul and a conscience, are completely justified: "And just then it crossed my mind that one might fire, or not fire—and it would come to absolutely the same thing" (p. 37). There is no moral question here, no question of will, and at least superficially the shot is ultimately meaningless.

In the first part of *The Stranger* the reader gets to know a man who lives in the present moment without any accounting and without any system of beliefs. In the second part of the book, after the murder on the beach, together with Meursault the reader undergoes a process of reflection and the construction of self-consciousness: "So I knew that all this time I'd been talking to myself" (p. 51).

As with the accusation of Josef K. in *The Trial*, the accusation of Meursault was never concrete: "a great deal was said about me; more, in fact, about me personally than about my crime" (p. 62). The court is not interested in the murder. In the age of the Auschwitz crematoria, murder no longer shocks anyone—and why should it? The court tries Meursault for having dared to release himself from the moralistic boa constrictor of Christianity, for having dared to stand up to Abraham, to Sarah, to God, and to Isaac, for having lived his life simply, for having gone to the beach and the movies without feeling any pangs of conscience. For having murdered from emotion and not based on a plan. Because, today, we find ourselves in the age of planned murder and any kind of emotional reaction is a sin, to act based on emotions and desires is not allowed.

At the trial, Meursault's acquaintances testify to his character, and ultimately he assimilates the judgment and admits to reflection and self-judgment: "I had an odd impression, as if I were being scrutinized by myself" (p. 54). Meursault stares at the audience and sometimes even identifies with them:

> For the first time I'd realized how all these people loathed me . . . It was then I felt a sort of wave of indignation spreading through the courtroom, and for the first time I understood that I was guilty (pp. 56–58)

Meursault is a formative character on the way to Kurtz *(Apocalypse Now)*, one that will choose absolute rejection of the notion of a trial, as will later become clear. Kurtz has a profound understanding of the implications of a trial for a free man. Death does not frighten Kurtz, only the idea that he will die after judgment has been passed upon him by the sick Western culture. Meursault appears to refuse to participate in the trial, which is no more than a game. He refuses to talk or to defend himself. Meursault prefers to shoot, and with this shot the dybbuk is released. The question then becomes—what kind of dybbuk is this? Every posttraumatic figure has a dybbuk that must emerge and be sanctified, a dybbuk that acts out uncontrollably. Kurtz has good reason to say the following in the movie *Apocalypse Now:*

> But we must kill them. We must . . . incinerate them. Pig after pig, cow after cow, village after village, army after army . . . and they call me an assassin. What do you call it when the assassins accuse the assassin? They lie. . . . They

lie, and we have to be merciful for those who lie...Those nabobs, I hate
them. I do hate them.

It is important to understand that Meursault's alienation is a matter of
choice. It emerges under the burden of the Nazi occupation and it
represents the choice not to be part of human society. This is perhaps
the last human choice that remains. How can a society that sends millions
of people to the gas chambers have the audacity (and the ability) to try a
man for a simple murder on the beach? The Western justice system is
based on a fraudulent and hypocritical set of norms in which terms such as
"justice," "guilt," "innocence," and "verdict" are nothing more than part
of a tragicomic scenario written in advance. Did people stop dancing in
Berlin while the crematoria operated at full capacity? Did the French stop
drinking wine? And considering the way things were, what exactly is
Meursault being tried for? Not for disregarding the distress of the other,
but rather for rejecting the hypocrisy demonstrated by Clamence in *The
Fall*. Meursault simply does not feel any guilt, and our society just cannot
accept this disdain for its norms, for guilt is the only product society has to
offer on the market today. Admit you are guilty and we will forgive you
and even worship you.

The truth is simple. Meursault commits murder because there is no real
reason not to murder. In the first part of the book, Meursault represents
the individual on the seam between the traumatic and the posttraumatic
states. Only after the trial does the posttrauma become permanent, *for it is
impossible to think about posttrauma without a sense of guilt. In turn, there
is no sense of guilt without reflection and introspection, that is, without self-
consciousness.* Perhaps that is the true purpose of the trial—to turn
Meursault into a posttraumatic man. To sacrifice him. To unlock and
develop a sense of guilt in him. It is interesting to discover that in the
transition from trauma to posttrauma Meursault does not relinquish his
alienation but rather preserves and extends it. Indeed, his salvation is
found in that very alienation.

By committing murder, Meursault is seeking a way to implement his
sense of guilt for not mourning the death of his mother. His quest is
problematic, not to mention theological. It appears that the first signs of
self-judgment were always hidden in Meursault's world, that Meursault
has his reasons, and that the murder was not without meaning. Rather
than being naïve, this analysis is decisive. Essentially, this murder must be
looked at differently. Meursault commits murder for no reason. He has no

reason to murder. Others are seeking a way to force causality upon nature. The death of the mother represent a whole different story. Yet no meta- physical or concrete sin leads Meursault to commit murder. The murder is committed out of unfathomable alienation—murdering simply because there is no real reason not to.

The topic of the mother represents another stratum in this layered story. Meursault symbolizes the final collapse of the nuclear family. He has no father and no siblings. He represents a world that has been orphaned of its father and that finds comfort in an absent mother who refuses to be there. This is reminiscent of how Christiane from Michel Houellebecq's novel *Elementary Particles* talks about herself with respect to her relations with her son: "If he had an accident on his motorbike and was killed, I'd be sad, but I think I'd probably feel relieved" (Houellebecq 2000, p. 177). If we think of Meursault as a character representing a collective story, like all the characters I have discussed so far, World War II symbolizes the transition from the traumatic to the posttraumatic condition and the death of the nuclear family. Meursault's generation grew up without fathers, or at least without anyone to fill the role of father. Their fathers died in World War II or were shell-shocked by the trench warfare. What we can understand from this novel is that the mothers are also no longer there. Meursault does not mourn his mother because from his perspective she was never there, not even at the outset. She did not prevent the *Akeda*. This was the case in the story of Isaac and also in Kafka's testimony in the letter he wrote to his father (Kafka 1971a). Meursault represents a world in which the family circle has collapsed and can no longer function as an anchor and a sense of home. It is therefore understandable that in the closing arguments at Meursault's trial the prosecutor explicitly mentions a father's murder:

> "This same court, gentlemen, will be called on to try tomorrow that most odious of crimes, the murder of a father by his son." To his mind, such a crime was almost unimaginable. But, he ventured to hope, justice would be meted out without paltering. And yet, he made bold to say, the horror that even the crime of parricide inspired in him paled beside the loathing inspired by my callousness. (Camus 1962b, p. 64)

The real story is that in the transition from trauma to posttrauma the hero loses the maternal-feminine aspect of his life, the possibility of a direct, diffuse, and dynamic relationship, whether with a mother, a spouse, or a character from his inner world. Abraham did not consult with Sarah when he set off to sacrifice Isaac.[3] As we will see, no reference is made to a mother figure in connection with Michael from *The Deer Hunter*, with Travis from *Taxi Driver*, and certainly not Kurtz or Captain Willard (Martin Sheen) in *Apocalypse Now*. After the death of the mother in Camus' novel *The Stranger*, there is no hope for consolation or comfort for the posttraumatic figure, and therefore no hope for true recovery. Meursault tells Marie that it does not matter whether they get married or not: "Marie came that evening and asked me if I'd marry her. I said I didn't mind; if she was keen on it, we'd get married" (Camus 1962b, p. 28). In this, he depicts the relations between men and women in the posttraumatic age, in which nothing departs from the realm of impersonality and arbitrariness. The man remains alone in a desert of ice. Relations can only be pornographic or paid for within a comprehensive economic system such as that described by Houellebecq in his novel *Platform* (2002). Like Meursault, Kurtz in the novel *Heart of Darkness* (1990) chooses to say "the horror, the horror" as his dying words and does not even hint at the existence of his girlfriend, despite her belief that he does, as is clear from his conversation with Marlow. Indeed, Meursault describes this situation precisely:

> Then she asked me again if I loved her. I replied, much as before, that her question meant nothing or next to nothing—but I supposed I didn't. "If that's how you feel," she said, "why marry me?" I explained that it had no importance really, but, if it would give her pleasure, we could get married right away. I pointed out that, anyhow, the suggestion came from her; as for me, I'd merely said, "Yes." Then she remarked that marriage was a serious matter. To which I answered: "No." She kept silent after that, staring at me in a curious way. Then she asked: "Suppose another girl had asked you to marry her—I mean, a girl you liked in the same way as you like me—would you have said 'Yes' to her, too?" "Naturally." Then she said she wondered if she really loved me or not. I, of course, couldn't enlighten her as to that. And, after another silence, she murmured something about my being "a queer fellow." "And I daresay that's why I love you," she added. "But maybe that's why one day I'll come to hate you." To which I had nothing to say, so I said nothing. She thought for a bit, then started smiling and, taking my arm, repeated that she was in earnest; she really wanted to marry me. "All right," I answered. "We'll get married whenever you like." (Camus 1962b, pp. 28–29)

In conclusion, Meursault appears totally liberated from the *Akeda* model. He does not yearn to be bound and does not have an obsessive need to bind. At least in the first half of the novel, he is released from the Kafkaesque guilt of which he has been accused—the lack of a sense of guilt.

During the trial, what Meursault has done is linked to patricide. This comparison can easily lead to the Freudian concept of patricide and the creation of a community of sons (Freud 1939, 1950). The murder takes place against the background of the cruelty of the father, an alpha male. It encompasses both an inverted model of the *Akeda* and the Kafkaesque model of guilt, in which the sons feel guilty about the father's murders', even if the murder took place in previous generations. The connection to patricide is clear. When the prosecutor in Meursault's trial refers to patricide, he claims that Meursault has murdered his mother and attempts to make Meursault adopt metaphysical guilt like the guilt of the community of sons described by Freud.

When the chaplain comes to Meursault before the execution, Meursault rejects him. Meursault does not believe in God, the question of God is of no interest to him, and the conversation with the chaplain is boring and meaningless. The chaplain claims that a sin is hanging over Meursault that he must renounce. According to the chaplain, God is the one standing in judgment over Meursault. Meursault disagrees, insisting that his sin has nothing to do with God. Humans are the ones who judged him and found him guilty, and God has nothing to do with the matter. Meursault categorically rejects the notion of a sin against God and rejects God's divine monarchy. By the end of the conversation, Meursault curses the chaplain and cautions him not to pray for him. Thus, we learn of the failure of society's attempts to force upon Meursault the first circle of the inverted *Akeda* together with the sense of guilt with respect to God (Kafka's third circle).

Meursault remains in the Nietzschean second circle, in which there is no connection between sin and sense of guilt. As noted, toward the end of the novel Meursault thinks he understands that his mother took a "groom" as a way of starting life over again. He too seems willing to start over. Nietzsche and the notion of eternal return reverberates through this statement, indicating that at least in some sense Meursault belongs to the circle of eternal return:

With death so near, Mother must have felt like someone on the brink of freedom, ready to start life all over again. No one, no one in the world had any right to weep for her. And I, too, felt ready to start life all over again. (Camus 1962b, p. 154)

CLAMENCE—POSTTRAUMATIC PARALYSIS

From the alienation and authenticity of Meursault we now move with Camus to the opposite pole, to Clamence, the hero of *The Fall* (Camus 1984). Clamence is a French lawyer from Paris specializing in defending the poor and wretched of society. At least in his own eyes he is the embodiment of ideal good, but all the good that he showers on others is nothing more than pretense, a charade, a show. In the reality of the day-to-day, Clamence is no more than an actor. Every action he takes is made with the knowledge that he is being observed. He is always self-conscious, indeed too self-conscious. The roots of his being lie in acting and reflecting upon how society regards him, and he is nothing more than a slave to a fraudulent image. Clamence is the absolute opposite of Meursault, and indeed it may seem that the punch Clamence receives from the motorcyclist has come from none other than Meursault. This punch exposes Clamence, and in the context of Clamence's show it is the first act in the play. This punch could have sobered Clamence, but he chooses to ignore it. Clamence's disregard for the cries of a woman who jumps to her death from a bridge over the Seine River late one night in Paris rips the mask off his face and leaves him no choice but to admit that he is a hypocrite and a liar. His image has been shattered, and from that point on Clamence will never again cross a bridge alone at night.

Clamence's lie is identical to the European falsehood regarding the humanistic approach to life, the culture that exalts the willingness to live for the sake of and the good of the other. In this sense Clamence, like Hans, represents the identity of the European. While Hans predates World War I, Clamence appears immediately after the war, representing the white man in Europe between 1939 and 1945 deep within the camps of horror and death. The knowledge and understanding that he is in fact incapable of taking the steps needed to enable him to help others does not allow him to continue to live this way of life. Clamence represents the failure to perceive the obvious during the years prior to and during World War II, while at the same time he represents our willingness today to look the other way in the presence of dark and shady regimes.

Clamence wanders through the European unconscious (Amsterdam). His endless circling around himself in Amsterdam is not only a trip through time to the unconscious of Western society but also a circular journey that cannot be escaped. The journey symbolizes the end of the road for the enlightened liberal European. Amsterdam is not a haven or a city of refuge but rather a hell on earth. As Shakespeare said, "Hell is empty and all the devils are here" (*The Tempest*: Act 1, Scene 2, Page 10). The circular wandering represents the condition of the lack of time and the collapse of space, a condition in which ultimately the only solution is evaporation, precisely like the Nazi solution for the "Jewish problem." Clamence is not capable of forgetting and therefore becomes paralyzed. The fact that he remembers paralyzes him as a human being. In the face of this paralysis we encounter laughter. This laughter that drives him out of his mind is of course the laughter we encountered in the *Vayera* Torah portion when God laughed at Abraham's expense and brought about the birth of Isaac. The laughter is intended to remind us that Clamence has not obeyed the legacy of Abraham to be human, to be first and foremost a *mensch*, even if a crazy one. Clamence is capable of feeling guilt, but that sense of guilt does not lead him to any action—this is indeed the biggest problem of Western culture. He is not capable of rebelling. Yet ultimately, this is the only thing that matters, for we are living in a world of results and not in a world of intentions.

It is important, however, to remember that there is no evidence of the woman's suicide and no evidence of her scream, which without a doubt can only be a product of Clamence's inner world. Yet this does not make it any less real. This is especially true for the posttraumatic figure. Indeed, the fact that the suicide is not mentioned elsewhere (e.g., in the newspapers) perhaps testifies to the woman's solitude but not to the possibility that the suicide never happened. The lack of any mention of the suicide in the newspaper provides a final excuse for inaction for a man who knows precisely what it is he does not want to know. The destruction of the Jews in Europe during World War II also received very little mention. Yet there was a scream, a cry for help in a world in which the absurd assumed control. Hence, there is sufficient reason to place the scream in Paris, in France, a country that despite having declared war on Hitler after the invasion of Poland remained largely inactive from the military point of view, not truly seeking to engage the enemy for the better part of a year, and then it was Germany that invaded France. The outcry was sounded only after the Nuremberg Trials. It continued to be sounded in Paris around a decade after World War II, and a few years later it was sounded again right before the construction of the Berlin Wall. Indeed, the outcry was sounded all the time. We simply chose not to hear it or not to respond to it.

The scream should have been a final warning signal, right before it was too late. The scream symbolizes the possibility for change. At the end of the novel, Clamence admits that the only solution from his perspective is to reenact the moment of the jump. Yet at the same time he admits that even if given the chance he would fail and not respond to the scream. This statement symbolizes the state of humanity just prior to World War II, and we cannot point to any real change since then. The condition described is of a physical site of imprisonment (Amsterdam) that represents a metaphysical prison. This is the condition of the posttraumatic individual—paralysis and the lack of any possibility of doing anything, a sense of perpetual captivity and entrapment, total helplessness that finds expression in Clamence's endless wandering around Amsterdam and in his resounding, ringing conclusion:

> O young woman, throw yourself into the water again so that I may a second time have the chance of saving both of us!" A second time, eh, what a risky suggestion! Just suppose, cher maître, that we should be taken literally? We'd have to go through with it. Brr...! The water's so cold! But let's not worry! It's too late now. It will always be too late. Fortunately! (Camus 1984, p. 44)

Clamence appears totally immersed in the Kafkaesque circle of guilt. Yet— and this is a critical point—this sense of guilt does not lead him to any action whatsoever. The scream is a cry that calls him to action, but Clamence is captive within his own world. In this hypocritical world, people discuss the need to be there for others but in practice, no one lifts a finger to help anyone else (and why should they?). The movement is circular and returns to the same point. In this context, the eternal return is the return to knowledge and the disregarding of this knowledge. It is a return to the refusal to be there for the other. Eternal return is submersion in life that is meaningless. Clamence's circular motion shows us that eternal return is an obsessive process of compulsive repetition of the same mistakes without being able to change your fate. This is true even when you are completely conscious of this, and perhaps precisely when you are too conscious of this. The circular motion is in effect the ongoing sense of downfall—not only for Clamence, but for Europe as a whole, as in Thomas Mann's novel *Death in Venice* (1980).

Yet even Clamence's sense of guilt is not authentic. His admission of guilt is nothing more than a tactic that enables him to live and enjoy his life, including his downfall and his consciousness of this downfall. Clamence tells us something more profound about our lives in the Western world. The discourse on guilt is a way of evading responsibility, for the sense of guilt is paralyzing. This sense of guilt is nothing more than a trick that enables us to live our pleasurable lives. Clamence seems to be telling us openly that when he was in a camp in North Africa, he took water from his dying friend because he felt he must preserve himself for the sake of others. Clearly, this is nothing more than a lie that Clamence tells himself, a lie which Clamence is very well aware of. Indeed, Clamence admits it openly.

Clamence understands that under the existing circumstances he cannot conduct himself as if nothing has happened. The Holocaust occurred and disregarding it is impossible. Therefore, he accepts the guilt in an exaggerated manner, but again this is only a game. In actuality, Clamence has not changed a bit. In his many confessions, which themselves are circular, he makes sure to change from "I" to "we" in order to tell his audience that they are all as guilty as he is. Because they are all in the same boat, he can still feel good about himself and continue living as he has lived. He can continue to move in the circle of self-guilt, which is nothing more than a mask that enables him to continue as usual. Every time Clamence can do something to change his fate, he chooses to do nothing. The final paragraph of the novel makes it clear to us that what was is what will be. Perhaps this is repetition compulsion in the posttraumatic condition— circles of guilt in which the individual returns to the same junctions and keeps choosing not to respond to the other. Even self-consciousness cannot change the foreseeable end.

Toward the Post-Human Era

He realized that he was now going to leave a world he'd never genuinely been a part of. (Houellebecq 2012, p. 167)

Daniel, hero of Houellebecq's novel *The Possibility of an Island* (2006), symbolizes the transition from the posttraumatic condition represented by Clamence to the post-human condition. In the posttraumatic condition "there is neither day nor night, the situation is without end" (Houellebecq 2006, p. 1), and "in the end there's just the cold, the silence and the loneliness. In the end there's only death" (Houellebecq 2000, p. 290). The posttraumatic era is an era without a home: "I've always lived as though I were in a hotel" (Houellebecq 2006, p. 222). The sense of alienation is total: he wondered "if he belonged to the human race" (Houellebecq 2012, p. 34). In such an extreme state, the origin of every cultural and historical condition, you cannot even love your own son. The posttraumatic individual knows that all there is at the end of the story is the *Akeda:* "On the day of my son's suicide I made a tomato omelette.... I had never loved that child" (Houellebecq 2006, p. 20). Similarly, Michel, the hero of *Elementary Particles* (2000) who shifts us from a posttraumatic to a post-human condition, understands:

> Bruno was right—paternal love was a lie, a fiction. A lie is useful if it transforms reality, he thought, but if it fails, then all that's left is the lie, the bitterness and the knowledge that it was a lie. (Houellebecq 2000, p. 140)

Not only does the posttraumatic individual live in an environment comprised entirely of relations between murderer and victim, binder and bound, accused and hangman. For the posttraumatic individual, emotion in and of itself is intolerable. Love is an emotion, and the posttraumatic individual is incapable of it or is no longer willing to feel it. Any emotion, whether positive or negative, awakens the physical memory of the traumatic experience. Indeed, the body itself is the traumatic memory. Therefore, in the posttraumatic state, humanity itself has become something that must be avoided. This leads to the emergence of a new generation that is terrified of all emotions, including love: "Esther did not like love, she did not want to be in love, she refused this feeling of exclusivity, of dependence, and her whole generation refused it with her" (Houellebecq 2006, p. 236).

Daniel as well, hero of *The Possibility of an Island,* ultimately does not really love Esther. Rather, he becomes obsessed by her young body. Daniel wants to become part of Esther's witless, foolhardy passion for life. Yet even in the case of Esther, it is not clear exactly what type of passion this is, if it is indeed passion at all. Esther, who naturally grew up without a father—or rather, with a father like Clamence who cannot be there for anyone—is not interested in love. Esther is the classical product of capitalist culture, the product of a culture that espouses negative philosophy, a culture that is not capable of coping with emotional pain, for such pain takes us directly to the trenches, to the beaches of Normandy, to the ice, to the jungles, or from the feminine perspective, to a reality of rape and inability to feel safe in a place where men are present. Indeed, even a father or a brother is not always a source of safety for the victims of sexual abuse. Hence, if emotion always leads to impossible pain, for "in the end, life always breaks your heart. . . . you still end up with your heart broken" (Houellebecq 2000, p. 290), it is better to live life without any emotion. Yet relinquishing emotion means relinquishing humanity. In the posttraumatic era concepts such as humaneness and love are nullified. The price of being human is trauma and therefore being human must be nullified as well. This is the reason that pornographic relations are the only possible relations between a man and a woman in this era:

> The centuries-old male project, perfectly expressed nowadays by pornographic films, that consisted of ridding sexuality of any emotional connotation in order to bring it back into the realm of pure entertainment had finally, in this generation, been accomplished. (Houellebecq 2006, p. 236)

We have already said that the posttraumatic condition is intolerable because from the perspective of the posttraumatic individual every environmental stimulus is painful. From the posttraumatic individual's perspective, only "inaction, more than ever, would cause him anguish" (Houellebecq 2012, p. 158), for any emotion turns into something that arouses the trauma. Therefore that same posttraumatic individual strives to cancel out emotions absolutely:

> It is the suffering of being that makes us seek out the other, as a palliative; we must go beyond this stage to reach the state where the simple fact of being constitutes in itself a permanent occasion for joy; where intermediation is nothing more than a game, freely undertaken, and not constitutive of being. We must, in a word, reach the freedom of indifference, the condition for the possibility of perfect serenity. (Houellebecq 2006, p. 260)

Clearly, then, in the post-human era, this is a situation in which indifference rules. "We no longer really have any specific objective; the joys of humans remain unknowable to us" (Houellebecq 2006, p. 5). The transition from the posttraumatic condition to the post-human condition is the shift from the human body to a body that is a machine: "Like them, we were only conscious machines; but, unlike them, we were aware of only being machines" (Houellebecq 2006, p. 326). So long as we remained human we remained with a body that always remembers, with a body in which the trauma is impressed and assimilated:

for we are bodies, we are, above all, principally and almost uniquely bodies, and the state of our bodies constitutes the true explanation of the majority of our intellectual and moral conceptions. (Houellebecq 2006, p. 151)

The shift to the post-human era obligates us to create a different kind of body:

If he was to keep on going they would have to change his artificial anus; well, he thought he'd had enough of that joke. And what's more, he felt pain. He couldn't bear it any longer, he was suffering too much. (Houellebecq 2012, p. 217)

The shift from the posttraumatic era to the post-human era seems to take place as a result of the inability of the posttraumatic subject and of posttraumatic society to go on with life. Posttraumatic subjects have no other alternative but to make present in actual reality what has for some time already been real in their inner world—the apocalyptic stratum that controls them: "No truly convincing theory has been formulated to explain what bears all the hallmarks of mass suicide" (Houellebecq 2006, p. 32).

Daniel, hero of *The Possibility of an Island,* the very same Daniel as in the story of Daniel's vision in the Bible, informs us that the human era has indeed come to an end. This same Daniel works as a standup comedian and is incapable of facing the laughter of his audience. This is the laughter that marked the beginning of the human saga, that bound Isaac at the very summit of its total absence, that knows that aging is the worst thing in this era: "In the modern world you could be a swinger, bi, trans, zoo, into S&M, but it was forbidden to be old" (Houellebecq 2006, p. 148).

Daniel represents the final product, the end of the process that began with the *Akeda,* where we learned that God represents the traumatic side of our lives and that that continued after we murdered God and took leave of the human side within us, just so that we would not become, as Nietzsche warned, "too human." Ultimately, as Kafka understood, all that we are left with are feelings of guilt. Yet this sense of guilt is empty.

Like Daniel, Michel, one of two sons of a hippie-type mother in the novel *The Elementary Particles,* is a scientist whose goal is to create a new species that is asexual and inhuman. Note that Jed, the artist in *The Map and the Territory* (Houellebecq 2012), chooses to take leave of everything that could possibly be considered human. These characters emerge against the background of the total collapse of a society that has lost its way. The post-human condition is not a matter of choice but rather of necessity—a Kafkaesque metamorphosis.

DESTRUCTION VERSUS INDIFFERENCE: THE END OF THE HUMAN ERA

As each of the chapters in this book contends, trauma is a cultural event. Meursault symbolizes the authentic character, the attempt to return to the body. Hence Western society judges him and sentences him to death. Clamence symbolizes the human being in the posttraumatic condition, trapped in the inability to do anything, trapped in this life. Daniel is not disconnected from these characters. He takes them a step further, to the end of the human era. As Bruno, another hero who symbolizes the end of the human era, in *Elementary Particles*, states at one point: "It's clear to me we have nothing—absolutely nothing—to do with this world" (Houellebecq 2000, p. 123).

It is important to understand that Daniel does not suffer from the same form of romantic despair as that experienced by Hans in *The Magic Mountain*. Daniel lacks any belief in God or in scientific progress. He is not authentic like Meursault, for Daniel ultimately still believes in love. He also does not suffer from the same pangs of conscience as Clamence. From Daniel's point of view, the family has no meaning. He is afraid of growing old. He is a step beyond Kafka's letter to his father, and ultimately he represents the individual in posttraumatic society, a society that attempts to cancel out every bit of humanity in him.

Ultimately, the posttraumatic society destroys itself out of its uncontrollable compulsion to recreate the traumatic moment repeatedly as a primal moment. Posttraumatic society is the result of a society that has internalized the notion that the ultimate fate of every emotion is inhuman pain, and therefore it is preferable to relinquish humanity and emotion as well. In this sense it is indeed possible that we are the last generation capable of passing the Turing Test. Indeed, we have already become too indifferent to do so.

Essentially, there are two alternatives in the posttraumatic world: indifference or destruction (of the self or of the other). To avoid destruction, individuals must consciously and intelligently choose indifference. Yet from this choice to the death of humanity, the road is short. In his essay on suicide, Camus (1975) indicates that on the morning after someone has committed suicide we must ask ourselves whether we had been indifferent to him. More than cruelty and brutality, indifference signifies the death of humanity. In a world in which a father sacrifices his son simply by his absence and indifference (and if they do meet, it is while waiting in line for a prostitute) and the mother is not silent but simply does not care, for she is indifferent, the sacrifice is even harsher than the *Akeda* of Isaac. It is a sacrifice made up of absence, a sacrifice with indifference at its core. In such a situation, there is no possibility of developing feelings of guilt. Under such circumstances, for Kafka's Hunger Artist (Kafka 1996) fasting is meaningless. It makes no difference to anyone whether he lives or dies, nor does it matter how he dies. Even the machine of destruction operates without any interest, as Ka-Tsetnik notes in his book (*Salamandra* series). Ka-Tsetnik remembers the guards yawning out of boredom while the Nazis sent people to die in the gas chambers. Indifference, whose roots are already apparent in Clamence, leads to infinite walking in circles whose center is absolute indifference. This explains the cloning of Daniel 3, Daniel 5, Daniel 11, and so on in the novel *The Possibility of an Island* by Michel Houellebecq. This is a case of eternal recurrence—the exact clone of a character that has collapsed into indifference.

It is important to understand the historical background of this circle. Daniel 1 attempts eternal return in order to disrupt the compulsive repetition of the posttraumatic figure, which always turns toward the destructive path out of passion and lack of control. The model of Daniel 1–25 creates a new eternal circle of indifferent characters. Even destruction does not elicit any emotion in them. This indeed is a successful solution—preventing destruction by turning it into a boring event. Even God eventually became bored with the extermination camps. And why shouldn't he. The Daniel 1–25 model yields the insight that every emotion will ultimately hurt us and that the response of the posttraumatic figure to this hurt will be suicide or murder. There is no middle course. The only alternative to indifference is pleasurable cruelty. Indifference should enable us to cope with the principle that there are those who derive pleasure from causing others to suffer, on the condition of course that this does not bore them. Again we see how cloning of characters detached from discourse about emotions and pleasure is nothing more than a solution in response to the posttraumatic world, in which reconstruction always leads to destruction (e.g., the story of Noah and the flood and the story of Sodom and Gomorrah).

Facing the passion to destroy are absolute indifference and emotional death. In each of Daniel's incarnations, his condition worsens—or improves, depending on the point of view—and Daniel becomes more indifferent and more isolated. Yet we must remember that the alternative is destruction. Indeed, destruction and indifference are two sides of the same coin. It is precisely within these circles that Clamence revolves, along with all of Western culture. The temptation to destroy and to impersonate God, if only for a moment, is almost boundless, and the posttraumatic figure cannot escape this repetition compulsion.

Notes

1. Altered states of consciousness are marked by the collapse of the system of logic, and therefore the relations between subject and object cease to be stable and the sense of self is undermined. In my view, what happens in altered states of consciousness is that due to various constraints (linked to cognitive load) the subject is unable to create a sense of time. This requires effort and this in turn generates an additional burden on the system. When this happens the entire architectural structure of consciousness crumbles. Indeed, in altered states of consciousness transparency crumbles and the subject is exposed to the structure of consciousness as productive consciousness in the sense that Bergson discussed. Exposure to the structure of consciousness brings up the gap between the individual as subject and the individual as object. That same gap manifests itself in that time as an objective dimension is exposed as the creation of the subject. This is why the dimension of time plays such an important role in altered states of consciousness. At this stage the subject understands the extent to which it, as subject, generates the illusion of objectivity. The subject understands the extent to which it is a creature of the world as a whole. The subject produces the content and thus transforms the world into what it is—a meaningful world. In altered states of consciousness, the process of spontaneous creation changes completely because the basis for our understanding of the world crumbles.

2. The fact that consciousness is rooted in the body means that the rational basis of thinking is the body. According to this approach, consciousness is not disconnected from the world. It is not merely a "presentation" of changing images, but rather part of the body and it exists in the world by means of the body. Perception is not simply the representation of a particular object in the world. Perception takes place via the body and ultimately what we perceive is absolutely influenced by the body. In effect, a very

specific body is required in order to perceive the world as we perceive it (Merleau-Ponty 2002; Noë 2004; Varela et al. 1991).

3. Try to imagine what kind of night Abraham must be having. God has told him that tomorrow he must set out to sacrifice his son. He spends the entire night tossing and turning in bed beside Sarah. What thoughts went through his head? What went through her head? Why did she remain silent?

CHAPTER 3

A Serious Man

Thou Shalt Have No Other Gods Before Me

Larry (acted by Michael Stuhlbarg), the central character in the movie *A Serious Man* (Coen and Coen 2009), is a Jew and indeed a serious man. He is married to a woman he loves and he is a devoted father to his son. He is also a professor of physics at a university, though he does not yet have tenure. The movie follows Larry from the moment his comfortable and boring life collapses. Throughout the movie Larry protests again and again that he does not understand what he has done to "deserve" all this: "Nothing! I didn't do anything." This is what he tells anyone and everyone who is willing to listen. For instance, when Larry describes his problems to the head of the university tenure committee, he gets the following definitive response: "Don't worry. Doing nothing is not bad. Ipso facto." Yet did Larry really do nothing? What Larry ultimately does not manage to understand is that as in physics and mathematics, in life as well there is no such thing as "deserving." That is just how it is.

At the beginning of *A Serious Man* Larry explains the Schrödinger's cat paradox to his students. This is a thought experiment in which a cat is both alive and dead at exactly the same time. This experiment makes it seem that humans have an impact on what happens around them. The central motif of the movie is based on the possibility of an individual influencing the world and on the implications of that influence. It is important to note that beneath the surface is the assumption that Nature will be revealed to

© The Author(s) 2017
Y. Ataria, *The Structural Trauma of Western Culture*,
DOI 10.1007/978-3-319-53228-8_3

us in a mathematical manner, or more precisely, that Nature can be perfectly represented through mathematics.

Larry is a rational (and a serious) man, a scientist who believes that the world is constructed and shaped in accordance with mathematical formulas. As he says, "The math is how it really works." Larry is a man of numbers and like Galileo, he is convinced that on the surface level of being life can be explained through math. To get right to the point, I would posit that the very notion that there are mathematical-physical explanations for the world is the prime accusation directed against the individual in monotheistic culture. As noted, in the case of Josef K. in *The Trial,* the accusation at the trial is one that cannot actually be expressed.

During the movie it becomes apparent that when it comes to life itself, the figure of the rational scientist does not seem reasonable at all, for as Freud claimed, on a certain level "practically all of us still think as savages do" (Freud 1959, p. 14). Thus if on the surface Larry appears to live in a rational-mathematical world, beneath the surface he still lives in the world of the Jewish accounting ledger, in a state of mind that can be described as "dry apocalypse" (Houellebecq 2000, p. 10). This is a world of constant anxiety.

Later in the movie the police, who represent the law in the broadest sense of national or divine law, arrive with Larry's brother Arthur, who has been arrested. They suggest to Larry that not only is his attempt to explain the world through mathematics a serious charge with respect to religion, but it is also a serious charge with respect to life itself. Any attempt to understand *everything* or even *something* ends in disaster. Being engaged in science is contrary to faith. Larry objects: "You can't arrest a man for mathematics!" Larry is implying that an individual cannot be put on trial for denying the existence of God. Yet by saying "It's just mathematics! You can't arrest a man for mathematics!" in referring to his brother Arthur, Larry is actually defending himself. In effect he is attempting to create a writ of defense, which he certainly needs. Larry believes, at least ostensibly, that he should not be accused just because he is engaged in calculations. Perhaps he, like his brother, is engaged in calculations regarding death. Yet as noted, mathematical calculations constitute a serious offense.

Physical theories undermine the Jewish perception of God and violate the First Commandment: "Thou shalt have no other gods before me." In Larry's case, the denial of God finds expression in being granted tenure and joining the club of science that rejects the existence of God. The tenure that Larry is to receive represents his passage from the world of the dybbuk, the world of God, to the world of science that denies the existence of God. Yet as later becomes apparent, such a passage is not really possible for the good Jew. Thus in the process Larry, like the classic Jew, becomes his own prosecutor and judge.

RELIGION AND SCIENCE: THE IMPOSSIBLE ENCOUNTER

Merely fact-minded sciences make merely fact-minded people. (Husserl 1970, p. 6)

It is impossible to bridge the gap between science and God, between the scientific-rational-physical approach and the accounting ledger of Nietzsche's God of all dark corners and places. Anxiety always remains. This is the lesson Freud teaches us in his book *The Uncanny* (1959):

Nowadays we no longer believe in them, we have surmounted such ways of thought; but we do not feel quite sure of our new set of beliefs, and the old ones still exist within us ready to seize upon any confirmation. As soon as something actually happens in our lives which seems to support the old, discarded beliefs, we get a feeling of the uncanny. (p. 17)

This is despite the absurd fact that those who believe seek reasons for every natural process that occurs and that in this absurd search they ultimately invent the reasons themselves. The system of scientific causality clashes with theological causality. This is an impossible encounter between the revealed layer of existence and the repressed world of superstitions (the world of the dybbuk) in which every event is seen as a type of "sign" signifying what is real. While the scientific approach seeks mechanical explanations, the religious way of thinking links Nature to values. The conflict between the two creates a volcanic system beneath the surface of Western culture. Thus it is with clear intent that in *Moses and Monotheism* (1939) Freud defines the Jewish God as a volcanic God. And every scene in which Larry argues for the scientific approach to life resembles a field court martial. He writes his writ of defense on the board, yet he does not understand that this is not a writ of defense but rather a writ accusing him of a crime. The equations used to explain the secrets of the universe are the facts and also the writ of accusation in Larry's trial. In such a situation Larry is not only a criminal but also an enemy who has been sentenced to death, as indicated by Alexander Solzhenitsyn in his extraordinary novel, *The First Circle:*

> Because of my way of thinking... there's a law which says that a person can be tried for his inner thoughts... Section 58, Paragraph 10 of the Criminal Code. (Solzhenitsyn 1968, p. 42)

The accusation does not need to relate to deeds actually committed. Thoughts are sufficient in order to convict someone. Indeed the Ten Commandments refer not only to actions but also to thoughts and intentions. Thus, even though Larry has apparently not done anything, he has done everything. He has lived a life that in essence denies the existence of God and thus he has become the enemy of a religion that believes in the record-keeping God of the accounting ledger and the never-ending accounting that goes along with this belief.

The movie *A Serious Man* moves along two axes: that of Larry's professional life and that of his private life. Along the first axis, Larry moves forward toward receiving tenure and establishing his status at the university. Along the second, Larry prepares for the bar mitzvah of his son, Danny, which symbolizes accepting God's authority, the imprint of Jewish anxiety, the burden of the commandments, and the mark of Cain. That is, Jewish history always takes place along two different and conflicting time lines: the rational versus the irrational. This is an impossible encounter that Larry, and every postmodern individual, must live and live with. On the one hand is the incurable anxiety that cannot be healed due to the chaotic and random character of Nature. On the other hand is the attempt, the need, to cope and to explain.

Thus the battle is between scientific experience on the one hand and Nietzsche's accounting ledger postulation on the other (Nietzsche 2002). Both cases involve a special mathematics. Yet it is precisely the inability to live without any explanation that makes the reality around us so traumatic.

ACTIONS HAVE CONSEQUENCES

Larry lives in two separate and contradictory worlds, the world of science and the world of the open accounting ledger that is in fact revealed on the classroom board and serves as the writ of defense of the individual in the postmodern era. The encounter between these two worlds is impossible and brings Larry, a character who represents the individual in the postmodern era, to total collapse. Larry lives in the Judeo-Christian environment, a monotheistic atmosphere that can be defined as life under an open accounting ledger, as expressed in Larry's words to his Korean student: "Actions have consequences. Actions always have consequences." Yet at this stage, after Larry's wife has announced that she wants a "Get" (i.e., a divorce according to Jewish law and via the Jewish Rabbinate) because she wants to live with Sy Ableman, Larry begins to doubt the validity of his own statements (e.g., actions always have consequences). On the other hand, if he chooses to maintain the notion that actions have consequences, he must accept the fact that he has done something and in order to cope with the problem he must understand what he has done, what he is guilty of. Yet he is unable to connect what his wife wants to do with her life to his own actions. Therefore he reduces the boundaries of validity for the notion that actions still have consequences. More than anything else, this step testifies to his guilt, for narrowing the field is a classic move in science when evidence begins to pile up that contradicts a particular theory. "In this office, actions have consequences!" Larry says to the Korean student. Essentially, the technique that Larry adopts in order to deal with his problem provides the strongest evidence against him. Larry is completely cut off from the covert and the hidden, that is, from the real part of his life, from the ever-present accounting ledger. He does not understand why his wife has decided to leave him. He sees no rational cause for this. As the movie progresses, Larry discovers more and more hidden layers in his life and attempts to explain everything that has happened in his life through his open account with God. This is indeed a different kind of mathematics.

Larry must undergo a radical change. He must remove himself from the world that can be explained by, and reduced to, physics and eventually to mathematical equations, from a rational world to a world that cannot be explained or, alternatively, a world that can be explained by a completely different kind of math. He must abandon physics. Without intending to do so, Larry clarifies this point in his classroom lessons. In the first lesson he discusses the Schrödinger's cat thought theory, which ostensibly offers humans the possibility of change and influence. By the second lesson he is already discussing the uncertainty principle according to which it is impossible to measure two properties of a quantum object simultaneously with infinite precision (Greene 2005).

Thus in certain senses religion and science operate in a similar setting in that both seek explanations. The shift to the uncertainty principle is a transition into a world that lacks a deterministic system of causality, and this is precisely the radical change that Larry refuses to make. Therefore, it does not matter whether you have "done something" or "done nothing." Things happen without any explanation. The human aspiration to explain is perhaps our greatest sin against ourselves, for the attempt to explain always denies the covert layer of life, that same layer which, as we have seen in the first chapter of this book, governs even God Himself—the dybbuk.

Dybbuk

A Serious Man examines the consequences of our actions and considers how these actions affect our lives and the lives of those around us. It would be more accurate to say that the movie attempts to reveal to us the extent to which we live as if our actions are being judged by God according to moral criteria, while God pays us back for these actions by means of natural disasters. This is part of the structure of *The Uncanny*. When Larry takes a bribe and changes the grade of Clive, his Korean student, from fail to pass, we as viewers cannot help but interpret all the misfortunes that subsequently befall him as divine retribution for a specific moral offense. Larry's doctor calls him to come to the clinic immediately to get the results of his chest X-ray (the very same X-rays that enabled scientists to discover black holes, one of the most important physical discoveries of the past century), and a tornado threatens his son, who has just celebrated his bar mitzvah. As we have already indicated, it is easy and natural to say that an urgent phone call from one's doctor and a tornado threat to one's son are divine signs. Indeed, we as viewers clearly sense this. Actions really do have consequences. As part of the sick Western culture, we simply cannot avoid this way of thinking. In that sense trauma could be a blessing.

The concept of reward runs as a theme throughout the movie, as it does throughout our lives. Earlier in the movie Larry asks: "What is Hashem [the name of God] trying to tell me, making me pay for Sy Ableman's funeral?" The notion that this is a sign from God indicates that even if we appear to be "enlightened" atheists devoid of superstitions, we still believe that God talks to us, even if only through disasters. Yet this is not the case. The temptation to think that there are divine signs in our lives has a clear purpose: to reveal that we observe the truth beneath the sterile talk. We live according to a very specific form of mathematics, an open accounting ledger that is never reconciled.

It is for good reason that the opening scene of the movie takes place in a remote Eastern European shtetl, the setting for a Hassidic tale. We can look at this from a distance, but in its closing stages the story takes place in our world. On the surface, Larry is an enlightened individual. Nevertheless, as the movie progresses we discover that this enlightenment cannot overcome the basic human feeling that there are things beyond our understanding. The real Jewish climate is the one we encounter in the opening scene. The setting may change, but the Jew always was and still remains in the world of the dybbuk. In this sense the Jew always searches for "signs from the Real." These signs are found in Nature, and as the first rabbi tells Larry, all you need to do is to "learn" to see them. Fundamentally, although the first rabbi seems liberal, this demand to learn to see the signs is in fact the most brutal and destructive demand made on this so-called enlightened individual.

In the early stages of the movie Larry cannot conceive of the notion of a dybbuk, that is, of the possibility that there is something beyond the physical world. He cannot admit to himself that he believes in the existence of a dybbuk and that the dybbuk (the accounting ledger) is what controls him. Larry looks for answers, looks for causes. He wants to understand what he has done. He wants his guilt to be concrete. Indeed Larry is not capable of accepting the notion that something crazy and uncontrollable can change his life haphazardly—a dybbuk. Yet as the movie progresses, we are exposed to the monotheistic-religious-messianic-apocalyptic side of Larry's life, the condition in which "the primitive beliefs we have surmounted seem once more to be confirmed" (Freud 1959, p. 17).

Larry, just like us, the viewers, must face the fact that even though he thought he had overcome the world of superstitions, this world is still governing him (and us). Ultimately, the attempt to articulate a clear cause, to formulate guilt, turns Larry into Josef K. from Kafka's book *The Trial.* Yet Larry does not understand that:

> a man did not necessarily have to be charged with the actual offence of which he was guilty: if he had fair hair he could be charged with having black hair, yet still be sentenced to the punishment due for being fair-haired. (Solzhenitsyn 1968, p. 555)

The dybbuk is not the spirit of someone who has died that has entered the body of a living man. Rather, it is the very attempt to find causality. The dybbuk is the search for explanation. This is what scientists are guilty of. This is what Larry is guilty of.

It is important to stress that this movie is not merely a comedy or tragedy of errors. It is the story of the modern Job. Each of us can imagine ourselves in Larry's place. What appeared to be the promising road to success in the monotheistic Western world (home, family, and a regular job) turns into a one-way road ending in a jarring crash. In this situation it is almost impossible not to be tempted to think that what happens to us comes from God or from some divine entity. This is Larry's struggle and this is worthy of being our struggle as well, as individuals and as a society— the struggle against the tremendous temptation to see signs of God in everything. There are, however, no signs. Nature is indifferent. Larry is the contemporary Job, Job in an era devoid of God, Job because he has been tempted to fall into the trap of the world as described by Nietzsche—the world of never-ending accounts to be settled (Nietzsche 1964). God does not give us signs. The signs are the product of human thought, of our inability to "receive with simplicity everything that happens to you" (Rashi).

Larry looks for signs in order to explain his condition to himself. Even though he has not done anything, like all of us he cannot help but think that things happen to him because of something he did. This is the dybbuk, the attempt to find "signs." This search reaches its high point when the chair of the tenure committee (Arlen Finkle)—who, like many other characters in the movie, can be considered to exist only in Larry's head—tells Larry that the committee has received anonymous letters stating that Larry is morally corrupt. Larry tearfully tells him: "I am not an evil man." It later becomes apparent that Sy, his wife's lover, is the one who sent these letters. Even though the committee disregards the letters, Larry attributes major importance to them because he does not know in what way he has sinned, if indeed he has. A man needs a concrete accusation. We prefer being accused of something rather than being left in a state of uncertainty:

> Nothing in its history has been as important as the need for rational certainty. The West has sacrificed everything to this need: religion, happiness, hope— and, finally, its own life. (Houellebecq 2000, p. 221)

How is it That We Seek Answers and Do Not Find Them

The first rabbi Larry consults claims that Larry's sad situation stems from his lack of belief in God and from his failure to see God in everything that occurs in Nature. Yet as we saw earlier in the quote from Rashi, we should always take matters as they are. God is not involved in what goes on in our lives. God, as Camus took pains to emphasize more than once in his essay *The Myth of Sisyphus*, is always silent. Larry flounders in his own helplessness. The religious perspective within which he experiences life does not enable him to cope with his problems because, contrary to what he really needs, it nurtures and encourages that which promotes fear and foreboding and threat. The subject finds himself strangled by snakelike tentacles that will not let him go. Larry's sister does say that Jews have the depths of tradition that are supposed to help them at such moments. Yet throughout the movie, it becomes clear that this statement has no foundation in reality. In fact, the opposite is the case—tradition is responsible for his situation from the outset. Larry is captive to the neighborhood in which he lives, to the Jewish community, to his job, to mathematics. He is caught between the accounting ledger and Schrödinger's cat, between spine-tingling terror and the thought that he has the ability to influence what happens in his life and to take control. No one can give him answers, not even regarding the property line between him and his neighbor, for the question of borders is not a technical question but rather an essential matter that defines one's sense of self. A lawyer cannot find the answer to this question. Thus, the lawyer whom he consults about this matter collapses and dies. We are alone in this world. No lawyer can help us. Only Larry himself can find the answers to his questions, and no rabbi can (or should) help him. As we saw in the novel *The Trial,* the ultimate goal is to try the accused directly, without any mediators. Guilt is personal and the payment is personal as well.

During the movie, we learn more and more about Larry's solitude and isolation. He cannot find a common language with any other character. He tries to reach the supreme court of law, to reach Rabbi Marshak. Yet as Josef K. in *The Trial* was told, this is useless. It is impossible to meet with the judges of the supreme court. Ultimately Rabbi Marshak would not have been able to provide Larry with any answers. Indeed the judges of Josef K. read porno magazines and chased the female clerks down the halls of the courthouse.

FROM REALITY TO HALLUCINATION—LARRY AND ARTHUR

As the movie progresses, Larry becomes less and less able to distinguish reality from hallucination. It is not clear whether Larry slept with his sexy neighbor or whether this was merely his fantasy. Indeed, it is not even clear whether this neighbor exists beyond Larry's inner world. Larry does not know whether or not he went outside to the motel pool with his brother. He is forced to clarify this issue with Arthur during the night, though it is not even clear whether Arthur himself exists or is also merely a figment of Larry's imagination. Freud defines such a state as an uncanny climate—a situation in which psychological reality replaces material reality.

If we examine the relations between Larry and Arthur in depth, we discover that it is Arthur, not Larry, who is the true scientist. Arthur does not give up on the attempt to understand Nature. Thus Arthur represents the deepest layer inside every scientist and within Larry as well. Arthur attempts to solve the question of the essence of the universe and of existence by means of totally unfounded calculations and sketches that he calls the Mentaculus. The Mentaculus is a probability map of the universe, or alternatively a writ of accusation against God Himself, no more and no less. That being the case, Arthur and Larry resemble one another. They are both engaged in an attempt to solve the mysteries of humankind, yet in so doing they are dismissing God. In addition to the attempt to solve the essence of the universe, Arthur is addicted to poker and is convinced that he has succeeded in cracking the code (for winning poker) using mathematics—again the same mathematics. But the only math for the Jew is the simple math of Jewish trauma, in which the Jew always pays dearly for his thoughts and deeds. Hence in another one of Larry's dreams, Arthur is shot while he is attempting to cross over to Canada by water. Having said that, we must again take into consideration the possibility that Arthur and Larry are actually the same character and it is not at all clear whether they can be referred to separately. Arthur is the suppurating and disgusting side of Larry. (He spends his nights draining pus from a wound on his neck.) In this sense Arthur represents the most profound truth of Larry's life: Despite the mask of scientific rationalism, Larry's life is governed by terror and anxiety. This is also what Arthur attempts to drain off at night—the most basic Jewish anxiety. Arthur thus represents Larry's most primeval fears. This is also the reason that Larry fantasizes about and wishes for his brother's death.

Thus, just as Josef K. in Kafka's *The Trial* does not understand what he is guilty of until he dies "like a dog!" (Kafka 2006, p. 271), so too Larry does not understand what he has done to deserve all that has happened to him. He goes from rabbi to rabbi in an attempt to understand. Just like Josef K., Larry too seeks order in the world. He must understand what he has been accused of. He refuses to accept things as they really are. Just like Josef K., Larry too cannot understand what Reb Groshkover says in the opening scene of the movie: "One knows when one isn't wanted." Larry, like the good, obedient, and faithful Jew at the moment before destruction, does not manage to internalize this notion. This is no wonder, for even Reb Groshkover understands this only after Dora stabs him. This is apparently the very nature of every good Jew. Yet the truth is harsher: It is impossible to understand that you are not wanted because we do not understand anything about the world around us. Interestingly, Rabbi Marshak actually has managed to understand this notion. He therefore chooses to quote a line from the song "Somebody to Love" by the rock group Jefferson Airplane: "When the truth is found to be lies" (Jefferson Airplane 1967).

SY AND LARRY: TRANSITION TO THE HIDDEN LAYER

A critical moment in the movie occurs when Sy Ableman, Larry's wife's lover, is killed at exactly the same moment that Larry is involved in an automobile accident in a different place. At this point, we can think about Schrödinger's cat: you can live, you can die, the boundary between when you are dead and when you are alive is narrow and unclear. From the moment the accident takes place, it is impossible to distinguish between Sy Ableman and Larry. This is a situation in which:

> one possesses knowledge, feeling and experience in common with the other, identifies himself with another person, so that his self becomes confounded, or the foreign self is substituted for his own—in other words, by doubling, dividing and interchanging the self. (Freud 1959, p. 9)

Larry asks: "Is Hashem telling me that Sy Ableman is me?" If so, Sy enters Larry's life in order to awaken him. It is my contention that Sy never existed except in Larry's head. In effect, Sy can be defined as Larry's inner judge. This finds expression in the letters Sy writes to the tenure committee. Sy is Larry's inner voice, which knows that being granted tenure in the physical world is a total denial of God. Hence, Sy writes anonymous letters to the tenure committee as a last attempt to save Larry from himself. Sy is Larry's anxiety. As we saw earlier, Arthur is Larry's festering wound. It is Larry's same anxiety that writes to the tenure committee out of Larry's genuine desire not to enter into the scientific world that denies the existence of the dybbuk. In essence, what goes on at night is not that Arthur drains the pus from his wound but rather that Larry writes those letters while hiding in the bathroom. Larry is unconsciously convinced that writing those letters will drain the pus, cleanse his inner filth.

Larry wants to return home, to the Jewish dybbuk, much like Kafka was entranced by the Yiddish theater. Therefore he writes those letters. Instead of writing a writ of defense like the one Josef K. is asked to write, Larry, like every good Jew, chooses to write a writ of accusation.

Sy and Larry thus represent the two perceptions in the world of Larry's mind, and they cannot exist together in one body. One of them must disappear. Sy's death in the automobile accident is a symbolic death, or more accurately, a murder Larry has committed in his inner world in order to survive. The automobile accidents of Larry and Sy, which take place simultaneously, constitute Larry's attempt to kill the dybbuk, the irrational voice, and to regain serenity, to return to a world of certainty. As James stresses in his important book, *The Varieties of Religious Experience* (1902), this is the central ambition of the religious believer.

On the surface level, this double automobile accident brings Larry to the pinnacle of the confrontation between the "scientist" and the man living his life under the influence of the ever-present "accounting ledger." Yet this is no coincidence. Simply put, Sy never existed. Throughout the movie Sy is depicted as a nightmare in Larry's head. The accident releases the dybbuk, but Larry does not learn the lesson. He attempts to go on living as if nothing has happened, and therefore throughout the movie more and more disasters are visited upon Larry, including the phone call from his doctor and the tornado threatening his son.

Larry is Job—not because God is testing him, but because he is torn between the rational approach to life and the dybbuk. As the plot of the movie unravels, the veneer of rationality is peeled away. Larry does not seek advice from scientific theories whose practical importance in our lives is inconsequential. Instead he seeks out a rabbi, though even the rabbi apparently has no answer. Larry asks, "What does that mean! Everything that I thought was one way turns out to be another!" In this question, he refers to the tremendous gap between the rational world in which we attempt to live our lives and the hidden layers in our lives that do in fact govern us: "What is essential is invisible to the eye" (De Saint-Exupery 1971, p. 48). As in the case of Abraham, for Larry too it is the inner insanity that governs him.

Larry in Kafkaesque Terms

To understand Larry, we must examine his brother Arthur and Sy, his wife's lover. These two characters represent the dybbuk and anxiety. They represent the trauma weighs upon life in this era in the monotheistic Western world. Arthur represents the obsession to understand everything and to express it through mathematical formulas. This attempt in itself arouses anxiety because it stands in absolute contrast to belief in God and is liable to activate the cruel automatic mechanism described in Chapter 1, as for example, in the case of the Flood and of Sodom and Gomorrah. Arthur can only be Larry's nightmare, as well as the prime example of a scientist striving to understand everything and leaving nothing in the dark. Such an ambition leads to a Kafkaesque sense of impossible guilt. This provides a basis for assuming that Larry is the one who wrote the anonymous letters to the tenure committee. Thus, the writ of defense Larry attempts to formulate (his attempt to understand what he is actually guilty of) turns into a defense of God and a bill of indictment against Larry.

Sy is Larry's wife's lover. He is a devoutly religious Jew, just what Larry's wife wants. They convey the message to Larry that he should become a believer, someone who does not seek to undermine God. Similarly, the court wants Meursault to be guilty of something, just so he will feel guilt. Larry can investigate but he should not attempt to understand the whole picture. In particular, he must give up his passion for formulating the world in mathematical terms that do not leave room for belief in God. He must relinquish the scientist within him, and especially the attempt to understand. Like Arthur, Sy is a consequence of metaphysical and unbearable guilt.

Hence we can say that Larry is trapped in the Kafkaesque model of guilt. He attempts to implement eternal return by wandering from rabbi to rabbi. This wandering leads him nowhere. It is nothing more than motionless spinning, frozen motion, eternal return in a spiral world drawn into the black hole of the basic and primal anxiety—the Jewish dybbuk. As someone who represents life in the posttraumatic era, Larry has not advanced even a millimeter from the Eastern European village portrayed at the beginning of the movie. The circular motion in the movie revolves around a frozen village in Eastern Europe. The Jew is frozen in time, and even if the scenery has changed, the anxiety remains the same.

As we will see in the next section, despite our natural tendency to reject this model, the attempt to escape this cycle can culminate in a cruel character like Chigurh in the Coen brothers movie, *No Country for Old Men*.

No Country for Old Men: The New Era

Human behavior is predetermined in principle in almost all of its actions and offers few choices, of which fewer still are taken. (Houellebecq 2000, p. 71)

Larry attempts to find the reasons behind what happens in life. Yet he remains trapped within the Western-monotheistic worldview. The truth, or to put it more correctly, reality, is much crueler. Nature is indifferent and there is no room for talking about any system of causality, including moral causality. This is what Larry refuses to understand. The tenure committee seems to understand this for it disregards the accusations of immorality. Pure physics has no interest in ethical matters. This is what the sheriff's uncle, Ellis, tries to explain in the movie *No Country for Old Men*, another movie by the Coen brothers:

Whatcha got ain't nothin new. This country's hard on people, you can't stop what's coming, it ain't all waiting on you. That's vanity. (Coen and Coen 2007)

There is no need for God. What is important is the automated nature of things, the insanity revealed in *No Country for Old Men*. The embodiment of God in this era as already defined in the *Akeda* bursts forth in the character of Chigurh (acted by Javier Bardem). As we understand from Carson Wells, the bounty hunter who had been a colonel in the Vietnam War, Chigurh is a man of principles. It is impossible to do business with Chigurh. He is never held accountable, not for the shirt the boy gives him after his automobile accident at the end of the movie, not even when he comes to kill Llewelyn Moss's wife. He makes good on his promises. The deal Chigurh proposes to Llewelyn is fair: If Llewelyn returns the money to him, Chigurh will still kill him but his wife Carla Jean will be allowed to live. This is a proposition worthy of the biblical God. Chigurh's arbitrariness is the only and absolute form of equality. Sometimes certain people are saved (e.g., Thomas Thayer, the storekeeper at the gas station); sometimes they are not. Chigurh is so frightening to us because of his mechanical ways, which at their core are so fundamentally fair. Chigurh does not discriminate among those he wants to kill. He does not need any particular reasons. That is who he is: psychopathic and fair at the same time. To put it more precisely, absolute fairness is what turns Chigurh into a psychopath: "Death is the great leveler" (Houellebecq 2000, p. 106). The automated mechanism is what is most frightening. What turns Llewelyn Moss into a man who cannot survive in this country is the fact that he returned to bring water to one of the wounded. He had pangs of conscience and the price of that, we learn, is death. Thus we encounter the same problem over and over again. In this life humanity brings with it a death sentence. There is no place for humanity in our reality.

It is important to understand that Chigurh has no need to be wronged by someone in order for him to kill that person. He kills in the most random, impersonal way possible. Indeed, it is precisely this randomness that grants meaning to death. The only nature that must really be feared is human nature. In a horrifying way, the bloody trail Chigurh leaves behind him is identical to the bloody trail Kurtz leaves behind him in the movie *Apocalypse Now*. In the tough and intransigent country in which we live, only blood speaks. The only possible language is the language of killing—the mathematics of blood.

While this may seem strange, the most frightening thing about Chigurh is that he is a free man. There are "no illusions about the depths to which the human animal could sink when not constrained by law" (Houellebecq 2000, p. 37). Chigurh has no need to provide explanations—first and foremost he is free with respect to himself—and therefore he enjoys absolute freedom. This freedom, turns Chigurh into the most dangerous thing on the face of the earth.

Chigurh's freedom is unique, a form of Spinozian freedom stemming from understanding necessity and not from a pathetic belief in free will.

> Far removed from Christian notions of grace and redemption, unfamiliar with the concepts of freedom and compassion, Michel's worldview had grown pitiless and mechanical. (Houellebecq 2000, p. 75)

In *No Country for Old Men* we learn that the greatest form of guilt is to have a conscience. Llewelyn is guilty of returning to bring water to the wounded. He knew he would have to pay a high price for that. He assumed he might die. There was no value in his action. It was only a matter of conscience, and for having a conscience in this era we must pay a heavy price. This era has taken leave of humanity. We are entering a new era in which one must pay for attempting to be human. Indeed, in this era nothing is more worthless and more unnecessary than to be human.

If the role of Sy Ableman is to awaken Larry, if for Larry he symbolizes the hidden stratum beneath the image of the rational scientist, then the role of Chigurh is to awaken every man. Chigurh is indeed the hidden stratum, the unrevealed level, of the posttraumatic man. Chigurh symbolizes a more advanced stage than Larry. He represents humanity after the conflict. More than anything else, Chigurh shows us what the world looks like without the conflicts that have seized and gained control of Larry. Larry is a lost, impotent, and even pathetic character. Yet Chigurh also shows us that no matter how much we feel that Larry is pathetic, his wretchedness is preferable to the truly liberated alternative—Chigurh. Chigurh seems to be engaged neither in scientific mathematics nor in the mathematics of the accounting ledger. He simply understands his true place in Nature: He embodies pure and natural violence in an era scarred by a sense of impossible guilt. At the gas station, for example, Chigurh attempts to win over Thomas Thayer, the clerk in the store, to his way of thinking and living through a coin toss, similar to the coin toss used by the Joker in the *Batman* movies (Goyer and Nolan 2008). The coin represents cruel and yet fair arbitrariness. Chigurh tries to convince Thayer that by tossing a coin he can win everything, including his life, but Thomas the storekeeper does not understand this.

Chigurh represents the posttraumatic man who lives the posttrauma without attempting to cover it up. He never tries, not even once, to explain. He does not attempt to regret. He is God in the story of the *Akeda* and he represents the hidden and traumatic layers of being in the life of an individual. He represents the terrifying automated and mechanical nature of things. Yet unlike God, Chigurh has completely given up on humanity, thus turning him into a truly free man. (God ultimately saves Isaac, even if only as a joke.) Chigurh is the picture of the day after the absolute *Akeda*, the world as it is after release from the unbearable feelings of guilt. Chigurh portrays the new era. Indeed more than anything, Chigurh is the person who understands that there is no accounting ledger and that any attempt to explain the workings of Nature by means of mathematical formulas is doomed to failure. This knowledge turns Chigurh into the freest individual on earth and thus also makes him immortal. More than any other character, Chigurh is the true superhero. In effect, he is Nietzsche's superman. He is someone who knows that there is no meaning to anything. That's just the way it is. This is the lesson Larry does not manage to learn. Larry's trauma, and that of any individual who is torn between the accounting ledger and science, has given birth to the new man, to Chigurh. The impossible conflict that Larry faces has begotten a person devoid of feelings, devoid of the need for a human environment, a person who acts in the name of the principle of the equality of death. Larry represents absolute impotence, the inability to decide between the different worlds. Chigurh represents the next stage—a person who has no compunctions about making decisions and carrying them out immediately. To ensure a lack of bias and absolute truth, Chigurh renounces the human dimension, turning himself into someone who is content with his lot and at the same time a man who is cruel to the extreme.

Chigurh shows no interest in social judgment. He does not take into account what society will think. He does not fear superstitions. He does not engage in fantasies, justifications, and moral preachings. He does not want to change the world. He simply lives the current moment. He lives his life without any question marks. Indeed, even Nietzsche could not have described his superman more accurately. Chigurh is the embodiment of freedom. Yet it recurringly becomes apparent that this state of freedom is much more dangerous than the condition of impotence to which monotheistic society has led us. Chigurh comes to remind us that if we despair of Larry's condition there is an alternative, but it is light years away from what we imagined, what we told ourselves it would be. An individual devoid of superstitions, devoid of fears, is in effect not a human being. And Chigurh is indeed not human. In a certain sense he is the perfect scientist for he has totally renounced the subjective dimension. He has totally adopted God's approach to this life. Black laughter. A never-ending saga. Chigurh's negotiations with Llewelyn Moss, who found that cursed suitcase, are identical to Abraham's negotiations with God. Yet Chigurh is fairer in his dealings than God. He is the metamorphosis of God's game of life with Abraham. Chigurh is no more than the other side of the coin—on one side is Larry, on the other side Chigurh.

When we despair of Larry, we must always remember that the alternative is Chigurh—a man with no hidden, below-the-surface, unrevealed level of being that governs him, a man with no inhibitions, no unattainable fantasies, no nightmares, no fears. Thus it becomes crystal clear that a truly free individual is the most frightening thing on this earth.

In order to understand what makes Chigurh so free and so dangerous, we must understand characters like Meursault. Chigurh is clearly the metamorphosis of Meursault. We must also understand the characters that developed from Meursault, such as Travis from the movie *Taxi Driver* and Kurtz from *Apocalypse Now*. The next chapter provides an in-depth examination of posttraumatic characters from the Vietnam War and its aftermath.

Unbridled independence is the consequence of the attempt to cope with profound and ongoing trauma. More precisely, in the Vietnam jungles the soldiers began to understand that they represented the generation of the sons and that they were not sacrificed against their own will, but that they have accepted their fate with enthusiasm. They also understood that after the *Akeda*, they, in turn, will be the ones doing the binding. The way to become liberated is to break down the *Akeda* model completely, to reject the sense of metaphysical guilt absolutely and to attempt to shatter the obsessive cycle of eternal return that motivates the repetition compulsion.

Before we can understand this process, we must see and perhaps even understand its outcome. None other than Chigurh is the perfect outcome of this process. Hence, we must understand that the character freed of society's chains is first and foremost a psychotic character. Perhaps, then, the impotent Larry—the metamorphosis of Clamence—is preferable.

CHAPTER 4

The Crisis of Manhood

TAXI DRIVER—TRAVIS

Travis (acted by Robert De Niro), the soldier who has returned home from the Vietnam War, who is clearly traumatized[1] and apparently was held captive as well, is steeped in violence. Travis is a solitary individual without a father, without even a friend in the world, lacking all ability to maintain intimate relations. At least on the surface level of meaning, Travis is the figure that the United States chooses to define as its new hero. Indeed, he becomes a hero after his insane/messianic journey of revenge. He is the one who will rid New York City of its filth. In effect, Travis, a typical product of American culture, is interested in just shedding a bit of blood in order to feel at home once again. Yet Travis is not interested in cleansing and purifying the city of its filth. Rather, he is a psychopathic killer who wants to maintain his own inner contamination and decay and to preserve his sense of alienation, voyeurism, disparateness, distorted sexuality, and violence (Morag 2009).

Travis does in fact attempt to resuscitate his body and restore his sense of self-efficacy. Yet he does not do this in order to recover his own self,

---

This chapter based upon the chapter: Ataria, Y. (2016). The Crisis of Manhood. In Y. Ataria, D. Gurevitz, H. Pedaya, & Y. Neria (Eds.), *Interdisciplinary Handbook of Trauma and Culture* (pp. 267–278). Springer.

but rather as part of a chronicle of psychopathology, indeed as part of a process of fixating upon the pathology. Travis does everything he can to sanctify, to enhance, to externalize, and mainly to stabilize the unconscious layers: the violence, alienation, messianism, distorted sexuality, and self-abhorrence, all of this being characteristic of an era lacking a God and lacking a father figure.[2] When Travis sets out on his crazed violent journey, he seemingly removes his civilized masks and decks himself out like a Mohawk Indian in order to return to a more primeval character, one that is pre-reflective and pre-Western. Travis wants to be reborn, not for the sake of inner purification but rather to preserve the horror and the trauma he has known. Travis does not "choose" to set out on a journey of killing, just as Kafka did not choose to write. He has no choice but to act as he does:

> The tremendous world I have inside my head. But how [to] free myself and free it without being torn to pieces. And a thousand times rather be torn to pieces than retain it in me or bury it. That, indeed, is why I am here, that is quite clear to me. (Kafka 1949, p. 288)

Travis is a captive of compulsive return. What, then, motivates him? His deeds cannot be viewed in terms of obsessive repetition of the *Akeda*. That is, while the killing spree in which he ostensibly saves the child prostitute Iris (acted by Jodie Foster) is not a reenactment of the *Akeda*, Travis can be likened to Isaac on the day after the *Akeda*. The generation of the fathers sent Travis to fight an unnecessary war in Vietnam. Like Isaac, he remained alive. Like Isaac, trauma was engraved and burned into his body, and he is ruled by this trauma.

Travis can also be thought of as the third model for the infinite sense of guilt, perhaps because of what he saw and what he did to little girls during his military service in Vietnam. Perhaps in his attempt to rid himself of that sense of guilt, he is pushed to save an innocent character—Iris—though their conversation at breakfast makes it clear that she did not really want to be saved.

There appears to be another way to understand Travis. In *The Fall*, Camus' main criticism of Clamence is directed at Clamence's indifference to the fate of the other. We operate on the baseless assumption that if we are there for the other, we will be freed. Yet from the perspective of the posttraumatic figure, Travis demonstrates what it really means to be there for the other. Travis seems to agree to the presidential candidate's request that he assume responsibility for cleansing New York City of the filth that has flooded it. Yet in Travis's demolished world, assuming responsibility is not what we wish or hope for him. While the posttraumatic figure does respond to the other, this response can only be in one possible style—violence ending in murder and suicide. Thus, Travis demonstrates the potential implications of breaking Clamence's hopeless cycle of eternal return—cyclical motion in a regression to the black hole of trauma, ultimately leading to apocalyptic catastrophe.

THE DEER HUNTER—MICHAEL

The dialogue between Travis (*Taxi Driver*) and Michael (Mike) Vronsky of *The Deer Hunter* is so straightforward that it cannot be ignored, and not only because these two characters are played by the same actor (Robert De Niro). While Travis wants to become a hunter, Michael is a hunter by his very nature. Sometimes it seems that Travis is Michael in another incarnation, or that he is a fantasy in Michael's mind. Yet the difference between Travis and Michael is fundamental. Michael understands that the model of the father has collapsed and attempts to save the model of the brother, though this does not succeed with Nick (Nikanor "Nick" Chevotarevich, acted by Christopher Walken), his old friend from back home who has become his brother-in-arms as well. Mike cannot go on with the game, cannot return to relations with a woman, to his affair with Nick's girlfriend Linda (acted by Meryl Streep). Nick himself is incapable of speaking to Linda, for "the surest of stubborn silences is not to hold one's tongue but to talk" (Kierkegaard inside Camus 1975, p. 19). He phones her from Vietnam but finds he is incapable of speaking. He never even gets past the telephone operator. He no longer wants to talk to her. He knows that he belongs in the insane asylum with Steve, the third friend, who was taken captive by the Vietcong. Returning to reality is impossible. Therefore, Nick prefers to maintain his silence. This silence is reflected in the life of Michael (De Niro) when he fails to have intimate relations with Linda. Indeed, Nick and Michael are actually the same person living in two parallel time dimensions, a condition that is quite typical of the posttraumatic experience in which the frozen element of time typifies the posttraumatic condition (Terr 1984). It is important to understand that from the perspective of the posttraumatic man, the woman is not attainable; she is situated beyond the trauma, beyond the frozen time dimension of the traumatic subject.

Michael allegedly decides to return to Vietnam in order to release himself from the dybbuk, to return to his genuine home, to flee the captivity of the counterfeit homeland, or, in the words of Captain Willard from *Apocalypse Now:* "When I was here I wanted to be there. When I was there, all I could think of was getting back into the jungle." Michael travels to save Nick in an attempt to save himself. He must keep his promise to Nick to safeguard him and take him home. His journey is a voyage into his own inner world. He does not want to relinquish the world, to give up on the other. He knows that only by rescuing Nick will he manage to save his own life. Yet the events that ensue are predictable, and on a deeper level he cannot save Nick. Indeed, he must destroy Nick. Nick represents Michael's trauma, his scar. Nick is in fact Michael's inner world. Michael knows that in order to survive he must murder the inner voice, that is, Nick. (As we will see later on, the dominant trait of Kurtz in *Apocalypse Now* is his voice.) This is in fact a zero-sum game. Thus, by definition the posttraumatic condition is the zero-sum game one plays with oneself—the mind and the body becomes enemies. In the posttraumatic condition, the mind and the body cannot continue to coexist. Hence, one of them must cease to exist.

That being the case, what begins as a game turns into horrifying reality. Because Michael understands this, he cannot tolerate Stan (one of their buddies who did not go to Vietnam) playing with a pistol. In one of the most important scenes in the movie, Stan threatens to shoot Axel (another buddy who did not go to Vietnam). Michael grabs the gun, puts a bullet into the chamber and recreates the game of Russian roulette that he, Steve, and Nick played while they were in captivity, uttering one of the movie's most important lines: "This is this, this isn't something else." Here it seems that replaying the game of Russian roulette has become an obsession for Michael as well. That is, compulsive repetition turns into dominant reality. In this situation Michael is close to choosing his inner world over the world outside, and if he were to do so, his fate would be identical to that of Nick. Michael also recreates the threat posed to him by Stan, making it clear to the viewers, and mainly to himself, how games can turn into an impossible reality. This is the moment at which Michael understands that the only way to save Nick is to play yet another round of Russian roulette. In order to recover, the posttraumatic individual must play the game out to the end, just like Abraham played out the game with God.

Michael is motivated by a sense of unbearable guilt. He promises Nick that he will bring him home, a promise he makes while he is naked and back-to-back with Nick. Interestingly, during the original Russian roulette game they are face to face. Yet even though Mike rescues Nick from captivity while being forced to play Russian roulette with three bullets in the gun, he does not bring Nick home. He pairs up with Linda, Nick's fiancée, knowing that even if he has saved Nick physically, Nick's soul is buried in Vietnam, as is Michael's own soul as well.

After Nick and Michael are rescued, they meet at a Russian roulette table in Saigon, where Nick seems to lose his mind. Out of a sense of obsessive repetition, Nick takes over a game between two locals and attempts to shoot the local player and himself, but he fails. In both cases the gun does not fire because the chamber is empty. Michael chases Nick, but Nick gets away. At this moment, the two characters seem to separate. One character (Nick) stays where he is, while the other (Michael) ostensibly moves forward. Thus, even if Michael gains Nick's physical release from captivity, he does not save Nick's soul. Nick obsessively continues to reenact his captivity, remaining captive in the deepest sense of the word.

APOCALYPSE NOW—CAPTAIN WILLARD

On one level, the voyage of Captain Benjamin L. Willard (acted by Martin Sheen) is a journey through American society as rerresented by Captain Willard's crew. On another level, it is a journey to the depths of the American ideal represented by Colonel Walter E. Kurtz (acted by Marlon Brando), the father who has gone insane, the man who "knows what is good and, despite himself, does evil" (Camus 1962a, p. 249). Ultimately Captain Willard must murder the myth. Indeed, according to Freud, the road to personal release passes through the murder of the father. Yet paradoxically Willard does not do this because he wants to—"Kurtz was turning from a target into a goal"—but rather because this is what Kurtz wants him to do—"Everyone wanted me to do it, him most of all." It is interesting to discover in the movie that Captain Willard understands the true nature of Marlow's task in the book *The Heart of Darkness* (Conrad 1990), upon which the movie was based. Kurtz wants to be murdered. He does not want to recover—indeed he rejects the very notion of recovery. He is not interested in indisputable facts and he certainly does not want to return "home" as a saint (like Travis). He is a graduate of the infinite games played by Michael (*The Deer Hunter*) and he understands that leaving the jungle will bring him back, just like Captain Willard, to the jaws of the dybbuk, to the trauma, to the recurring, infinite, and uncontrollable game. Kurtz knows that there is no place to return to and no point in returning: "Droll thing life is—that mysterious arrangement of merciless logic for a futile purpose" (Conrad 1990, p. 65).

Kurtz is not a violent sadist by nature. His uncontrolled outburst of violence stems from his exaggerated humanity and compassion, from his ability to see the other in all of existence. Hence, he can say the following to Captain Willard:

> I've seen horrors, horrors that you've seen. But you have no right to call me a murderer. You have a right to kill me. You have a right to do that, but you have no right to judge me. It's impossible for words to describe what is necessary to those who do not know what horror means.

In Captain Willard's eyes, Kurtz is a saint, or even perhaps a martyr or a prophet, because Kurtz has not ceased to be an ideal. In choosing to die at the hands of a fellow soldier—one who served together with him in the Green Beret Special Forces and who is like a son and a brother to him—Kurtz symbolizes the new God. He is the genuine Superman, saturated in trauma and in violence stemming from the other, from a perfect vision of the other within the self. Kurtz deals with the *Akeda*. But no less than that he also deals with the story of Cain and Abel in that he attempts, in his own twisted way, to make amends while wondering "What cry would ever trouble them?" (Camus 1962a, p. 243).

Alternatively, if we want to claim that Kurtz preserves the model of Cain and Abel, we must then say that Abel yearns for death, thus shedding new light on Judeo-Christian passive/aggressive relations. Kurtz looks at the other and discovers the new God of anarchy within himself. In his life and in his death, Kurtz is in control of his fate, of nature. He does not judge himself according to Western values. He does not accept his guilt like Meursault in *The Stranger*, and in the overt layer of meaning he is far from the Kafkaesque characters. He does not sink into himself like Clamence in *The Fall*. He is not convinced that he has a home on the faraway white continent. He is submerged in this very moment, in the present. He returns to his deeper roots and discovers the true ideal that accompanies the American narrative: "The horror! The horror!"

Kurtz attempts to break the model of the first *Akeda* by means of a contradictory *Akeda*. He wants to be the initiator of his own binding and to force Captain Willard to murder him without renouncing himself as the father image—as the new god. In addition, his goal is to smash the third model of the sense of guilt. He is absolutely convinced that he cannot be blamed for anything. He totally rejects external judgment by someone who was never inside. As noted, Freud (1950) discussed the murder of the father and the creation of a community of sons who are consequently overcome by a sense of guilt. Since Kurtz in effect leads Captain Willard to murder him, he attempts to abolish the sense of unbearable guilt over the murder of the father. This is a reconstruction of the historical murder as an act of repair and working through and not as the result of compulsive repetition.

Kurtz understands that he has become a god. At the same time, he knows that he must refuse to be a god because in his position as a god he will be a captive of repetition compulsion that will ultimately end in murder and destruction. He knows that as a god he will not be able to avoid eternal return. Trauma will govern him, and he will repeatedly reconstruct that which he opposed. He knows that if he remains alive, eventually he will bind. Like in the case of God, matters are not under his control. Only the end of his existence can release him, and it is to this end that he recruits Captain Willard. There is an attempt here to break all three cycles at once, to save Captain Willard, and to charge him with the real task: to understand and execute the message and then to pass it on, mainly to Kurtz's son. Thus, Kurtz can be seen as the God of Abraham who, a moment before the *Akeda,* understands the potential repercussions of his acts on humankind as a whole. Therefore, he decides to commit suicide and in so doing bequeaths us a directive for a new history.

When Captain Willard leaves the temple after having murdered Kurtz, in one hand he holds a knife and in the other a book. When everyone bows down to him, he throws down the knife and refuses to become a god. Like Kurtz, he understands the implications. He keeps the book and brings it to Kurtz's son, to Isaac, to explain why his insane father had to die, why we must get rid of the father to create a new history. This explanation is meant to prevent an additional *Akeda* from occurring out of absence. As noted, the son grew up without a father but only with an impossible myth of his father, and this myth is more than sufficient to cause a sacrifice to be made. Captain Willard was sent to the son, perhaps to serve as an alternative father or perhaps simply to explain and prevent the son from continuing the *Akeda* cycle because he lacked a father figure. Hence, this is an attempt to break the three cycles, including the cycle of eternal return. Kurtz wants to start history anew. In the next chapters, we will see that even this step may have grave repercussions.

The Posttraumatic Figure: Travis, Michael, and Captain Willard

This chapter has attempted to describe the posttraumatic male figure. We encountered several aspects of this figure, each expressing a different attribute of the posttraumatic hero—the son that was sacrificed and who has retuned to what was once home but is now a cold and hostile place. Travis (*Taxi Driver*) represents the eternal cycle of trauma as compulsive repetition, which does not offer release but rather reconstructs the trauma. Travis' response to the other emerges from his apocalyptic world, and the result is a massacre. In contrast, Michael (*The Deer Hunter*) is submerged in a sense of infinite guilt. Even though he tries to return to his former sane life, he too is condemned to compulsive repetition of the traumatic moment in an attempt to save his friend Nick (perhaps the other side of himself) who remained at the site of the trauma. Indeed, Travis can be seen as the metamorphosis of Michael, who has returned home—that is, to the place that once was home. Both of these characters are imprisoned in their chaotic apocalyptic world.

The third movie, *Apocalypse Now*, also features a dual character: Kurtz and Captain Willard. Kurtz attempts to shatter the model of the *Akeda* and the model of guilt. He understands that the posttraumatic figure's perennial return is an obsessive reproduction of the traumatic moment. Hence, he attempts to break the cycle of return and to restart history through Captain Willard. He forces Willard to murder him, perhaps as the beginning of a possible solution.

The next chapter examines whether Kurtz's attempt to shatter the model of the *Akeda* is a good solution or whether it has graver repercussions.

NOTES

1. In a conversation with the manager of the taxi stand, he demonstrates signs of posttrauma. His use of pills also supports this assumption.
2. An important aspect in understanding the lack of a father figure is Travis's encounter with the presidential candidate in the taxi. This conversation underlines for Travis that there really is no one that can be depended on to clean the city of its filth.

CHAPTER 5

The New God of Anarchy

The Binding of Isaac

Sarah laughed, Abraham understood, God did not, and since then the relations have been clear: Out of total insanity, the father binds his son, and the mother remains silent and thus cooperates with the father and his craziness in an extremely bizarre way. Insanity totally dominates our lives. The son is an orphan even while his parents are still alive. Perhaps he himself merely longs for death, and his father has done his bidding. This is the way it is from generation to generation. Relationships are forced upon us. You love someone simply in order to sacrifice him out of an internal struggle, a dybbuk. This disease that has been discussed so much, perhaps even too much, does not loosen its grip—it remains relevant. For some time now this has not been merely a matter of guilt as posited by Jaspers (2001). It is not merely a Christian or Jewish question, and no clear, unambiguous beginning or end point can be designated. Each of us is Isaac and also Abraham, but each of us is also and always Sarah—the one who understood God as a psychotic figure better than anyone else. The inner struggle creates the purest form of insanity, which leads to automatic outbursts that cannot be controlled, as in the case of Sodom.

Today we know that Kafka himself wrote the short story "In the Penal Colony" and we are relieved to learn that "one of us" (someone of flesh and blood) so accurately described the reality in which we live. Yet this is not the case with respect to the story of the *Akeda*. One could

© The Author(s) 2017
Y. Ataria, *The Structural Trauma of Western Culture*,
DOI 10.1007/978-3-319-53228-8_5

surmise that in another incarnation Kafka wrote the *Akeda*. Yet Kafka undoubtedly would not have allowed Isaac to remain alive in this story. Precisely here it seems that we are the butt of the joke—that the great parody is always at our expense. Leaving Isaac alive is worse than K.'s death like a dog in *The Trial*. The biblical author, however, is much crueler than Kafka. He lets Isaac live, and hence a culture that is absolutely traumatic is unleashed on the world: on Abraham for his willingness to butcher his son in order to take his revenge on God, on Isaac as the one who is bound for sacrifice, and on his mother who said nothing. (Not to mention Hagar, and her son, Ishmael, who was banished merely for chuckling.) Sarah, the mother, disappeared and has yet to return because we all know where inappropriate laughter can lead. She could have stopped Abraham from binding Isaac. The fact that Isaac remained alive enabled, in fact forced—as if by a dybbuk—the generation of the fathers to bind the generation of the sons over and over again.

Kurtz and Tyler Durden both understand, each in his own way, that there is only one way to be released from the burden of this difficult reality: to kill the father and all that he symbolizes. To use Freud's (1939) words: "A hero is a man who stands up manfully against his father and in the end victoriously overcomes him" (p. 18).

APOCALYPSE NOW—KURTZ

Kurtz understands very well that the father binds his son without having any real choice in the matter. It is the father's inner dybbuk that leads him to sacrifice his son. Correspondingly, Kurtz no longer recognizes the system of values created by the white/Western/Christian world. He is not willing to be judged. He has no problem dying so long as he is put to death by a man that understands that the ethical system according to which we live has no validity. Perhaps it would be more accurate to say that Kurtz yearns to die but he is not willing to die at the hands of hypocrites who in the morning lecture on justice and morality and at night rape and plunder, who speak in terms of justice and act by dropping napalm bombs, which is the smell of victory.

It is clear that Kurtz no longer has a place in this life and in dying he wants to be released. For once he wants to choose. Kurtz understands that in the existing system "man's greatest achievements were based on murder" (Houellebecq 2000, p. 208). He is able to choose his own death, as part of an idolatrous rather than a monotheistic setting, a system in which guilt is separate from redemption. More profound observation reveals that not only does Kurtz release himself. Thus, he also releases Captain Willard. From Kurtz's point of view, there is only one way to achieve release, and that is by binding his father according to the Freudian model. Kurtz does this in the same way in which the Vietnam War is being conducted. He does this when, like Abraham with God, he enters into a head-to-head confrontation with the country that sent him to battle for "just causes." The impossible paradox is that we always believe that just causes require sacrifices. This is precisely the model at the basis of the experience of disaster in which we live. Kurtz received an assignment and demonstrated to his metaphysical fathers the meaning of sticking to these objectives at all costs. He managed to meet every objective placed before him. He did so without a mask, which he stressed by painting his face as if to say "this is who I really am." Kurtz follows in Abraham's footsteps. He takes matters to their bitter end just to prove to the other side, to God, that words spoken and decisions made in air-conditioned rooms while drinking a glass of red wine, like at the Wannsee Conference, have repercussions.

Kurtz is obligated to humanity, not to God, obligated forever, and thus he allows Captain Willard to murder him. It would be more accurate to state that because he is obligated to humanity he demands that Captain Willard murder him in order to release Captain Willard as well. Kurtz is the "first man" and at the same time the "rebellious man." For this reason, he demands that Captain Willard kill him only after Willard himself has undergone a process of sobering and release—a process enabling him "to learn to live and to die, and, in order to be a man, to refuse to be a God" (Camus 1962a, p. 245). Release always comes from inner insanity. Kurtz knows he must die, for "Lucifer also has died with God" (Camus 1962a, p. 264). Kurtz has internalized that he himself, by his very nature, constitutes the lesson of Western monotheistic culture. He sacrifices himself out of deep metaphysical insights. He is totally rational. He knows that the system, by its nature and its methods, has gone insane. It is important to stress that Kurtz is not a product of the system in the way that Private Leonard Lawrence (nicknamed Gomer Pyle) in the movie *Full Metal Jacket* (Kubrick and Harlan 1987) is a product of the system. Kurtz understands the system very well, indeed better than it understands itself. He understands the system in the way that Abraham understands God, or to be more precise, as Sarah understands God. For that reason he places himself in a position of changing the system from within in the most radical way possible. Kurtz understands that reports like those he himself had written in the past will not help. Just like God, the system, in order to change, needs blood, lots of blood:

> In ancient times the blood of murder at least produced a religious horror and in this way sanctified the value of life. The real condemnation of the period we live in is, on the contrary, that it leads us to think that it is not bloodthirsty enough. Blood is no longer visible; it does not bespatter the faces of our pharisees visibly enough. (Camus 1962a, pp. 243–244)

This is exactly what Kurtz intends to supply us with. Every man who reaches Kurtz on his journey will discover along the way the extent to which the system has become faulty, has gone crazy. For Kurtz represents the collapse of the system. This is his goal—to reveal the absurdity of the system.

Thus, only when the individual who has come to kill Kurtz comes from a place of total refusal to be part of that automatic-mechanical-destructive system will Kurtz be willing to die at the hand of this individual. This *Akeda,* this self-sacrifice carried out by your son who is at the same time your brother and who also understands the collapse of the overall system, is the height of rebellion, because as Kurtz sees it, this *Akeda* releases both the binder and the one who is bound, thus setting a new starting point for human history.

Kurtz's vision is accurate. The posttraumatic individual is a cultural product. Thus he has forgotten how to speak using words and can only conduct himself in the system by means of games of death and killing, a system that can only speak in terms of bloodletting and the dead. Kurtz chooses to kill in the way that he does so that there will be no doubt. He knows (following the mass suicide of the Sicarii rebels at the Masada fortress) that fresh blood is the best way to talk to, and to arouse God. Thus he attempts to beget a superman. Hence, in Kurtz's view, Captain Willard has been released from the chains of the system because Willard kills Kurtz out of abhorrence for the system and out of an understanding of its implications. On his journey Willard comes to understand that the generation of the fathers has betrayed him, and upon arrival at his destination, he is charged with the task of killing Abraham himself. Captain Willard, who in essence is the incarnation of Isaac, kills Abraham at the behest of Abraham (Kurtz). Thus Kurtz tries to save himself in his death as well as to atone for Abraham's deeds. Kurtz's aim is to restart history all over again. He attempts to save one soul, the soul of his son who is also his brother: Captain Willard. In this, he seeks to unify (and integrate) the model of Cain and Abel. With the model of the father who sacrifices his son, and then he tries to dismantle both these models.

FIGHT CLUB—TYLER DURDEN

The movie *Fight Club* (1999) is an attempt to show how it is that insanity has become the only way to cope with what Marcuse (1964) refers to as the One-dimensional man. Insanity and the one-dimensional man are two sides of the same coin. While the one-dimensional man represents the set of values that collapsed with the defeat of the white male, insanity represents the new story that has emerged out of the void.

The author of *Fight Club* chooses to show us the conflict by means of the dialogue between the unnamed protagonist of the film (acted by Edward Norton) and Tyler Durden (acted by Brad Pitt), his alter ego. Like a prisoner in a concentration camp the protagonist remains unnamed, and the only clue to his name is in sentences like "I am Jack's cold sweat." Durden says:

> The things you own end up owning you... You're not your job. You're not how much money you have in the bank. You're not the car you drive. You're not the contents of your wallet. You're not your fucking khakis. You're the all-singing, all-dancing crap of the world... It's only after we've lost everything that we're free to do anything. . . .

Kurtz could likely have said the same thing: "Have you ever considered any real freedoms? Freedoms from the opinion of others...even the opinions of yourself?" Tyler Durden makes us confront that fact that even if we have not "murdered God,"

Our fathers were our models for God. If our fathers bailed, what does that tell you about God? . . . You have to consider the possibility that God does not like you. He never wanted you. In all probability, he hates you. This is not the worst thing that can happen . . . We don't need him! . . . Fuck damnation, man! Fuck redemption! We're God's unwanted children.

Tyler exposes our one-dimensional and one-use reality. As the hero of the film (Norton) says: "Tyler, you are by far the most interesting single-serving friend I've ever met."

Insanity grows from within. It stems from the alienated and hollow existence. Indeed, Foucault (1965) states that there is insanity in all of us. Similarly, the hero of *Fight Club* says: "It was on the tip of everyone's tongue. Tyler and I just gave it a name." Indeed, on the journey into the horror of Vietnam, insanity is found in each of us. This cannot be denied—it is a result of living in the gray area in which each one of us can become the prey or the predator—or both (Agamben 1998; Levi 1959). The insane person states the truth: God, even if He exists, hates us. The alternatives we have created, the pornography and the shopping channels, are nothing but a choice of emptiness. We have simply forgotten what Sarah has always known—life is a form of black humor. Life has been planned in order to wreak havoc on everything that is important and to leave nothing of us behind. Even before we die we have already been turned into dust.

This being the case, in the beginning Tyler Durden constitutes the model of ultimate release. He responds to the cries of a woman attempting to commit suicide (Marla), and in responding to the distress of another he ostensibly solves the problem put forth by Camus in *The Fall*. Yet the problem is more serious. Tyler (Pitt) is the other side of the hero of the movie, someone who is at least partially insane. Despite the sense that Tyler is a model for life and for salvation, he is not real. The one who responds to the woman's cries for help is not a man who is levelheaded in his thinking but rather insane.

Like Kurtz, Tyler Durden wants to grant the world new hope. The hero of the movie, the narrator, ultimately does not want to destroy the world if the price is taking human lives. When Tyler erases the names of the members of the cult (the hero of the movie has no name while the crazy one does), the nameless hero of the film shouts out the name "Bob" after Bob has been shot. The duplications are inspired by Kafka's story, "In the Penal Colony": the exchange of roles between victim and accuser, the self-flagellation of the hero of the movie, the perpetrator who now becomes the one who is later sentenced—he is the judge, the prosecutor, and the mourner. Ultimately insanity becomes automatic (i.e., with its source in the divine) and thus gains control over our lives.

The hero of *Fight Club*, a member of a generation that grew up with posttraumatic fathers (his father abandoned him when he was six) and that served in the Vietnam War, tries to revive his brother-in-arms. In doing so he discovers that this brother-in-arms, captive and shell-shocked, does not want to return to the existing system (like Nick). He wants to destroy it and begin again. In a certain sense this is the only option for him and for the posttraumatic survivor. The posttraumatic man in the postmodern era understands that he must respond to the other, yet this response is not according to the model of Levinas. To respond to the other, to the stranger within yourself, is to return to your body; to a pre-reflective condition. To go back to being an animal. This is the way to dismantle the murderous traumatic mechanism.

To be a "rebellious individual" is first and foremost to rebel against yourself. To help the other means to help him discover the animal within him, the murderer within himself, the insanity within him—to awaken him from the coma of consumerism. Tyler understands this and thus makes the following statement:

All the ways you wish you could be, that's me. I look like you wanna look, I fuck like you wanna fuck, I am smart, capable, and most importantly, I am free in all the ways that you are not.

Tyler represents a state of mind according to which "it's only after we've lost everything that we're free to do anything."

At the end of the movie we understand that Tyler is the observer and the new God of anarchy. The protagonist of the movie, an ostensibly sane character, is a Don Quixote battling today's windmills: the credit card companies, the undisputed masters who are stronger than God and reason—the ones who determine the truth. We should remember that Don Quixote dies when he sees and recognizes reality as it is, but Tyler Durden offers us an alternative—one that is violent and whose price is human life. In this sense the difference between Tyler Durden and Franz Fanon (1968) becomes blurred, and the question is whether we are really interested in yet another violent revolution, for ultimately Tyler Durden does not oppose murder. Rather the opposite is true—he encourages it.

On another level we learn from the story of Tyler Durden how big and beautiful ideas ultimately lead to uncontrollable and uncontrolled acts of murder, like God's outburst in the story of Sodom. In view of the dominant posttraumatic experience, the problem is that it is not certain whether there is another choice, a nonviolent path for the posttraumatic individual to follow.

There is a great deal of similarity between Meursault (*The Stranger*) and Tyler Durden (*Fight Club*). They both experience Kafkaesque emptiness. They both conduct their lives on the margins of society. They both are fed up with one-dimensionality and with hypocrisy. They both are totally authentic. Ultimately they both attempt to remove the mask, a crime whose punishment is death. Hence they both must be killed. Society has no other way of containing them. Yet can the machine in the story "In The Penal Colony" decide what word to carve on their bodies?—"courage," "daring," "innocence," "authenticity," or perhaps "misery" or simply "Mom." What should be carved on Kurtz, when all he can say is "the horror, the horror"? The machine does not know what to carve. Anarchy controls everything.

CURSED DUALITY: SELF-ANNIHILATION AS DYBBUK

The protagonist of the movie *Fight Club* is nameless. He is a man who slowly stops knowing when he is asleep and when he is awake, when he is himself and when he is Tyler, when he beats up on himself and when he is being beaten up by others, when he is alive and when he is dead, when he is the victim, and when he is the victimizer. He is exactly like someone who has undergone a trauma. After experiencing trauma, an individual lives in two separate and distinct dimensions that clash with one another. One of the characters always moves along the path of murderer and the other along that of victim, though it is never clear "which is which and who is who" (Pink Floyd 1973). As I claimed, this is the case with Captain Willard and Kurtz in *Apocalypse Now*, who are actually the same character. This is also the case with Michael and Nick in *The Deer Hunter*. That same eternal sense of sin binds the monotheistic individual, the one who constantly battles the accounting ledger, who must always be his own judge and must examine himself constantly. Thus we are always accompanied by the same judge, the same hangman, the same observer (the mirror in the opening scene of *Taxi Driver*). This incongruity erupts during trauma. Indeed trauma is the result of overdeveloped consciousness. That is, trauma is the illness of consciousness. In the traumatic condition we constantly examine life from afar and therefore never live life to the fullest. Absolute trauma contains only observation, without any point of reference, without an observer (Ataria 2014a, 2016c). There is no body to grab onto, and it is clear that the sense of self has collapsed.

The hero of *Fight Club* does not attack himself but rather attacks the one observing him. He attempts to rid himself of that judgmental character. Kurtz, too, is not willing to die at the hands of the judge. He is only willing to die at the hands of Captain Willard and only at the last minute does he totally identify with him. The posttraumatic character cannot go on living with this duality, with this sense that more than one person inhabits the same body—structural dissociation (Nijenhuis et al. 2010). The posttraumatic condition is one in which the split has become too manifest, indeed insufferable from the point of view of the individual experiencing it. The solution is always the death of one of the characters. Thus, in *The Deer Hunter* the director gives us the impression that Michael shoots Nick rather than Nick shooting himself (Morag 2009). Yet they are the same character. Whether Nick shoots himself or Michael shoots Nick does not much matter. This same duality also represents the condition of the posttraumatic individual who is always embroiled in some sort of impossible conflict. This conflict is between the different characters within himself, characters whose desires diverge more and more as the conflict deepens, the gap widens, and the two characters distance themselves one from the other more and more.

The present era is characterized by an impossible inner conflict that is worsening each and every moment of our lives. This paradox, when it erupts, always does so in the form of an apocalyptic dybbuk. In the case of Travis in *Taxi Driver,* the dybbuk emerges in a semi-messianic act. In the case of Gregor Samsa in Kafka's *Metamorphosis,* the dybbuk erupts when the character turns into a cockroach and only ends when he relinquishes his "human" existence and remains only with the core truth—he is a cockroach: "We are transformed into the phantoms glimpsed yesterday evening" (Levi 1959, p. 21).

Death, and only death, speaks to the posttraumatic individual, the one who cannot but see, who always finds himself at noontide, and who knows that the attempt to cope with the judgmental system always leads to dying like a dog. The posttraumatic individual can only speak the language of blood and death. Michael, the hunter, understands this. He understands that words in themselves represent the prevaricating systems in which we are situated and therefore he can only attempt to save Nick by playing Russian roulette.

Words have no meaning. Therefore, Meursault (*The Stranger*) chooses to remain silent during his trial. The posttraumatic individual understands that there is only one way—to return to the old playing board, and not just to change the moves played but first and foremost to change the rules of the game. Michael, the hunter, attempts to do this and fails. Tyler Durden from *Fight Club* is convinced that by means of the collapse of the economic system this is possible. Perhaps. He also knows that the only way to succeed in this assignment is to adopt God's methods. Therefore, when the sane side of Tyler Durden (the character played by Edward Norton) attempts to stop the process, he cannot. Tyler predicted that his humanity would suddenly appear and therefore gave a specific order: From the moment the operation begins, it must not be stopped, even if he himself gives an order to that effect. Tyler Durden thus adopts God's automatic course. He understands that this is the only way to take matters to the end—with the indifference of the Kafkaesque machine. Meeting the goals requires acting in a cold and emotionless manner. Only thus is it possible to lead us back toward the Big Bang, to return to the starting point, to begin all over again.

From the perspective of the posttraumatic individual life itself has no meaning and therefore death has no meaning either. Death is preferable to life without a home, a life of total alienation. When Travis, the taxi driver, returns "home" he understands this, and he cannot tolerate the inner filth. The filth on the streets of New York symbolizes his inner world as well as the collapse of the world of values he had once believed in. Like Captain Willard and like Kurtz, Travis returns to a bestial state. All the heroes understand that the human condition does not allow one to be human. It is necessary to take a step back, to a prehuman bestial state. In such a state violence is not a matter of choice but rather an uncontrollable dybbuk. In that world, there is no longer room for humanity. Clamence (*The Fall*) is proof of this. Clamence tells the story of human beings in this era, of the self-conscious that leads nowhere apart from impotence, thus resulting in the need for a total revolution. A slap does not help, nor does crying out (as in the case of Clamence). Only a pistol pointed at the temple. Only an unending stream of the dead can generate any change whatsoever.

BACK TO THE BODY—FROM REDEMPTION TO DISASTER, FROM RECONSTRUCTION TO WORKING THROUGH

This chapter moved from a consideration of post-Vietnam films to an examination of the movie *Fight Club*. I believe *Fight Club* is a direct continuation of the post-Vietnam films and I treat it as a film about the sons of posttraumatic fathers from the Vietnam War—the heroes of *Taxi Driver*, *The Deer Hunter*, *Apocalypse Now*, and others. The characters in *Fight Club* are the posttraumatic sons that returned from the Vietnam War.

A central motif in *Taxi Driver* and *Apocalypse Now* is the attempt to return to the bestial body. In the final scene of *Taxi Driver*, Travis appears with a crude haircut and his face covered in blood. Captain Willard paints his face, and in other scenes Kurtz appears with a painted face as well. Painting the face is not intended to hide their identities but rather to expose their true character, their allegiance to the bestial body.

As we will see in the next chapter, the reason for this is that in a more profound sense the posttraumatic hero must reject his body in order to survive. I believe this is the reason that the hero of *Fight Club* beats himself up. He attempts to revive his body, to bring his dead body back to life. At the most extreme point, the only way to do this is by administering violence to the body in the same way that electric shocks are administered to revive the heart.

The next two chapters consider two issues that are essentially the same issue seen from different points of view. Chapter 6 examines the sense of hostility toward the body that develops in captivity and the extensive implications of this hostility. The hostility creates a form of intolerable duality. Chapter 7 examines this duality in Kafka's novel, *The Castle*.

The Body in the Postmodern Era: A View from Captivity

CAPTIVITY AS A STATE OF MIND

Prisoners of war (POWs) cannot feel at home. They feel they are no more than objects; they can no longer control their own lives; they do not understand the things that happen to and around them; nothing makes any sense any more. Futility governed by a sense of emptiness, randomness, and chaos rules their lives. POWs' bodies are no longer their own, but rather belong to the captors. The values, ideas, and beliefs held by the POWs before their captivity have collapsed.

If the POW wants to survive, he must adapt. In practice, this means that the POW must find a way to disconnect from the present moment, from the unbearable pain, from the endless sense of loneliness. He must disassociate himself from his own body and begin living in a bodiless dimension, a disembodied dimension. When the POW is in a state of total isolation, all the components of our lives that we take for granted—time, space, body, logical thinking, the ability to distinguish between wakefulness and dreaming—dissipate as if they had never existed. The POW must strain to maintain his very sanity. This is a battle that finds expression in his struggle to think clearly. To that end the POW must shift to a different state of mind, an altered state of consciousness (Herman 1992).

The state of mind of the various characters in Kafka's works is similar to that of the POW: These characters suffer from absolute alienation, anxiety, detachment, lack of a sense of home. In addition, the body of

© The Author(s) 2017
Y. Ataria, *The Structural Trauma of Western Culture*,
DOI 10.1007/978-3-319-53228-8_6

the Kafkaesque character has ceased to be his own—a body cut off from the self. Furthermore, these Kafkaesque characters suffer from an inability to speak out and explain themselves. In fact, Kafkaesque figures feel they are strangers to language and are located outside the language. Thus, in this situation language becomes the other in the most brutal fashion (Deleuze and Guattari 1986). Josephine the Singer, or the Mouse Folk, for example, feels that while words are uttered they do not say anything (Kafka 1952). Gregor Samsa in *The Metamorphosis* (Kafka 2002) is another example of the state of mind of the Kafkaesque (anti)hero, the same state that characterizes the POW.

According to POWs' testimony, entering into captivity is accompanied by the total absence of logic, as expressed by Gregor Samsa when he wakes up with the body of an insect:

> One morning, when Gregor Samsa woke from troubled dreams, he found himself transformed in his bed into a horrible vermin. He lay on his armour-like back, and if he lifted his head a little he could see his brown belly, slightly domed and divided by arches into stiff sections. The bedding was hardly able to cover it and seemed ready to slide off any moment. His many legs, pitifully thin compared with the size of the rest of him, waved about helplessly as he looked. (Kafka 2002)

From this patently impossible opening scene, Kafka continues with a logic of sorts that is totally insane. Things happen on their own without any control. The experience of Y, a released POW, is similar.[1]

> There are some very traumatic moments when you feel like your brains are being electrically grounded to the floor. For a long time, don't ask me how long, I felt absolute stagnation, my brain did not work, I felt I was simply unable to activate my brain, and I remember saying to myself: "concentrate, think, concentrate, think." I know exactly when that happened. I knew, I came to the understanding that I'm stuck, everything is totally automatic and I felt I could not stop, and you ask yourself "why?", you tell yourself to "concentrate, think," and there's no response, everything happens without knowing, without any discretion, it just happens to you, you don't know how. And again you tell yourself, "concentrate, think," and your head is totally empty, you don't know what to do, loss...termination...you see stars and you again tell yourself, "concentrate, think," you want to control something, your head is totally empty and that's a terrible feeling of absolute helplessness, of uncertainty, of the

futility of nothingness, I don't know how to define it. A time when things happen and you don't control them—that's one of the worst things I remember from captivity. (Y)

It is important to understand that the sense of captivity described by Kafka is the result of looking soberly at what is defined as "home." Home is the culture (the language, the set of perceptions and beliefs, and all the rest) that you grew up with and into. It is the society to which you belong. At the moment of trauma society is revealed as what it truly is— rotten to the core. Society for its part cannot contain clear and sober observation. Therefore it has no choice but to destroy, in one way or another, everyone who has been exposed to its true nature. Kurtz and Captain Willard (*Apocalypse Now*) agree that there is nowhere to return to, there is no home, and thus the very concept of *home* has collapsed. This is not because America does not want to embrace them but rather because in the jungles they discovered the true face of America and of the set of values they were raised on. They know that now that their eyes have been opened and the truth has been revealed to them, they cannot return to the true captivity at "home." Deep in the jungles, they have killed their fathers in order to survive. This murder takes place when the soldier understands that the generation of the fathers has sacrificed him to the dybbuk, has bound him to the altar of vague and cruel "divine law." This same *Akeda* is repeated again and again using innovative, varied, and vicious methods.

What seems to be common to Kafka's stories and to the condition of the POW is that everything we are used to taking for granted in our lives collapses in a single moment, to the point that the sense of self loses meaning and disintegrates. The Kafkaesque world lacks an anchor, as does the world of the POW, as manifested in the separation of the self from the body. That being the case, the main thing missing for the POW is the body as anchor, that same body that serves as a bridge between consciousness (the inner world) and the world outside. Through our bodies we perceive the world and act in it (Husserl 1989; Merleau-Ponty 2002; Noë 2004). By means of our bodies we understand the world. Thus in effect, without the body the world lacks meaning. Kafka's characters frequently exchange their bodies with those of animals. The reason for this is related to the inability to remain in one's body in this world. Replacing the body is not a choice but rather a necessity in view of the emotional condition of the Kafkaesque characters, who feel absolutely alienated from their bodies and from the world. This is also true for humankind in the postmodern era.

ABANDONING THE BODY

From the perspective of POWs, the body becomes the source of suffering. Therefore they prefer to be in a bodiless dimension. I argue that this is also our condition in the current era, as reflected in different forms and dimensions of culture, for example in movies like *The Matrix* (Wachowski and Wachowski 1999) and *Fight Club*. The idea behind a movie like *The Matrix* emerges directly from "The Allegory of the Cave" in Plato's *The Republic* (Plato 2000): We live in a world of illusions and we do not see "things as they are" (Irwin 2002). Life is an illusion. Our bodies are virtual and we are never in contact with what is real. Our lives in the current era are virtual lives. The body in and of itself, its reality, can only be doubted for it is questionable. Our lives are analogous to the life of the POW. Therefore, more than being a nightmare *The Matrix* is a fantasy. In contrast, and for exactly the same reasons, the hero (Tyler Durden— Brad Pitt) of the movie *Fight Club* attempts to revive and revitalize his own body, exactly as POWs often attempt to do through pure violence (acting out). In this context it is interesting to examine the testimony of M, another released POW:

> I had a really good technique. I didn't know what to do with myself. I saw I was on the verge of a nervous breakdown, that I was . . . going crazy, that you are about to explode, you think you have been left alone. So I would start hurting myself in a place where I was injured from the investigations. That's my technique, to hurt myself where I was hurting. You are busy with pain. That way you are not busy with questions, you enter a different niche, a niche of pain, no longer bothersome questions, you go with yourself into the pain in order not to ask and not to think. And all the time I would hurt myself, day and night, worse than their torture, in order not to keep asking those never-ending questions. The pain lets you think about what was, what will be and what is, you know what you have, you have the pain, you know how to cope with it, it hurts but you cope. This is very important at times of stress, it keeps you quiet, hurting but quiet. My psyche hurt me more than the wound. (M)

In the current era, following a history in which the body has been cut up, burned, melted, and subject to all sorts of other horrors, humans have lost their bodies. Tyler Durden, the hero of *Fight Club,* is a man with a body we all dream about, but it does not really exist. The body becomes nothing more than a computer game, a form of virtual reality. The overwhelming success of computer games in which the miserable, weak Kafkaesque body is converted into a perfect body is the only fantasy in this era, in which not only have we lost what is real, but we have also lost our bodies as something real. With the disappearance of the body everything that is otherwise taken for granted collapses. Nothing is left to hold onto, there is no anchor. In this situation the only way to revive the body is through violence, sadism, and pornography, that is, by annulling the real body and creating a new and patently inhuman ideal.

In this era human beings cannot tolerate their bodies. This is the result of Western culture, which has turned life on earth into captivity. Plastic surgery has become routine, and men fantasize over artificial breasts and abnormal penises. Men remove body hair because it is not "aesthetic." Michael Jackson is not just another example of these trends but rather the North Star of the future of humanity, a prophet of sorts. The goal is not to be more beautiful but rather to cease inhabiting the true, the imperfect human body. Women want a different face, a different nose, new skin. The ideal of beauty has become in essence an ideal that rejects the very notion of the natural body. This does not turn us into devotees of the higher, transcendent soul. All that is left is the contemptible body, for this is an unrelenting negative philosophy with no positive attributes. In turn, the ideal of beauty has become an ideal that by its very essence rescinds, eliminates, does away with the natural body, the body that is always just a bit crooked, that is most certainly not perfect, that sometimes hurts us, that snores at night and falls asleep on the bus, drooling all over itself.

Thus, in this era the human body has become both the object of contempt and an agent of that contempt as it despises itself. Our bodies are the garbage can of the world, and the world is insufferable. It is a basic error to think that in this era beauty and aesthetics are sacred, for the opposite is the case. In this era it is the counterfeit/operated-upon/reshaped body that is sacred—everything one cannot be. This is an era without a body, or better put, an era in which the body must be rejected.

In turn, when the natural body is rejected, the world itself is rejected as well, and that is because we perceive the world through our body.

The symptoms of the loss of the body and the shift to an altered state of consciousness find expression in a sense of alienation: "He knew he would always feel as though he were staying in a hotel" (Houellebecq 2000, p. 292). Human beings in this era are captive because their bodies no longer serve as their home: "Already my own body is no longer mine" (Levi 1959, p. 34). Captive because they are nothing more than an object that is moved from place to place. Trapped because their thoughts have no anchor to facilitate clarifying them.

MARGARITA

In Bulgakov's masterful novel *The Master and Margarita* (Bulgakov 1997) we also encounter the motif of the lack of desire to remain in the human body as a type of escape and disconnection identical to the disconnection sought by the POW. On the one hand, the book deals with the crucifixion of Christ and is thus directly connected to Christian sources of abhorrence for the body, while on the other hand it deals with the totalitarian regime that has de facto turned its citizens into POWs (Arendt, 1973). In this novel, all the main characters attempt to escape this life by replacing their bodies. The main characters, those who have been at least ostensibly released, all have relinquished the human body. Woland is Satan, a tall man of foreign origins with one green eye and one black eye. Koroviev/Fagotto, Woland's assistant, is described as a tall man dressed in a checkered garment, wearing a checkered cap and cracked eyeglasses. In the chapter in which the entourage of Satan leaves Moscow, Koroviev's true form is revealed—a dark purple knight with a frightening countenance. Behemoth, an enormous black cat, is capable of walking on two legs and speaking. At the end of the book he gets into trouble with the secret police and is shot. But then he drinks a bit of kerosene from the Primus stove and recovers. In the chapter in which the satanic entourage leaves Moscow, Behemoth's true form is revealed—a demon pageboy, the best clown in the world. Azazello is a short broad-shouldered man with red hair, horrifyingly loathsome and ugly with a prominent fang protruding from his mouth. Azazello is the one who gives Margarita the cream that turns her into a witch, and he also poisons her and the artist at the end of the book. In the chapter in which the entourage leaves Moscow, Azazello's true form is revealed—a pale-faced demon-assassin. Margarita, who alters her body without hesitation and thus in effect is redeemed, represents the notion that the human body is despised and that any redemption whatsoever nullifies the natural human body: "After all, we are divided, aren't we, divided in our nature?" (Boell 1976, p. 301). Unlike Margarita, Nikolayevich Ponyryov, her downstairs neighbor, relinquishes the opportunity to be reincarnated as a pig. He does not have the courage to totally abandon the human body (the source of all our sin). He ultimately laments having renounced unification with Venus in exchange for a note certifying that he did indeed attend Satan's ball. We have already seen that in the postmodern era there is no difference whatsoever between reality and hallucination. Throughout the book, there seems to be no law that can reliably distinguish between lies and the truth. Not only has the boundary been blurred—it simply does not exist. In the background is an assumption that is perhaps the most central assumption of Western culture—*redemption cannot be achieved through the human body.* Redemption is nothing less than a new body:

> The human body, which was only lent and did not properly belong to them, must be kept clean, just as the servant has to keep clean the livery given him by his master. Every uncleanness had to be put right; this meant that the Israelite had to recognize, by sacrificing something or other which he called his own, that to change another's property was a presumption and an illegality and that he himself owned no property whatever. But what wholly belonged to their God and was sacrosanct to him, e.g., booty and numerous products of conquest, was given him as his full possession by the fact that it was completely destroyed. (Hegel 1948, p. 192)

HUMAN BEINGS IN POSTMODERN SOCIETY

The individual in postmodern society has lost his body. This is not to suggest in any way that the physical dimension is not important. Indeed, the opposite is the case. Today we worship a body that is everything except the human body. People prefer to die rather than live with a defective body: "Nothing—not even death—seems worse than the prospect of living in a broken body" (Houellebecq 2000, p. 247). For the posttraumatic being, death is preferable to life in a body that has betrayed itself, a body that is reminiscent of the trauma. But the body that was traumatized remains injured forever—the trauma is burned into it. It is important to stress that the loss of the physical dimension is among other things the result of a culture grounded in the Christian perspective on life. Thus, after 2000 years in which bodily abuse has been sanctified in the name of an account that can never be settled, the body is torn apart and nothing remains of it.

Humans abhor their bodies and do everything they can to renovate them by means of external components. It is as if they want to replace all their organs and become a "brain in a vat." The condition of Johnny in *Johnny Got His Gun* (Trumbo 1997) reliably represents our condition— life that is severed from the body. But we cannot really separate ourselves from our bodies, and the body, for its part, never forgets trauma (Van Der Kolk 1994). It only gets older and the trauma is fixed permanently within it to the point that it becomes the reflection of emotional trauma in a physical form.

When the posttraumatic individual passes a certain stage, every encounter with the world jars the trauma awake. Therefore, any physical experience whatsoever awakens the trauma within us, for a physical experience is nothing more than the way we are present in the world and experience it. Hence, every encounter with our body reawakens the traumatic experience again and again. In consequence the body is also transformed into a metaphysical prison for us.

This is the reason that posttraumatic Western culture denies the body. This culture believes that perhaps by denying the body it can avoid re-experiencing the trauma again and again—the trauma that in essence is the result of the encounter with this world. Hence, post-traumatic societies, which are capable of dropping an atomic bomb without asking too many questions, act only in one direction: to infiltrate every area of life and, by generating a distorted ideal of beauty, to annul the physical and human dimension in order to create a buffer zone with the world. But this goal will never be attained. In the tremendous effort to create new spaces that are free of trauma it destroys everything in its wake and thus in essence perpetuates the trauma. In other words, in an obsessive attempt to avoid stimuli (for the posttraumatic entity avoidance is a major symptom), posttrau-matic society must destroy every stimulus that awakens that trauma, that bleeding and uncontrollable open memory. The goal of plastic surgery, it seems, is to replace the trauma-laden body with a new body, one that trauma cannot adhere to. From the perspective of society in general, destroying the stimulus that arouses the trauma is nothing more than destroying the entire social and ecological environment. Ultimately, for posttraumatic society every stimulus reawakens the trauma, so that the only solution is total destruction. As we will see, there are other ways to cope with the traumatic experience. Yet when no process of coping and recovery takes place, the need to destroy the social order erupts. Trauma is essentially the result of a particular culture, a particular *Akeda*, a particular social order. The posttraumatic subject is convinced that by destroying the social order he can perhaps begin anew. From this it is also clear why Tyler Durden from *Fight Club* sets out to destroy the core of posttraumatic society, for it is impossible to draw distinctions between capitalism, consumerism, the annulment of the body, and the posttraumatic condition.

This is a critical point indeed. The response to the body described in *Fight Club* is identical to the response to the capitalistic system. The diseased and polluted body contains within itself the motif that guides monotheistic capitalistic Western society. Furthermore, the body has turned into the system itself. The body has turned into the law. Essentially, something must be dismantled before it can be rebuilt. This is true when it comes to the body that has ceased to be human and true when it comes to the system that has ceased to be human. In essence, this is what leads Tyler Durden to take apart the body in order to rebuild it in a more natural way, and this is also his objective with respect to the economic system.

LENI PFEIFFER AS A POSSIBILITY FOR REDEMPTION

The Nazi ideology that strove to elevate and sanctify the Aryan race was essentially unable to reconcile itself to physical defects and therefore destroyed everything it came into contact with. If not for the fact that the Nazis were defeated, they would have eventually destroyed themselves as well, for every individual's body has defects. This is what makes us human. Even the Nazis, to their great regret, were flesh and blood and therefore defective in one way or another. The eruption of the automatic and cruel killing machine was among other things a reaction to the trench warfare of World War I in which the body, even the Aryan body for that matter, wallowed in mud, blood, and excrement. Thus the trauma is etched into the body, which does not forget. This same trauma developed and erupted again and again in World War II in the form of endlessly repeated and uncontrollable games. Men who were defeated, downtrodden, and depressed needed an apocalyptic solution, and that is what Hitler knew how to provide them with.

Thus there is a good reason that Leni Pfeiffer, the character showcased in Heinrich Böll's novel, *Group Portrait With Lady*, prominently displays a man's body and organs in her home. Leni understands that it is not really possible to be reborn in a new body. Therefore it is also not possible to forget (or to repress) what the body remembers. The road to recovery passes through acceptance of the shattered, crushed body at the height of its wretchedness and not through an attempt to make the body into something that is not human. Leni places the internal organs on display. She displays what is hidden, which is the most real thing there is. She does not attempt to present herself as a rational person. She is nothing like that "rational individual" who constantly claims that he cannot be accused of a "lack of humanity." Leni is simply who she is: a person who has totally accepted her own body:

> Any analysis of human behavior, however rudimentary, should take account of such phenomena. Historically, such human beings have existed. Human beings who have worked—worked hard—all their lives with no motive other than love and devotion, who have literally given their lives for others, out of love and devotion; human beings who have no sense of having made any sacrifice, who cannot imagine any way of life other than giving their lives for others, out of love and devotion. In general, such human beings are generally women. (Houellebecq 2000, p. 92)

Leni is a particularly important character when one considers the fact that at the end of *The Master and Margarita* we discover that the characters we thought were free are actually bound and imprisoned, each in his own way, within the terms of the accounting ledger from previous incarnations. Again the fact that humans are an historical entity prevents us from being liberated. This is because the cultural approach within the Judeo-Christian system of beliefs ultimately posits the belief "that we have only one conscience—and that a crippled conscience is as irretrievable as a lost life" (Solzhenitsyn 1968, p. 345).

Leni, then, is a woman who is completely comfortable with her body because she lives without the Judeo-Christian accounting ledger:

Leni is not bitter, and she is without remorse, she does not even feel remorse at not having mourned the death of her first husband. Leni's lack of remorse is so absolute that any degree of "more" or "less", in terms of her capacity for remorse, would be beside the point; she probably does not even know the meaning of remorse; in this—as in other respects—her religious education must have failed or be deemed to have failed, probably to Leni's advantage. (Böll 1976, p. 13)

Leni is the one who expresses ecstatic yearning for the holy bread, but when she tastes it she is repulsed by it. She is disgusted by the fact that Christian culture, by her definition, sanctifies the abuse of the body. Later Leni becomes a devotee of a nun who has grown sick of the convent and even tries to save her life. Here, again, it is clear that Leni is totally liberated from the world of Christian sin. Leni sees the people and not the method. She takes no interest in politics but only in people. She does not care that Boris is a Russian. "Through Leni's brave deed Boris was simply made a human being, proclaimed a human being—and that was that" (Böll 1976, p. 189).

Thus Leni, the one named as the most German girl in her elementary school, the one who considers Kafka's story "In the Penal Colony" as appropriate educational material for her son who is not even eight years old, inadvertently answers the following question: "If you wanted to put the world to rights, who should you begin with: yourself or others?" (Solzhenitsyn 1968, p. 425). Her answer is not philosophical but rather embedded in life itself. Philosophy never rescued anyone. It always appears after the fact, when it is much too late. Leni understands that being unable to accuse someone of lacking humanity still does not make that individual more human. Leni is the answer to the machine of destruction in that she simply lives her life, thus reconciling herself to the finite and crumbling human body. Leni represents the possibility of a liberated individual who is not Chigurh (*No Country For Old Men*). She represents a positive model. The reason for this appears to be related to the fact that Leni is a woman. This notion is tied to a central statement in this book: The posttraumatic male can no longer continue. The solution must come by creating a new feminine discourse, one that is completely dissociated from Sarah.

Leni from Nazi Germany, who later turns into Lola, heroine of the movie *Run Lola Run,* offers an alternative: simply to live this life without feelings of guilt, to live for the moment without superfluous accounts, more than anything else not to feel ashamed of her human body. Thus Leni places the human body on display, both its inner and its outer parts. Leni is a character born out of a profound insight: the posttraumatic man cannot continue to live in the world, cannot remain in his body and therefore acts to destroy everything around him. Leni also understands that the way to cope must be feminine and inclusive and has no room for words but rather must include a return to the human body: "The unity of man has not yet been broken; the body has not yet been stripped of human predicates; it has not yet become a machine" (Merleau-Ponty 1965, p. 188). The body must be returned to a condition in which it indeed exists in the world. So long as the body remains that which separates the sick mind and the chaotic world, the traumatic experience will continue to spread.

ONE'S BODY AS ONE'S CAPTIVITY

The primary claim of this chapter is that the posttraumatic condition is characterized by a sense of impossible captivity and that conventional tools cannot be used to liberate oneself from this captivity. Captivity drags the characters depicted in this book into playing recurring and never-ending games with a dybbuk that represents the only way to escape from infinite slavery into some sort of freedom. Another possibility is to protest violently against society and against the foulness of the world.

The individual in the postmodern era exists within a state of absolute collapse of all systems. He desperately cries out for help, which has disappeared together with Sarah's echoing silence. The individual in this era cannot sleep, cannot rest, cannot feel comfortable, leading him to a need to seek constant escape, though it is unclear from what he is fleeing and it is most surely unclear to where he is running. He has simply taken the advice of Pink Floyd: "You better run" (Pink Floyd, "Run Like Hell," *The Wall*). This is a general state of abstention and of threat without any genuine origin. What is clear is that this individual can no longer remain in one place. Moreover, in this times the world appears to be smaller than ever: "I never imagined that life would be so constrained, that there would be so few opportunities" (Houellebecq 2000, p. 272). The individual in this times cannot go beyond the boundaries of the cell: "One thing seemed clear to him: no one knew how to live anymore" (Houellebecq 2000, p. 120). He is all alone. From time to time food is tossed at him through the opening in the cell door. From time to time he hears the screams of his

neighbors: "And we have learnt other things, more or less quickly, according to our intelligence: to reply 'Jawohl,' never to ask questions, always to
pretend to understand" (Levi 1959, p. 29). But no more than this. The
only way to cope with this state is to return to the human lived body with all
of its insufferable defects, to its reverberating finiteness.

In this chapter, we examined the hostility toward the body as it has
developed in the current era. As stated previously, this hostility leads to an
unbearable duality and a sense of being captive in one's own body. The
next chapter examines Kafka's novel *The Castle* to explore how this duality
reaches new heights in the posttraumatic era.

NOTE

1. All quotations from released POWs are from Ataria (2010).

CHAPTER 7

K.'s Fatalistic World

The Posttraumatic Experience: The Divided Consciousness of K.

In wandering through the village, K., Kafka's protagonist in his novel *The Castle*, wanders through the unconscious of the posttraumatic survivor. In these ramblings there is no possibility of distinguishing between dream and reality. For the posttraumatic survivor, to sleep means to be in a nightmare. Indeed, it is well known that for those who suffer from posttraumatic stress disorder (PTSD) sleep is a threatening experience that must be avoided. The posttraumatic survivor lives life in a state of constant exhaustion, existing in a twilight zone between wakefulness and dreaming: "So he played with his dreams, and they with him" (Kafka 2009, p. 133). Thus, already at the beginning of the book when K. arrives at the Bridge Inn, he falls asleep, and from that point forward there is no way of knowing whether the entire book is nothing other than a dream within a dream or whether its events take place in reality. Indeed, Kafka himself lived within a world of "relentless insomnia" (Kafka 1974, p. 317).

In the world of the posttraumatic subject, the lines between dream and reality are blurred. Nevertheless it appears that under these surrealistic circumstances it is precisely during sleep that K. comes to his senses: "K. was asleep. It was not real sleep; he could hear what Bürgel [secretary of a castle official] was saying perhaps better than during his early period of wakeful exhaustion, word after word came to his ear, but his troublesome consciousness was gone; he felt free" (Kafka 2009, p. 231). In the

© The Author(s) 2017
Y. Ataria, *The Structural Trauma of Western Culture*,
DOI 10.1007/978-3-319-53228-8_7

posttraumatic state of mind, one is neither awake nor asleep but rather in a twilight zone of sorts, at the margins, on the edge. For instance, when the hero of the movie *Fight Club* (Edward Norton) goes to sleep, the other character (Brad Pitt) within him comes to life. This duality is precisely what exists between K. and Klamm. In essence, this is the duality experienced by the posttraumatic survivor. In a personal confession, Kafka makes the following shocking statement: "But for me in particular it is a horrible double life from which there is probably no escape but insanity" (Kafka 1976, p. 38).

The posttraumatic state of being is a condition in which all memories are nothing more than *memories from the ghetto*. It is a condition in which the world is a threatening and dangerous place: "How uncertain and menacing everything there must seem if he dares not even open his mouth to ask an innocent question! When I think of that I blame myself for leaving him alone in those unknown rooms where such things go on that even he, who is reckless rather than cowardly, probably trembles for fear there" (Kafka 2009, p. 161). The lie controls everything: "It was just for show" (p. 194). The world is devoid of hope: "But this last small, vanishingly small, almost non-existent hope is the only hope you have" (p. 100). It is a world in which the apocalyptic end is inevitable: "So what could have been foreseen but not prevented had happened" (p. 207). Clearly, "there'd be nothing we could do to improve matters" (p. 108). Yet the world remains the same physical world that does not exist for the sake of anyone. This is the posttraumatic survivor's interpretation of a world that has become impossible. Thus it is reasonable that K. hears the following statement: "You take everything the wrong way, even a silence" (p. 161). It is important to understand that it is human beings that confer meaning upon the world. From this we can deduce that the nature of the subject's mental wound expresses itself in the distorted meaning the posttraumatic survivor imposes upon the world. As indicated, we know that the world from the perspective of the posttraumatic survivor has become threatening and intolerable. This is because the wounded survivor projects his own unseen injury upon the world and thus turns it into an impossible place to live. Thus, when the survivor who suffers from posttrauma attempts to avoid being part of the world, attempts to abstain from it, he is actually avoiding himself, for the world is nothing more than a reflection of the self. That is to say, in the world one finds nothing but oneself.

Through an examination of the novel *The Castle*[1] as well as Kafka's autobiographical writing in his dairies,[2] this chapter examines the implications of the traumatic experience on the life of the survivor. To be more specific, this chapter describes how posttrauma compels the survivor to exist in two unconnected worlds, on two separate planets, that rule out and deny one another: the inner world and the outer world.

THE CASTLE AND THE VILLAGE

Duality is a predominant theme in *The Castle*, expressed through the castle and village, K. and Klamm, Artur and Jeremiah (K.'s assistants), Olga and Amalia (the sisters), the Bridge Inn and the Herrenhof Inn (the pub), Klamm's Frieda and K.'s Frieda, Frieda and Pepi, and other pairings as well. Two worlds exist in the novel: one is the world outside that cannot be reached, the world of the castle: "Even up on Castle Mount the air must be quite different" (Kafka 2009, p. 130). The other is the inner world, the world of the village.

The castle and the village are disconnected, separate entities, while at the same time they are obsessively connected with one another and in a kind of sadistic yet sanctimonious relationship characterized by self-justification. It is unclear who derives more satisfaction from the relationship, the master or the slave. The encounter between the village and the castle is a meeting marked by unfinished legal proceedings, messengers delivering meaningless messages, first and second secretaries incessantly recording minutes that will never reach their intended targets. K. asks: "Very well, Mr. Secretary . . . will Klamm read these records?" (p. 102). The answer is direct, predictable, and clear: "'No,' said Momus, 'why would he?' Klamm cannot read all the records, in fact he never reads any of them. "Oh, don't come pestering me with your records!" he often says'" (p. 102). Despite this, nothing can be hidden from the masters of the castle. They know everything: "This village belongs to the castle" (p. 5). Indeed, in his letters to his friends, Kafka describes man as a castle comprising an infinite number of rooms, not all of which are familiar to him (Murray 2004). The castle would like to cut off all contact with the village—simply not to know about the village—but it cannot achieve this goal, which is beyond its control. In effect, the castle misses and yearns for the village and cannot restrain itself from entering the village and spending time there:

> It's as if the official mechanism could no longer stand up to the tension and the years of attrition caused by the same factor, which in itself may be slight, and has made the decision of its own accord with no need for the officials to take a hand. (Kafka 2009, p. 63)

Therefore the connection will never be direct and sincere. The castle will always remain distant and unattainable: "There was nothing to be seen of Castle Mount, for mist and darkness surrounded it" (p. 5). K. wanders around in an impossible attempt to reach the castle: "although [the castle] moved no further away from the castle, it came no closer either" (p. 13).

All the interests of the village are focused on the castle. The villagers admire the masters of the castle. The castle, for its part, is repulsed by the village experience. Nevertheless, at the same time it is drawn toward the life of the village, to the world of the instinctual, of the base, of urges, and of desire:

> Down here too we find traces of that attitude among the servants, but only traces, because otherwise it's as if they were transformed by the fact that the castle regulations don't apply to them so much here in the village, where they are a wild, unruly set, ruled not by the castle regulations but by their own insatiable desires. (p. 194)

For the villagers, the laws are everything, while they mean nothing to the people of the castle. Therefore the very existence of the village threatens the castle. There is no place further from the castle than the village, while at the same time there is no more intimate, basic, sexual, and scandalous connection than that between the village and the castle. The relations between the village and the castle therefore represent the relations between the inner world and the outer world in the climate of posttraumatic existence.

K. AND KLAMM

Fundamentally the chasm between Klamm and K. is impassable and cannot be bridged. This is not because they are two separate people but rather because they are two faces of the same individual. Among other things, Kafka hints at this through their names—K. and Klamm. In one of the most important and deceptive sentences in the book, K. states: "I can't help thinking of myself at the mention of Klamm" (p. 72). This is not only a hidden passion to be a strong and dominant master (alter ego), for very soon it becomes evident that Klamm is someone who likes to sleep and does not want to meet anyone. He is a depressive individual, a Kafkaesque version of Kafka himself. K. and Klamm represent the split in an individual who has been shaped in a traumatic climate and whose life is conducted in the shadow of posttrauma: "I doubt whether I am a human being" (Kafka 1974, p. 287). Yet on the other hand Kafka feels alive only within this posttraumatic-dissociative climate: "I am awake only among my imaginary characters" (Kafka 1974, p. 245). Kafka makes an even more extreme statement: "My life, my existence consists of this subterranean threat" (Kafka 1953, p. 201). Kafka identifies precisely why the split is necessary. The split, as I elaborate below, generates vitality.

K. and Klamm are two characters representing two worlds. The same character, it seems, is unified in the castle itself, yet at the same time it endlessly scrutinizes itself. Therefore, when K. looks at the castle, he senses that someone is also simultaneously examining him. In effect this is a reflective process in K.'s divided world:

> When K. looked at the castle he sometimes thought he saw someone sitting quietly there, looking into space, not lost in thought and thus cut off from everything else, but free and at ease, as if he were alone and no one was observing him. He must notice that he himself was under observation, but that didn't disturb him in the slightest, and indeed—it was hard to tell whether this was cause or effect—the observer's eyes could find nothing to fasten on, and slipped away from the figure. (Kafka 2009, p. 88)

The castle as well, so it seems, does not constitute a unified structure: "If you hadn't known it was a castle you might have taken it for a small town" (p. 11). The castle is not really one whole structure, just like there is no one coherent self. Instead, the castle is scattered, disassembled, and split. Thus, the castle represents the divided self: "as if drawn by an anxious or careless child" (p. 11).

Throughout the book, K. longs to meet Klamm: "If that is the case, then I'm prepared to answer all your questions at once. Yes, if it comes down to that I am ready for anything" (p. 101). Yet K. does not know why he is so interested in such a meeting: "but it's difficult to say just what I want of him" (p. 78). The picture soon becomes clear. K. simply wants to stand facing Klamm and to lay bare Klamm's very existence:

> First I want to see him at close quarters, then I want to hear his voice, and then I want to know from the man himself how he feels about our marriage. Anything else I may ask him depends on the course of the conversation.

There could be a good many subjects for discussion, but what matters most to me is to see him face to face. (p. 78)

From the very first moment, it is clear that there is no real chance for this to happen: "I'm waiting for someone," says K., and he continues, "just on principle rather than hoping for any success now." In turn, the gentleman replies to this statement as follows, "Go or stay, you'll miss him anyway" (pp. 93–94).

Klamm appears only when K. disappears—two separate characters in one body. The posttraumatic survivor cannot contain both characters at the same time. One must die. In certain cases these characters are not aware of each other's presence and yet they despise one another. For this reason it is clear that the answer to K.'s question "Perhaps he [Klamm] was looking for me" (p. 98) is negative. Nevertheless, the relations between the two are quite complex, for the very fact that Klamm comes to the pub shows that he has come toward K. Descending from the castle is taking a step inward. Klamm is incapable of doing anything more than this. The posttraumatic survivor is paralyzed, frozen.

In order to better understand the relations between Klamm and K., it is important to understand the concept of structural dissociation (Nijenhuis et al. 2010). This form of dissociation is a condition in which there are two personalities: an apparently normal personality and an emotional personality. The apparently normal personality totally denies the trauma, while the emotional personality is managed from within the trauma. The trauma is burned into the body; in turn, the emotional personality appears in flashbacks, a condition in which the trauma suddenly appears out of nowhere and is experienced in the here and now. Accordingly, Klamm represents the world facing outward— the ostensibly normal world of the castle. K., in contrast, has not yet been liberated from the trauma. He remains frozen in the time of the trauma—an individual detained in a transparent, "see-through" prison. "Just as this condition prevents me from talking naturally, eating naturally, sleeping naturally, so it prevents me from being natural in any way" (Kafka 1974, p. 262). The flashbacks and the involuntary memories control the entire field of existence and do not leave room for the apparently normal personality. Yet the more the apparently normal personality—that is, Klamm—is engaged in denying the traumatic memories, the more profound and vivid the traumatic memories become. Klamm's goal is to prevent K. from reaching the surface and taking over the center of existence. Yet as time passes, this task becomes more and more difficult, for the trauma—and this is an essential point—becomes physical and inevitably floats to the surface as part of the physical experience of existing in the world. The solution, then, is total severance of the self from the body.

It is clear why K. is not wanted in the castle, why he must continue to be disregarded. Yet the castle's intense loathing for K. will not lead to an open struggle against him: "that if there were any disagreements it would be the fault of K.'s recklessness—it was said with delicacy, and only an uneasy conscience (uneasy, not guilty) would have noticed" (Kafka 2009, p. 25). In any event, despite K.'s longings to be in contact with the castle, he has an even greater desire—to remain in the world of alienation: "I really do believe I am lost to all social intercourse" (Kafka quoted in Canetti 1974, p. 32). In K.'s world, a sense of discomfort and dissatisfaction replaces a sense of home: "He was disappointed, for he had expected someone new, not these old acquaintances who were such a nuisance to him" (Kafka 2009, p. 105). To put this in the words of Kafka himself, "the timid faces of so many of my acquaintance who suddenly gave me a wide berth" (Kafka quoted in: (Pawel 1984, p. 44)). This is the reason why K. wanders end-lessly from place to place. K. seeks to be a stranger or even the Stranger, the other. In fact it may be that K. wants to be thrown out by the law: "Someone like K. Someone who would set himself above everything, above the law, above the most ordinary human consideration for others" (Kafka 2009, p. 248). Yet K. does not do this deliberately but rather out of "dull indifference and lethargy" (p. 248), from a place of emotional death: "K. was ruthless" (p. 120). But not only does K. lack compassion. Rather, as Frieda accuses him more than once, he also has no love in his heart. Kafka describes this condition, in a letter he wrote to Felice several years before writing *The Castle*, as "dull indifference." This dullness—mentioned in *The Castle* as well—is the consequence of the emotional death experienced by the posttraumatic survivor, someone who moves between absolute indif-ference and the fear of death: "Fear, next to indifferences, is the basic feeling I have towards people" (Kafka 1974, p. 286). K.'s alienation is not a matter of choice but rather a matter of uncontrollable necessity, and his rejection by the village satisfies his profoundest ambition to be an outsider, to be estranged. Indeed, the more he is hated, the more K. feels "at home." K. himself admits that he never intended to stay in the village. In effect, had he not been rejected he would have left after a day or two:

> K. could have gone there during working hours, could have said, as the situation required, that he was a stranger here, a travelling journeyman who had found a bed for the night with a certain resident of the parish, and was probably going on in the morning unless he found work here, improbable as that might be, work for only a few days, naturally, on no account would he stay any longer. (Kafka 2009, pp. 146–147)

Yet as soon as he is rejected, he decides to stay there forever: "'Yes,' said K. 'I'm here indefinitely'" (p. 210). Only in exile can the stranger feel at home: "He had not come here to lead a life of peace in high esteem" (p. 136).

Unlike the hated and intolerable K., "well, of course Klamm was indispensable in the castle and the village alike" (p. 212). Yet the question is not why Klamm is necessary in the castle, for he represents the seemingly normal personality (versus the emotional personality—K.). Rather, the question is why Klamm is necessary in the village. We have already seen that Klamm never really goes down to the village. He always stops at the pub, the way station. The Herrenhof Inn is the main meeting point between the people from the village and the residents of the castle. It is the place where the villagers go to give an account and where the officials go to give free rein to their darkest cravings and desires. The pub is located in the twilight zone between the outer and the inner worlds, the point at which the two worlds meet and where it is possible to engage in some sort of dialogue, even if the discourse is entirely distorted. Klamm's arrival at the pub (twilight zone) represents arriving at the meeting point with the inner world of the other. Yet Klamm does not dare go outside the pub. He arrives there and withdraws, as if the pub is a hospital for mental patients. And of course we know that Kafka spent time at various convalescent facilities of this sort (Murray 2004).

Klamm is K.'s prison in that he ties K. to life and does not allow him to sink completely into the world of hallucination and relinquish the outside world. So long as Klamm exists, the outside world is present in the experience, for Klamm carries with him the outside world while K. is present only in the inner world. We know that someone who suffers from severe posttrauma is liable not to leave the house in order to avoid a world in which everything arouses trauma. Detachment from the world is the solution. Yet this is only a partial solution, for it entails relinquishing the possibility of living. This is also the reason that K. is desperate about the possibility of total detachment from Klamm: "But at the same time—and this feeling was at least as strong—he felt as if there were nothing more meaningless and more desperate than this freedom, this waiting, this invulnerability" (Kafka 2009, p. 95). The posttraumatic survivor's detachment from the world ultimately leads to absolute insanity. This is a battle for life in which two characters seek to destroy each other, yet at the same time understand that it is a two-edged sword. The death of one will lead to the death of both. Returning to Kafka's letter, we discover the following:

> In me there have always been, and still are, two selves wrestling with each other. One of them is very much as you would wish him to be, and by further development he could achieve the little he lacks in order to fulfil your wishes. None of the things you reproached me with at the Askanischer Hof applied to him. The other self, however, thinks of nothing but work, which is his sole concern; it has the effect of making even the meanest thoughts appear quite normal; the death of his dearest friend would seem to be no more than a hindrance—if only a temporary one—to his work; this meanness is compensated for by the fact that he is also capable of suffering for his work. These two selves are locked in *combat*, but it is no ordinary fight where two pairs of fists strike out at each other. The first self is dependent upon the second; he would never, for inherent reasons never, be able to overpower him; on the contrary, he is delighted when the second succeeds, and if the second appears to be losing, the first will kneel down at his side, oblivious of everything but him. (Kafka 1974, p. 438)

In *The Castle*, Klamm is apparently the more important of the two characters. The barmaid relates to him as if he were God Himself: "I have only one request. Do not mention Klamm's name. Call him 'he,' or something else, but don't call him by his name" (Kafka 2009, p. 78). K., in contrast, is described as follows: "You're not from the castle, you're not from the village, you're nothing. Unfortunately, however, you are a stranger, a superfluous person getting in everyone's way, a man who is always causing trouble" (p. 46). Furthermore, the villagers again and again attempt to convince K. that he is not real.[3] Yet we can look at this differently and see K. as the more positive character of the two. For example, Olga, one of the two sisters (Olga and Amalia), asks K.: "... but then why does Barnabas doubt that the official who is described there as Klamm really is Klamm?"

(p. 155). In addition she claims that no one in the village really knows Klamm: "You can find people in the village who would swear that Momus is Klamm" (p. 160). It is impossible to identify Klamm, for he is emotionally dead, absolutely indifferent, and therefore makes no kind of gesture even remotely connected to humanity, not even the smallest of gestures expressing life. Indeed, he is devoid even of facial expressions. Klamm is a living dead person, precisely like the posttraumatic survivor, and for this reason in order to avoid coping with the traumatic and anxiety-filled experience reflected by K.'s psyche, Klamm chooses to sink into absolute indifference. In effect, a rereading of *The Castle* shows that Klamm avoids every encounter with human beings, exactly like the posttraumatic survivor who sits in a darkened room without any desire or ability to see the world. Avoidance is the only possibility. Klamm represents the posttraumatic survivor who attempts to evade his inner world. And this evasion paralyzes him so he is unable to communicate with the world in general. Therefore Klamm is observed through a peephole in the door. He cannot tolerate human beings, for humans immediately elicit in him the physical dimension of the trauma, as Kafka wrote in his diary on November 22, 1911: "a major obstacle to my progress is my physical condition" (Kafka 1948). Perhaps, then, this is what leads K. to make the following admission: "Whether he really speaks to Klamm is a matter of life and death to Barnabas. 'It's the same for me,' said K." (Kafka 2009, p. 156). K. attempts to reach Klamm in order to wake him up, for if Klamm dies this is also the end for K.

FRIEDA AND PEPI

The relations between K. and Klamm run along several channels. For good reason Frieda is situated in the Herrenhof Inn at the meeting point between the two worlds, for she is clearly the main channel. Frieda herself grumbles to K.: "I am valuable only to you because I was Klamm's lover" (Kafka 2009, p. 138). Frieda's beauty in K.'s view and in the view of the entire village[4] derives from her relationship with Klamm: "It was the proximity of Klamm that had made her so ridiculously enticing, and enticed as he was, K. had swept her into his arms, where she was now withering away" (p. 121). Thus, as Pepi admits, K. fell into Frieda's arms only because she had been Klamm's lover.

Pepi's testimony is particularly important, for as we will see Pepi is extraordinarily familiar with Frieda:

> Isn't he ashamed of himself? What did he see in Frieda? He could admit it now. Could that thin, sallow creature really have appealed to him? Oh no, he didn't even look at her, she just told him that she was Klamm's lover, that was interesting news to him, and he was lost. (p. 121)

Frieda is the bridge joining between K. and Klamm, the last possible means toward a sane dialogue between the two parts of the divided character. Yet matters are never fully explained in Kafka's books, and the truth is a superfluous concept: "You don't need to accept everything as true, you only have to accept it as necessary" (Kafka 2006, p. 263). Reality is the encounter with an infinite number of contradictory versions of reality, all of which are equally possible and impossible. Reality loses its importance relative to interpretation—a world of interpretations upon interpretations. One of the versions belongs to Bürgel, one of the officials at the pub. He tells a sleepy K. that once Frieda "brought Klamm his beer. There seems to be another girl there now. The change is of no significance, of course, probably not for anyone and certainly not for Klamm" (Kafka 2009, p. 238). The reason for this lack of significance from Klamm's perspective once again relates to his emotional numbness. Klamm is in a profoundly depressive state, totally indifferent and emotionally blunted. He does not want to leave his room and does not want to meet anyone from the village. This becomes clear in additional descriptions that continue the same line of thought, in which Klamm represents the outside world that Kafka knows nothing about: "My novel is the cliff on which I am hanging, and I know nothing of what is going on in the world" (Kafka 1953, p. 264). Alternatively, Klamm represents an individual in a state of awakening, and in this case K. represents the world of dreams. Thus from Pepi's description of the outside world we learn that this is a world of absolute stagnation:

> Oh, winter here is long, a very long, monotonous winter. But we don't complain of that down there, we're safe there from the winter. Well, some time spring will come, and summer too, and they have their own time, but now, as we remember them, spring and summer seem as short as if they weren't much more than two days long, and even on those days snow sometimes falls in the middle of the finest weather. (Kafka 2009, pp. 271–272)

Klamm's world, the outside world, is always rainy and snowy, always frozen. The weather outside represents Klamm's mood. It is the climate that the posttraumatic survivor lives within.

Returning to the K.-Klamm-Frieda triangle, we see that Frieda is not torn between two men but rather between two identities belonging to one man in one body. This may be Klamm of the outer world versus K. of the inner world, or perhaps Klamm represents the state of wakefulness while K. represents the condition of sleep. In any case, the discrepancy between reality on the one hand and imagination and hallucination on the other does not really exist. For this reason, Frieda is positioned at the inn, at the meeting point between the inner and the outer worlds, in the twilight zone, or alternatively, the therapeutic zone. In any event, the nature of Frieda's relationship with Klamm is not clear. It is even possible to think that Frieda is a caregiver and perhaps a jailer. Frieda says to K.: "There's a little peephole there; you can look through that" (p. 35). You look at a prisoner or the inmate in an insane asylum through a peephole, but not at a lover. When Frieda is enticed by K. (and it is not clear who is the one doing the tempting and who is being tempted), she is attracted to the other side, that is to the inner world, of Klamm. Thus she too must become divided. In this context, Kafka writes the following in his diary: "This is how it is, Felice. And yet they are locked in combat, and yet they could be yours; the trouble is that they cannot be changed unless both were to be destroyed" (Kafka 1974, p. 438).

Thus what she says to K. can be understood: "As for you, I know everything about you. You are the land surveyor" (Kafka 2009, p. 37). Through Frieda's acquaintance with Klamm—whether she is his lover or his caregiver or his fantasy—she meets K.: "for who can keep anything from Klamm" (p. 102). This can be explained as follows: If Klamm knows K. who thus knows Frieda through his acquaintance with Klamm, she then is also acquainted with K. As noted, the fact that Klamm refuses to meet with K. does not indicate that they do not know one another. In fact, the opposite seems to be true. Klamm cannot meet with K. based upon his deepest acquaintance, and thus too he cannot meet with Frieda while she is with K. This is a total division. Yet within this state of being divided and of lack of acquaintance there is nevertheless some sort of intimacy, for the two identities share the same body.

Frieda's acquaintance with the other side of Klamm is not sufficient. In order to be with K., Frieda too must be divided. Thus, when Frieda says to K. that "being close to you, believe me, is my dream, that and only that" (p. 222), she is not speaking metaphorically. Frieda understands that her meeting with K. can only take place during the division, only when she leaves the Herrenhof Inn and goes to the village. It can only happen when she is in a dreamlike state of consciousness. Here I permit myself to be quite clear in making this statement—at least to the extent that one can be clear in the context of Kafka—because while K. and Frieda are making love at the Herrenhof, K. suddenly hears "a cheering sign of dawn when a voice from Klamm's room called for Frieda in a deep, commanding, but indifferent tone" (p. 40). All the while they are at the Herrenhof Klamm is present, for this is the site of the encounter and if Frieda wants to be with K., she must leave the inn. Only outside the inn can she be with K. From this we can understand that K. is not Frieda's Dream with a capital D. Rather he is possible only in a dream, only in an inner world totally cut off from the outside world. Klamm belongs to the castle, while K. belongs to the village. Therefore, in order to belong only to K. Frieda must leave the twilight zone and go to the village, to the desolate environs throughout which K. roams.

Pepi is the other side of Frieda. When Frieda "descends" she releases Pepi, who ascends: "I've been working here with her [Frieda] for several years, we always shared a bed, but I can't say I was close friends with her, and I'm sure she doesn't give me a thought any more" (p. 89). This lack of closeness between them also stems from the structured dissociation theory. The divided characters do not know each other and even despise one another. Yet at the same time they know each other in the most intimate way possible, for they share one body. This abhorrence leads Pepi to describe Frieda as follows: "an unattractive thin girl not as young as she used to be, with short, sparse hair, a sly girl too . . . her face and body were undoubtedly a miserable sight" (p. 253). Pepi tells K. that all she wants is to be his lover, and thus in effect to replicate Frieda obsessively, over and again, as in Frieda's relationship with Klamm, and to replace the loathsome Frieda once and for all:

And then Pepi had dreamed that when she had the position herself K. would come to plead with her, and she would have the choice of either listening to K. and losing the job, or turning him down and rising higher. She had worked it out that she would give up everything and lower herself to his level, and teach him the true love that he could never know with Frieda, the love that is independent of all the grand positions in the world. (p. 254)

Pepi is Frieda's undesired shadow, just as K. is Klamm's cold sweat. K. and Pepi are in the lower world, the world of desires and dirty dreams. They both long, though only seemingly, to enter the light. Yet they both actually prefer to remain in the cellars, in the village, in the world of dark desires. This is the reason that on the one hand Pepi suggests that K. go down to the lower world, to the young maids, to the world of murky urges and instincts: "We've both been betrayed, let's stay together, come down to the other maids with me" (2009, p. 268). We know how much Kafka loved this world, as he wrote in this diary in 1910: "I passed by the brothel as though past the house of a beloved" (Kafka 1976, p. 12). From this perspective we understand that K.'s attempt to be Frieda's lover and even her husband is an attempt to break out—something that has no chance of succeeding. Frieda for her part is not capable of truly penetrating the inner world of Klamm, who as noted represents K. She belongs to him only in the outside world. Indeed, Klamm does not actually allow her to penetrate inside. Not her and not anyone else. This is the nature of the posttraumatic survivor—blunted emotions, emotional death, craziness, and inner anxiety that can be neither remedied nor relieved.

The Assistants

There is another point of interface between the castle and K. and between K. and Frieda: Artur and Jeremiah, K.'s assistants. It is important to note that it is not at all clear whether K. is really a surveyor or whether he had assistants along the way. The way in which the word "surveyor" is written in German indicates someone who makes errors in measurement. Nevertheless, in the posttraumatic state of being we cannot distinguish between hallucination and reality. Thus, we do not know who K. is, and even K. himself does not know, as becomes evident from K.'s telephone call to the castle representatives: "'Who am I, then?' asked K." (Kafka 2009, p. 22). Of course from what the mayor says we know that the telephones in the castle are not connected:

> Down here, we hear that constant telephoning as a rushing, singing sound on the line, and I'm sure you've heard it too. But that rushing, singing sound is the only real, trustworthy information that the telephone conveys to us down here, and everything else is just an illusion. *There is no telephone connection to the castle, there's no switchboard passing on our calls;* if we call someone in the castle from here, the telephones ring in all the lower departments, or perhaps they would if, as I know for a fact, the sound was not turned off on nearly all of them. (pp. 66–67, my emphasis)

Who, then, was K. talking to? K.'s assistants are sent to him from the castle. Later it becomes clear that Galater, another official who represents Klamm, sent them and ordered them to reassure K.: "When Galater sent us to you he said...you two are going to be the land surveyor's assistants...the main thing is that I want you to cheer him up a little. I hear he takes everything very hard" (p. 204). Thus the role of the assistants is to cheer K. up. Indeed, the assistants are K.'s caregivers. Later we learn that Jeremiah is a chamber man at the Herrenhof, that is, one of the staff of caregivers at the convalescent home. But to K. these are neither caregivers nor assistants but rather jailers. K. says to the Bridge innkeeper: "These are my assistants. You treat them as if they were my guards instead, and your assistants" (p. 50). This is quite clear in light of the fact that caregivers at insane asylums are guards of a sort.

The duality of the assistants represents, and thus replicates, the duality of K. and Klamm. When K. first meets his new assistants he immediately asks them: "Well, so who are you?" and they reply: "Your assistants" (p. 19). He continues to muse out loud, asking as if he does not expect a reply: "Do you say you're my old assistants who were coming on after me and whom I'm expecting?" (p. 19). At this point a number of possibilities arise. The clearest one is that K. is not a land surveyor and he has no assistants on the way. Another possibility is that K. is indeed a land surveyor, even though there is no evidence of this at any point in the story except perhaps in the following question that K. asks: "'Do you know anything about land surveying?' 'No,' they said. 'But if you claim to be my old assistants, then you must know something about it,' said K." (p. 19). Yet from this question it is still impossible to conclude that K. is a surveyor, but rather simply that he expected that if the castle was already sending him assistants they would know something about land surveying, for K. is thought to be a land surveyor. But the castle knows everything about K., and even that he is not really a land surveyor. Therefore the castle sent him emissaries suitable to him.

There is also a third possibility. K. does not know whether or not he is a surveyor. K. does not believe himself. In the posttraumatic reality, the subject loses the ability to distinguish between hallucination and reality, between lies and truth. Therefore, K. simply does not know who he really is. He is lost in a thicket of identities and dualities. "'I'm going to have a hard time with you two,' said K., comparing their faces yet again. 'How am I to know which of you is which?'" (Kafka 2009, p. 20). Immediately afterwards he speaks harshly to them: "'The only difference between you is your names, and apart from that'—he hesitated—'apart from that you're as like as two snakes'" (p. 20). The mission of the assistants is to reflect the duality in which K. is imprisoned. This is how they "assist" K. Their role is to help K. understand his divided identity. At this point we should remember that it is K. and no other who declares that he has precisely two assistants (not one and not three). It is K. who constantly thinks in terms of dual images. Thus it is no surprise that K. immediately understands this. He understands the situation precisely: "I can't distinguish between you with those. So I shall treat you as a single man, and call you both Artur" (p. 20). Yet when it comes to him and Klamm, he continues to refuse to understand that he and Klamm are actually the same person. K. refuses to accept this even though, as we have seen, on a certain level he understands it very well.

The assistants precisely reflect K.'s condition as a dual figure. He is blind to the situation on the one hand and totally conscious of it on the other. For example, when K. sees one of the assistants hanging onto the fence trellis, dead tired, he says to himself: "I must say . . . he's a model of intransigence" (p. 143) and immediately adds a profound insight that he cannot project onto his own life: "it could freeze him to that fence" (p. 143). This is a reflective statement, for it is clear that the assistant's condition represents that of K. Later that evening he admits that he used to drive along the same road that one of his assistants drove along. K. confirms the comment made by Amalia (sister of Olga and Barnabas): "I once heard of a young man who was busy thinking about the castle day and night, he neglected all else, there were fears for his sanity because his whole mind was up there in the castle" (p. 180). In response K. states: "I think I'd like that man" (p. 180). a) That is, even though he despises the stubborn assistant who could lead him to his death, he tells Amalia that he actually likes a similarly stubborn character she has spoken about. In this sense it seems that he yearns for death more than for any sort of life. K. knows that this stubbornness will end in death and yet he consciously chooses this approach. In effect he yearns for death.

K.'s dialogue with the assistants continues to be inconsistent, marked by a mixture of disgust and admiration. For days the assistants cling to K. while he makes sure to abuse them constantly. Then he suddenly turns to Jeremiah, who has been waiting for him at night on the path outside Olga's house, and says to him: "but in spite of the respect I feel for your person, even if you feel none for mine any more" (p. 208). K. says this to Jeremiah immediately after meeting him, after having previously decided to sneak outside in order to surprise Jeremiah and beat him up. This follows what happened the previous night when K. pummeled Artur, the other assistant. At a certain point after that night during which K. beat up Artur in his sleep in the schoolroom (the night prior to the meeting between K. and Jeremiah outside of Olga's house), Jeremiah and Artur part ways. Artur goes to complain at the castle, while Jeremiah stays with Frieda. At this point, after Jeremiah and Artur have parted, when K. meets Jeremiah outside of Olga's house he does not recognize him:

> "But who are you?" asked K. suddenly, for it didn't seem to be the assistant after all. He seemed older, wearier, his face fuller but more lined. "Don't you know me?" asked the man. "Why, I'm Jeremias, your former assistant." "You are?" said K. He walked slowly, limping slightly, with a pernickety and sickly air. (p. 204)

K. answers him: "But you look quite different" (p. 208). The dialogue is reminiscent of the nature of the relations between Don Quixote and Sancho Panza. Panza is nothing more than the rational voice in the head of the crazy, impractical knight. Similarly, Jeremiah symbolizes a final sane voice amidst absolute insanity. The moment K. sees Jeremiah as he really is represents his confrontation with reality, with what truly exists. This is the genuine encounter with Klamm, for the meeting with the castle takes place without K. recognizing it. This is the meeting K. longs for, but when it occurs he is not capable of understanding it. It would be more accurate to say that K. avoids understanding it, for he later claims that Jeremiah is nothing other than a little Klamm. The meeting with Jeremiah is an encounter with an impossible reality. Jeremiah represents the reality in which the posttraumatic survivor is sick and worn out by the endless inner struggle between different identities. Jeremiah represents Klamm, and hence also the relationship with Frieda. In any event, the fact that Jeremiah is a form of Klamm explains why K. beats up on Jeremiah and at the same time admires and respects him.

For the posttraumatic survivor, duality is the secret to maintaining some semblance of vitality. Jeremiah's exhaustion bursts forth and is revealed only when he is separated from Artur. Polarity is what provides the posttraumatic survivor with the strength to live. Therefore, immediately after Artur disappears from the scene it becomes apparent that in fact Jeremiah is not so young after all. K. even describes Jeremiah as a lump of flesh, someone who has lost all that is vital in himself: "a specimen of humanity who sometimes gave the impression of not being properly alive" (p. 207). The radical alteration in Jeremiah's appearance after his separation from Artur shows us that for the posttraumatic survivor, who cannot cope with reality as it is, division of the self is the only way to cope with life. Dividing the self is what makes it possible to live in an impossible world, for coping with reality is out of the question. Nevertheless, while the divided inner world constitutes a defense mechanism of sorts, the situation in the outside world is in reality totally different. The bifurcated individual is exhausted, weak, and sick, exactly how Kafka was in his own life.

As already noted, the assistants reflect the condition of the individual with a divided identity. Among other things this finds expression in the similarity between K.'s description of Jeremiah and the way in which the castle is perceived by K.: "The castle, its outline already beginning to blur, lay as still as always. K. had never seen the slightest sign of life there" (p. 88). Indeed, not only is K. describing Jeremiah. He is also describing the man within whom he is imprisoned—Klamm—lame, fatigued, old, and sick.

To conclude this section, I wish to note that the assistants' dialogue with K. represents the dialogue between Klamm and K. Jeremiah represents Klamm in the dialogue between K. and Klamm, while the duality of Jeremiah and Artur represents the divide between Klamm and K. Among other things, this becomes clear through the dialogue between Frieda and K.'s assistants. Frieda has a special relationship with the assistants in general and with Jeremiah in particular, a relationship marked by sexual attraction and rejection. This is apparent throughout the book. K. refers to it time and again while Frieda does not attempt, is not able, or does not want to deny it. The relationship between Frieda and the dual assistants represents her dual relationship with Klamm and with K., who are, as noted, characters with dual identities. Therefore, when Frieda pleads with K. to free her from the burden of the assistants, she is really asking for the impossible. She asks K. and Klamm to conjoin and unite into a single character with one identity, not two. This is nothing other than an impossible fantasy for Kafka the author. The relationship between Frieda and the dual assistants is a reflection of her relationship with K. and Klamm. Hence Frieda is attracted to the assistants. And indeed, when Jeremiah arrives at the inn on the last night, after K. has attempted to surprise him and beat him up, he naturally lies down to rest in Frieda's bed. K. then says:

He doesn't feel a trace of love for you, he told me so openly, as Klamm's former lover you seem to him, naturally, someone to be respected, and settling into your room and feeling like a little Klamm for once must be very nice, but that's all. You yourself mean nothing to him. (p. 220)

After this statement, there is no longer any room for doubt (to the extent that this can be said in reference to Kafka). Jeremiah is indeed a small version of Klamm. Artur and Jeremiah represent the duality of K. and Klamm. Jeremiah represents Klamm, who is in effect an old and weak man, sick and powerless, and also Frieda's lover.

THE DUAL CHARACTER AS A KEY TO UNDERSTANDING POSTTRAUMATIC CULTURE

The novel *The Castle* represents the condition of the posttraumatic survivor—the divided state of being: "There have always been, and still are, two selves wrestling with each other" (Kafka 1974, p. 438). This is a condition in which the outside world is intolerable, so the subject submerges himself, dives, and plunges deep into his inner world and creates another self there. *The Castle* provides a unique phenomenological description of the world of the posttraumatic survivor. This is a person who is divided and broken apart. Not only is his inner world cut off from the outside world, it is also engaged in a constant struggle with the outer world. In this condition the conflict is an impossible one. Therefore, the posttraumatic survivor is absorbed by a never-ending inner struggle that turns this world into hell on earth.

As we have seen, the struggle between two characters that are one finds expression in movies such as *Fight Club, The Deer Hunter,* and *Apocalypse Now.* I believe that understanding the sources of this split is critical not only to understanding the split posttraumatic figure but also to understanding the divided posttraumatic society.

Kafka remains the focal point throughout the novel, and this is no coincidence. One of the most difficult issues when it comes to the posttraumatic figure is the difficulty in depicting the trauma—the difficulty in depicting the lacuna, the excess, the silence. The next chapter provides an in-depth examination of the issue of silence and an attempt to understand the importance of creating a new language that will allow for processes of working through the trauma. So long as language imprisons us and preserves our silence, the posttraumatic victim and posttraumatic society are imprisoned by an obsessive compulsion to repeat the traumatic moment. In other words, so long as we are unable to break the silence, we are condemned to wander like K. in the castle. Yet as we will see in the next chapter, even though Kafka does not enable working through to occur, he does invent a new language that emerges from within the silence.

NOTES

1. Kafka apparently began writing *The Castle* in January 1922, in a second wave of creativity (the first was in 1914) at a snowy vacation resort. Kafka admits that he was in a condition that was nothing less than a world war: a sense of impossible persecution with increasing self-accusations, in an extremely precarious emotional and physical state, a sense of threat that became more and more substantial from day to day. He continued writing the novel at the home of his favorite sister Ottla in the village of Planá, where he apparently wrote the last nine chapters of the novel. During that period he had at least four serious nervous breakdowns. In March of 1922 he read the first chapter to Max Brod. Evidently he continued writing the book through August of 1922. According to Brod, the novel was meant to end with K.'s death. Immediately after that an emissary from the castle would arrive to give the message to K. that he could remain in the village.

2. In the case of Kafka, it is impossible to separate his autobiographical writing from his literary writing, "for it is through writing that I keep a hold on life" (Kafka 1974, p. 138), and he further adds: "I have no literary interests, but am made of literature, I am nothing else, and cannot be anything else" (p. 304).

3. This is a recurring motif in Kafka's writing: "What is it that makes you all behave as though you were real? Are you trying to make me believe I'm unreal?" (Kafka 1971b, p. 61).

4. We can understand this from K.'s dialogue with Pepi, the chambermaid who replaced Frieda for four days while she went to live with K.

CHAPTER 8

This is the End: A World of Silence

SILENCE IN THE POSTTRAUMATIC ERA

One of the major issues in the study of trauma touches upon the possibility of describing the traumatic experience—an experience that by definition is almost beyond words, and is certainly beyond words if we adopt the Lacanian approach. This issue becomes particularly critical in view of Felman's definition of the twentieth century as the posttraumatic century in her groundbreaking book *Testimony* (Felman and Laub 1992). In this book Felman and Laub focus primarily on the matter of testimony and on the witness. Reading this book raises disturbing questions. On one level it asks what, if anything, the witness' story tells us about the traumatic experience. On another level it raises an even more disturbing question: Is trauma something that can be "talked about" or "talked out"? Or to put it more radically, can trauma even be represented? The answers to these questions have far-reaching implications, not only with respect to our ability to "trust" (e.g., from the legal perspective) the survivor testimony of a particular trauma victim, but also regarding the way we understand our own traumatic past as individuals and as nations. This is particularly the case in view of the customary notion that accurate memory of traumatic events in the joint and collective past is an important component in the legitimization of civil society (LaCapra 2001). Therefore, if trauma cannot be accurately described or represented (LaCapra 1994), we clearly find ourselves in a

© The Author(s) 2017
Y. Ataria, *The Structural Trauma of Western Culture*,
DOI 10.1007/978-3-319-53228-8_8

situation in which the writing of history, for example, cannot in any way rely upon the testimony of those who survived the inferno.

Yet perhaps there is another possibility—the possibility of silence as a means of expression, silence as a fissure through which we can understand trauma. I seek to show that silence is a major attribute of the traumatic experience (Laub 1995) and that both as researchers analyzing trauma and as artistic creators we are responsible for representing this silence and remaining faithful to it.

In this chapter, I attempt to examine the relatively radical notion that extreme traumatic experiences are not only beyond the ability of survivors to describe verbally but are also beyond their ability to describe in any "familiar" or existing language. In addition, I also argue that turning trauma into a narrative account—even if from the survivor's point of view this is essential on the road to "recovery"—in effect constitutes the erasure of the traumatic experience and its trans-formation into just another story. Furthermore, I maintain that LaCapra's "middle voice"—a voice that is not completely in the past yet not completely in the present—disregards the most important component of trauma: the silence that in particular characterizes the subject who suffered from dissociation during the trauma and now lives in a dissocia-tive climate.

LaCapra—Basic Concepts

Excess

"Excess" is a basic concept in LaCapra's philosophy. Excess is *that thing* in the traumatic experience that diverges from every symbolic and/or verbal representation. Excess creates an emptiness that cannot be filled by sym-bols or representations, even when the victim describes the traumatic event in great detail. Thus, in the posttraumatic survivor's attempt to fill the emptiness, a repetition compulsion develops in which flashbacks, nightmares, and the like find expression.

Acting Out/Working Through

LaCapra points to two major means by which a particular individual or society copes with traumatic events, or more specifically with the excess of the traumatic experience.

(1) Acting out is a process of uncontrollable and unconscious repetition on the part of the posttraumatic survivor, who is relentlessly oppressed by the past even to the point of being captivated and confined within it. This finds expression in the compulsive repetition of recurring traumatic scenes. In this condition the dimension of time collapses and the individual feels as if he is returning to the past and reliving the traumatic scene over and over again.

Acting out is related to repetition, and even to the repetition compulsion—the tendency to repeat something compulsively. This is very clear in the case of people who undergo a trauma. They have a tendency to relive the past, to exist in the present as if they were still fully in the past, with no distance from it, as in the following:

> They tend to relive occurrences, or at least find that those occurrences intrude on their present existence, for example, in flashbacks; or in nightmares; or in words that are compulsively repeated, and that don't seem to have their ordinary meaning, because they're taking on different connotations from another situation, in another place. (LaCapra 1998, p. 2)

(2) Working through can take place on the individual or the institutional level. In this process the traumatic event is to a certain extent controlled and contained, and is even represented, if only partially. This process is likely to somewhat limit acting out and compulsive repetition, for it leads to creating a distinction and separation between the current moment and the traumatic event. Thus the traumatic subject is capable of returning to the traumatic moment without uncontrollably sinking into that moment itself. That is, the subject recalls the trauma but at the same time continues to be present in the here and now:

> In the working-through, the person tries to gain critical distance on a problem, to be able to distinguish between past, present and future. For the victim, this means his ability to say to himself, "Yes, that happened to me back then. It was distressing, overwhelming, perhaps I can't entirely disengage myself from it, but I'm

existing here and now, and this is different from back then."
(LaCapra 1998, pp. 2–3)

It is important to understand, however, that despite the theoretical distinction between these two processes, acting out is certainly likely to be an essential condition for working through. In effect, then, acting out and working through are intimately linked to one another. Yet nonetheless, LaCapra underlines that working through and acting out are indeed *distinct* processes. Based on this dialogue between acting out and working through, LaCapra suggests a middle ground:

> Acting-out and working-through, in this sense, are a distinction, in that one may never be totally separate from the other, and the two may always be implicated in each other. But it's very important to see them as countervailing forces, and to recognize that there are possibilities of working-through that do not go to the extreme of total transcendence of acting-out, or total transcendence of the past. (LaCapra 1998, p. 6)

LaCapra—Major Difficulties

LaCapra, like other major scholars, does not refer to one factor that is central to the study of trauma: Dissociation during trauma is the number one risk factor for the development of posttraumatic symptoms (Ozer et al. 2003). Therefore, if as a result of World War II we are indeed living in a posttraumatic century, as Felman and Laub have suggested (1992), we must take the following possibility into consideration: We are living in an era marked by strong dissociative characteristics (as this book has suggested). With this in mind it is essential to distinguish between trauma survivors who do not suffer from posttrauma and those who do. As we have seen throughout this book, those who suffer from posttrauma live in a dissociative climate, in which, as elaborated below, any process of working through demands annihilation of the traumatic figure within them. That is to say, working through processes are those in which the trauma victim relinquishes the silence marking the trauma in favor of the word and the narrative (e.g., "just another story"). Yet in a deeper sense, the word does not touch upon the silence and thus by definition cannot represent the trauma. Consequently, it can be said that not only is the story not faithful to the traumatic experience, but also in some sense the story negates the traumatic experience.

Dissociation—A World that Denounces Itself

Definition

Under conditions of dissociation, events that are usually connected one to another become disconnected, detached, and distinct one from the other. Conscious parts of the "self" become separated from each other and endowed with a sense of their independence, "selfness," and separateness. Moreover, dissociative states are often marked by emotional numbness (emotional apathy). In more severe cases the individual may feel as if he is being controlled by outside forces, and the subject finds himself operating in a way that does not really work for him without being able to object and desist from following through in this manner. Many researchers believe that dissociation is a defense or coping mechanism activated during trauma that enables the organism to survive (Herman 1992; Van Der Kolk 1987; Van Der Kolk and Van Der Hart 1989; Van Der Kolk et al. 1996). In a situation in which there is no possibility for fight or flight, only one option remains—cutting oneself off from reality and from the suffering body. However, given that dissociation at the time of trauma is the number one risk factor for the development of posttraumatic symptoms, it is quite clear that we cannot overlook dissociation in examining the climate in which the survivor lives after the trauma. In the context of this book, then, we cannot ignore dissociation as a feature that stands at the very core of the posttraumatic society.

Dissociation During Trauma and the Question of Memory

One of the major problems when it comes to understanding the dissociative experience during trauma is related to the following question: How, if at all, does the subject remember the traumatic experience in general and the dissociative experience during trauma in particular (McNally 2003)? This question is inherent to understanding the dissociative experience. Shattered memory and dissociation during trauma are two sides of the same coin (Van Der Kolk 1994; Van Der Kolk and Fisler 1995). Some studies do show that dissociative-traumatic memory is often shattered and even unreliable, yet opinions are divided regarding the reasons for this. According to one approach, due to dissociation during the trauma the experience is not encoded, so *that from the subject's perspective it does not exist—it is absent.* According to another approach, however, the experience itself is encoded but the subject *does not have access* to the memory in the present—the traumatic memory is cut off from the narrative. Each of these possibilities has different and far-reaching implications with respect to our understanding of the dissociative experience and the way in which we remember it, if at all. A third approach merges these two approaches, claiming that some parts of the experience are not encoded and therefore are absent, while other parts are encoded and not accessible, but can be reconstructed (Spiegel 1997).

Moreover, studies have shown that a decrease in the intensity of posttraumatic symptoms is accompanied by a memory of the traumatic experience that is less shattered. In other words, "recovery" from trauma finds expression in a more organized, though not necessarily more genuine, narrative memory of the traumatic event (Kindta et al. 2005). To this point it is important to add that a more organized narrative memory is not necessarily a more "genuine" or more "authentic" memory. In effect, the opposite may be true: the process of recovery is accompanied by structuring a memory that the subject *can live with* (Yovell et al. 2003), and therefore by definition one that covers up more than it reveals (Ataria 2014b).

In a situation in which memory is not absent, another important characteristic is the subject's inability to willingly and intentionally recall the memory of the dissociative experience during the trauma (Ehlers et al. 2004). This leads to the conclusion that the dissociative experience remains cut off from the autobiographical/narrative sense of self in the present (Van Der Kolk and Fisler 1995). Some researchers claim that this is again a type of defense mechanism (Sutherland and Bryant 2008).

Hence, it is possible to suggest that one of the major characteristics of dissociation during trauma is the lack of narrative memory on the one hand and the presence of a physical, intrusive, uncontrollable memory of the event on the other. The importance of this attribute cannot be exaggerated for it constitutes the basis of the posttraumatic, chaotic/destructive symptomatology: a narrative memory that is missing, absent, or inaccessible versus a strong and uncontrollable physical memory (Van Der Kolk 1987). At this extreme point, this mechanism can lead to structural dissociation.

Structural Dissociation

In direct consequence of the above, dissociation during trauma can develop into structural dissociation, a condition in which the survivor has two different and contradictory personalities that are not conscious of each other: the "apparently normal" part of the personality and the "emotional" part of the personality (Nijenhuis et al. 2010; Van Der Hart et al. 2004). Under such circumstances the subject on the one hand feels totally disconnected from the traumatic event to the point of not even remembering it, while on the other hand he can experience the trauma anew in the here and now, usually as a result of environmental stimuli of which he is totally unaware. This re-experiencing of the trauma finds expression in nightmares, flashbacks, and the like (Ehlers and Clark 2000). In extreme cases these two personalities become enemies and even attempt to destroy one another, as we have seen in previous chapters.

It would not be an exaggeration to state that this is one of the most problematic mechanisms of the posttraumatic survivor, and it stems *directly* from dissociation during trauma. The major cause of the need to destroy oneself or rather the outside world is the extreme traumatic event that not only remains unprocessed cognitively but also is impossible to describe in any way. To use LaCapra's terminology, we can define this indescribable phenomenon as excess—an experience that exists far beyond the boundaries of the possible and hence remains beyond the boundaries of language as well. One reason the traumatic experience eludes proper expression is that it is deeply imprinted within the body and hence does not undergo high-level cognitive processing. In effect, the body is charged with trauma to the point of becoming totally identified with the traumatic experience. The bodily memory is unrepresented and completely uncontrolled, and as a result it erupts powerfully in the physical dimension, causing the posttraumatic survivor to feel time and again that he is present at the moment of trauma (Ehlers et al. 2004). Under such conditions, trauma apparently does not turn into "memory" but rather remains in the "here and now." In the posttraumatic survivor's attempt to cope with the physical nature of the traumatic memory, a total division is created between the two personalities: the apparently normal on the one hand and the emotional-physical on the other. Clearly under these circumstances a dialogue between the two is impossible, for on one side there is a world comprised totally of language, words, and symbols while on the other there is a world that by definition rejects language. This point is discussed in detail in the next section.

The Need to Destroy the Trauma

As we saw earlier, both Kurtz (Brando) and Captain Willard (Sheen) from the movie *Apocalypse Now* as well as Mike (De Niro) and Nick (Walken) from the movie *The Deer Hunter* represent the posttraumatic survivor that suffers from structural dissociation. These figures (Kurtz/Willard and Mike/Nick) are in fact the two sides of a fragmented posttraumatic subject that cannot live together in the same place, in one body, and therefore attempt to destroy each other.

In *The Deer Hunter,* Mike and Nick are really the same character. At the end of the movie Mike goes back to Vietnam in order to "save" Nick, but in effect he goes back to play the final game in a series of never-ending games. In this game Mike is destined to destroy the other that is within himself, or to be more accurate, to destroy the body that remembers the trauma, indeed that is loaded with trauma. As we are led to understand, Nick (Walken) obsessively and uncontrollably recreates, over and over again, the game of Russian roulette he played against Mike (De Niro) while they were Vietcong prisoners of war. Nick is completely loyal to silence and to trauma. Thus—and this is a critical point—he dies as soon as he utters his first word since his release from the Vietcong prison. This word, which is the strongest representation of the difficulty built into the situation of the posttraumatic survivor, is of course "Home." Immediately after uttering this word, he grabs the gun and again, for the last time, reconstructs the game of Russian roulette. In this game, he "loses" to his best friend Mike, who tried to save him and by so doing save himself as well. As noted, Nick is the other side of Mike and therefore knows exactly what Mike experiences in returning "Home." Therefore, Nick's use of the word "Home" is not naïve. In essence, he is telling Mike, and us as well, that the posttraumatic Vietnam soldiers no longer have a home and cannot have a home. More precisely, Nick is telling Mike that both of them are already at home in Vietnam, in a game of Russian roulette, and that no one can fool him. The major and most important insight emerging from this film is that the posttraumatic figure has no home other than in a traumatic and frightening world. Only there can the posttraumatic hero feel at home.

Yet when we analyze this scene from a broader perspective, we understand that in effect this is not a loss. Indeed Nick's so-called suicide (as we saw earlier, it is possible to treat Mike's attempt as suicidal by its very nature) is part of his attempt to return to life, to what he defines as "home." To do so he must destroy his inner world by wiping out the trauma that has been branded onto his body like the marks of shooting heroin are branded onto Nick's hands. This is the only route that a survivor living in a dissociative climate can take. Thus, when Nick allows himself to speak, he in effect relinquishes the traumatic experience itself.

Hence, in the case of the relationship between Nick and Mike speech represents the "relinquishment" of loyalty to the traumatic experience for the sake of "recovery" and "returning to life." This relinquishment finds expression in the destruction of the physical level of the trauma for the sake of the word, which always tells a lie.

A similar process occurs in the film *Apocalypse Now*. Despite the preliminary dialogue between Kurtz (Brando) and Willard (Sheen), here as well they are the same character and the murder is inevitable. The purpose of Willard's journey is to destroy the part that he cannot contain within himself Hence at the end of the movie Willard murders his inner world—Kurtz. A critical point to be noted in the images at the end of the movie is the fact that Sheen is holding a book in one hand and a knife in the other. In murdering his inner self—Kurtz—he in essence enables the story to take place. Only by murdering the inner world, the physical and nonverbal layer of the trauma, can the story of the traumatic experience be told. In this sense, in order to transform the trauma into a story, the excess in it, that is, the central attribute of the traumatic experience, must be destroyed.

Back to LaCapra

Severe dissociation during trauma can find expression in a totally split identity that cannot engage in dialogue with itself. Thus, any attempt at working through is impossible. In such extreme cases, the only technique for coping with the *excess* that LaCapra refers to is by destroying the other within the self. In this sense recovery processes do not contain the trauma but rather negate it. Any attempt to continue to live must involve creating a narrative that one can *live with*, and in order to do so the survivor must attempt to destroy the traumatic dimension within himself. If this process succeeds, then the self "recovers." But as noted this is not a real recovery. Instead, the individual in a sense has denied the existence of the trauma. The story can be told, but this story does not involve representing the trauma but rather inserting it into a particular pattern of kitsch or melodrama. In such a process the dimension of silence is not represented but rather is repressed or even annihilated. In relinquishing silence the survivor suddenly is unable to stop speaking and telling, yet the narrative does not describe the traumatic experience but rather something completely different. The narrative is an ongoing process of fleeing from the emptiness, using speech as an escape from the paralyzing silence.

This being the case, LaCapra's distinction between acting out and working through is correct and accurate. Furthermore, in LaCapra's model the processes of acting out and working through merge. Yet, it seems that at least in some cases, particularly cases of complex trauma or dissociative subtypes of PTSD and complex PTSD, this merger of acting out with working through is not possible. Moreover, it is possible to suggest that in many cases working through exacts the very high price of negating the unique nature of the traumatic experience and turning it into just *another story*. In this sense, working through in effect covers up and hides the trauma, transforming this experience from a unique event of encountering what is real into "a story one can live with." In effect, I would like to suggest that the posttraumatic survivor is faced with the possibility of "all or nothing"—to be silent and remain faithful to the traumatic event that defies representation, or to "sell out" for the sake of a bogus recovery. In the dissociative climate, this bogus recovery is nothing more than the destruction of the other inside oneself. Indeed, many researchers repeatedly stress the importance of silence to testimony.

THE CIRCUS OF WORDS VERSUS SILENCE

As we have seen, dissociation during trauma and shattered memory are two sides of the same coin. Nonetheless, the following two states must clearly be differentiated: the state of *absence* in which events *have not been encoded* due to circumstances and the state of *loss* in which the memory has been encoded but is not accessible. In the not-encoded case of absence, any attempts at working through lead to a narrative that has no connection whatsoever to the traumatic experience. This is a profound crisis of testimony, for processes of working through in a state of absent memory create a barren witness. In contrast with events that have been encoded but are not accessible in the present, at least in some cases working through, if it indeed takes place, is a process in which the trauma undergoes normalization and standardization of the worst kind. That is, the dictates of kitsch, melodrama, and a Hollywood happy ending are applied to the trauma. Total silence is exchanged for words that seem to bear significance, and as such they immediately fall into an infinite whirlpool of "word games" and deviate from the essence of the traumatic experience. Here again the traumatic experience loses its singularity—its burning silence. At the moment that the posttraumatic survivors verbalize their trauma they in essence relinquish it, for in this era glorious and dazzling silence is the only authentic option. Yet it is possible to suggest another way to cope. The silence no longer chooses the survivor. Rather he or she is the one who chooses to remain silent. In this powerful turnaround, the survivors remain authentic and committed to silence, but unlike in classic acting out processes, they rebuild themselves as silence and out of silence, hence remaining faithful to silence. Thus the posttraumatic survivor who chooses silence makes the only authentic choice possible in a world lacking any reasonable choices. Indeed silence can be considered to be a real choice made in an impossible world lacking in choices. Moreover, as Camus indicates, for certain victims this is the only possible choice other than suicide:

> The only coherent attitude based on non-signification would be silence—if silence, in its turn, were not significant. The absurd, in its purest form, attempts to remain dumb. If it finds its voice, it is because it has become complacent or, as we shall see, because it considers itself provisional. (Camus 1954, pp. 7–8)

Trauma is a totally impossible condition. It is a liminal state between nightmare and hallucination, a condition in which legal systems, beliefs, expectations, and hopes have all collapsed. By definition, then, there is no way to explain or interpret trauma. The posttraumatic survivor represents a condition in which truly there are no words, and this is not simply a metaphor. The words do not pierce what encases them; they constitute a set of symbols that is absolutely cut off from the experience. Any attempt to insert a word into this world—a holy world of mystics who have become submerged in dark nights—desecrates the holiness, desecrates the individual. More specifically, during trauma words become foreign so that in the posttraumatic condition it becomes impossible to use everyday language to describe the world behind the screen—the so-called REAL world. Words do not describe, do not explain. Words obstruct and obscure. Testimony harms the intimate relationship between the witness and the original experience. Speech turns what is impossible into just another story and thus destroys it in the most fundamental way. Words are only a step on the road to a "documentary film" and then to a commercial break.

Moreover, in the context of the circus that is Hollywood, speaking is tantamount to cooperating with the system, which as we all know is not only cynical but also always leads to the concentration camps in one way or another. In a deeper sense, spoken words are the first step toward cooperating with the simplistic and dangerous pattern of guilt-atonement-redemption. Words transform the trauma into story, narrative, or history. From the perspective of the posttraumatic survivor, words will always be a lie, will always conceal and sell out and market more than they reveal. Words will always remain within the realms of self-betrayal. Every word is a fraudulent self-branding. Every form of speech, even inner speech, represents the willingness to stand trial as victimizer or victim. Every form of speech is an admission and acceptance of the verdict, which ultimately, within the Kafkaesque reality, means that the entire accusation boils down to a single word engraved on the body, as it is in the case of "In the Penal Colony."

While in many cases words are a condition for recovery (Laub 1995), in the case of trauma, recovery is nothing more than the generation of a story that in some cases never was, a story that can be lived with and that has nothing in common with reality. For trauma, at least in certain cases, is not just another story that can be lived with. Trauma represents the total emptiness found beyond the words and beyond the ability to create a story. On another level this is the world that wants to move forward, forcing survivors to speak for it rather than for themselves. Victims continue to be victims. They speak so that we, the society that sacrificed them, will feel good about ourselves, so that we can listen to a good story, be shocked, have a good cry, and then move on again to sacrifice, to injure, to disregard what we do every day to the helpless and susceptible people in our closest circle. The story of extreme trauma enables us to continue to disregard the present and in this sense allows for the dismal routine of our everyday pornographic lives. Trauma stands at the center of the circus. This is a major insight in understanding posttraumatic culture. As Kafka understood in his story "*A Hunger Artist,*" trauma is not merely part of the circus. Indeed, it is necessary for the circus to exist.

Silence is the only possible way to rise up against trauma in a world in which words arrange everything. It is the only possible response in a world in which horrors are laundered and turned into some sort of slogan whose only function is to nourish and reinforce the model of the *Akeda* or Binding of Isaac—a model in which a *father weeps over his son who is weeping over his father* and at the same time continues to bind him. For the posttraumatic survivor within this circus, time is frozen. The survivor is disconnected from the body and from reality, while on the initial physical and pre-reflective level he or she continues to experience the impossible: screams, screeches, brutal rapes, skulls being smashed, teeth being extracted, the abuse of children and those who are helpless. And in the midst of this impossible situation, the victim stops shouting based upon a profound understanding that shouting is tantamount to admitting that there is a God, that there is order, that there is meaning. By shouting, the victim admits he still has expectations. In turn, if the victim still has expectations, he acknowledges his vulnerability. Therefore, as a first step the victim stops emitting the expected screams and is no longer willing to cooperate with the system. In a certain sense this is a declaration of having reached the lowest possible point on earth. The survivor walks around like a dead man among the living, in the state of consciousness of the *Muselmänner*. (*Muselmänner* was a slang term used among captives in the Nazi concentration camps to refer to those who suffered from a combination of starvation and exhaustion and had become resigned to their impending death.) To be more accurate, the survivor resembles someone living among the dead. Under such circumstances, it is impossible to testify without betraying the experience. Can anyone envision a situation in which a *Muselmann* can return to the world of words? This is patently impossible (Agamben 1999; Levi 1993). Some situations are irreversible and beyond description, situations where an attempt to talk about them is a sin in a godless world.

In silence, you return to a pre-reflective, pre-judgmental, pre-human state. You return to your body and to your initial contact with the world. This is the reason why Travis (De Niro) in the movie *Taxi Driver* applies face paint before he sets out on his killing spree. This face-painting makes a declaration that he is returning to a wild, authentic state. This posttraumatic survivor paints his face not to hide anything but rather to expose who he really is. For the same reason Captain Willard in *Apocalypse Now* paints himself before he sets out to kill his real father—Kurtz. The unwillingness to speak is the choice not to participate in yet another game. Silence is one clear and ongoing statement of "NO!" As Camus puts it, "[t]here is no fate that cannot be surmounted by scorn" (Camus 1955, p. 90). This is the reason why Meursault in Camus's novel *The Stranger* chooses to remain silent at his trial, for the very act of speaking is an admission, cooperation, willingness to be part of the impossible horrifying game of the bidding circus. Words rape you into becoming part of the pornographic circus of death, which photographs very well. In this sense, if these are indeed the rules of the game, then Ivan Karamazov in Dostoyevsky's novel *The Brothers Karamazov* (1992), in one of the most spine-tingling dialogues ever written, understands that it is simply preferable to remove oneself from the game: "If you are the dealer, I'm out of the game . . . If you are the dealer, let me out of the game" (Cohen, "You Want It Darker," 2016). Silence is the first step in this direction.

To use words is to create meaning, to create a story, to construct a beginning, middle, and end. A word will always mediate and even neutralize. A word is nothing more than a single opaque X that reveals nothing. The use of words is an attempt to create a world of causes and consequences. Yet the world of trauma is fundamentally different. It is a world of pure and banal evil, evil for the sake of evil. Evil without words. The posttraumatic survivor understands this very well, knows that words are nothing more than a cover, knows that even as we define we are covering up and concealing. The moment of pure trauma cannot, and should not, be placed into a pattern or frame.

The traumatic experience is a one-time encounter with the alien and indifferent world, an encounter with what is truly authentic (Evans 1996; Žižek 1991). For this reason Friedländer, whether consciously or perhaps unconsciously, chooses to open his monumental book *The Years of Extermination* (2007) with a quote from the journal of Stefan Ernest ("The Warsaw Ghetto," written in hiding in 1943 on the Aryan side of Warsaw): "Even the mightiest pen could not depict the whole, real, essential truth."

From the perspective of the posttraumatic survivor, the word itself in its nakedness forces the choice between life and death, for the word does not exist in the liminal state. This is the reason that Nick in the film *The Deer Hunter* must kill himself as soon as he first manages to hear a word—to hear Michael (De Niro). Michael is ostensibly the one who is attempting to go on. Like Klamm, Michael is the "man on the outside" who is "apparently normal." It seems that Michael is attracted to his inner world—to Nick (K.)—for in essence Michael cannot find himself in the world outside. Hence, Michael too does not have the ability to feel at "home." Nick represents Michael's inner world. From a state of purification, Nick is not ready or perhaps is not able to talk with himself. Therefore, when the narrative-self (Michael) insists on addressing him (Nick), he puts an end to his life. This is the reason that in the last scene Michael seems to be shooting at Nick (Morag 2009). This insistence on addressing the inner world of a posttraumatic survivor in words is tantamount to murder, for from the moment words enter the world of the posttraumatic survivor the experience is transformed from an experience lacking yet, in the same time, full of meaning, an authentic and one-time experience, to just another story—another statistic.

Posttraumatic survivors who remain true to themselves and to their initial experience of the encounter with absolute evil cannot move from the world of silence to the world of words, for this move by definition requires that they relinquish their own truth—and there is no truth other than this. In this sense the beautified term "recovery" proposed by Herman (1992) is nothing more than an existential break from the real thing. Any attempt to talk to posttraumatic survivors in any language whatsoever generates a violent response, whether internal as in *Apocalypse Now* and *The Deer Hunter* or external as in *Taxi Driver*. Authentic posttraumatic survivors that remain faithful and true to themselves will prefer death to talk—even inner talk. This indeed has its own absolute logic. Posttraumatic survivors continue to communicate, but in a much clearer and more direct way using the language of flesh and blood. Posttraumatic survivors seek only silence for themselves, but if silence is not allowed, they are faced with two either-or alternatives: either the other or me, either kill the individual facing them or kill themselves. From their perspective, there is no difference—as can be learned from the character of Travis (*Taxi Driver*). Thus, in his book *The Rebel*, Camus (1962a) describes suicide and murder as similar states. In a world of total indifference, neither has any meaning.

KAFKA: WRITING FROM WITHIN THE SILENCE

If we return to Felman's definition of the twentieth century—and there is no reason to exclude the twenty-first century from this definition—as the posttraumatic century and take into consideration that the risk factor for developing posttraumatic symptoms is dissociation during trauma accompanied by all its singular characteristics, it appears that we are indeed trapped in a crisis of testimony. That is to say, in the best of cases those "horror stories" we hear on many occasions cover up more than they reveal. In a worse case, they do not represent the traumatic experience itself, and in the worst of cases they simply cannot be a reliable source—neither in the research context nor in the legal context. The question then becomes whether it is indeed possible to talk from within the traumatic silence.

I wish to propose that the traumatic silence can be expressed. To do so we must think in terms of infinitely open allegory. According to the immortal formulation of Quintilianus (Quintilianus 1953, pp. Book 8, Chapter 6, Section 44), "allegory says one thing and means another" (Fletcher 1964, p. 2). Inspired by Kafka, we can also think of a very different category of allegories, those that are empty and hollow, that point at a world that is empty and lacking in meaning, a world of signifiers that signify nothing. In a world of such infinitely open and essentially hollow allegories, signifiers have no significance whatsoever. The signifiers lead us to a dead end. We have no possibility of understanding or interpreting a work through allegorical understanding, for the allegorical world does not lead us to an organized and rational world or a world of significance, but rather leads us cruelly and indifferently to our inner world of emptiness. The infinitely open allegory is a signifier of sorts that does not lead us to a real world but rather to another signifier. We move from one signifier to another without being exposed to any significance whatsoever. In this sense at some point we are forced to relinquish the concept of "significance" or "meaning" and then to relinquish the "concept" itself. The words of the posttraumatic survivor signify total emptiness, and Kafka's writing gives expression to the experience of someone who speaks with words lacking any kind of meaning—even imaginary.

Kafka had good reason to want to burn all his writings. Through this desire, this passion, Kafka calls upon us to expose the emptiness in his works. Kafka writes out of and about absolute nothingness. In this sense the burning exposes the emptiness. The burning destroys the work yet exposes its significance, or to be more accurate, its lack of significance. The burning of Kafka's works would be a disaster. Can we even imagine our world without Kafka's writings? Yet burning these writings would also be meaningless, just as the burning of bodies is at the same time a disaster yet also lacking in all significance—apart from Holocaust tourism as part of Uncle Sam's great circus. The law of the conservation of energy, according to which the total energy of an isolated system cannot change, has not been violated. The physical world has not been shocked. In fact, physical equations could not care less about being alive or being dead. And after all, we are pure physical entities.

Kafka fantasizes about destroying and thus nullifying his writings, for in so doing he exposes his work as an act that is at the same time uncontrollable but also a type of impossible choice in a world lacking choices for the posttraumatic survivor. Thus, the posttraumatic survivor creates out of a yearning to destroy his work and to expose its lack of meaning. By doing so Kafka tries to create a new world. Essentially, this seems like the only alternative for the posttraumatic survivor—to create a complete and perfect world, a new world that is not in any way dependent upon the real physical world, a world rooted in the dissociative climate. This new world represents the inner world of the posttraumatic survivor who knows that silence is the only authentic coping option. In the Kafkaesque world the concept of truth has no meaning whatsoever, nor does the concept of testimony. It is for good reason that in *The Trial*, Josef K.'s trial will never take place. For Kafka the witness, along with the witness's story, is meaningless.

Fundamentally, then, the infinitely open allegory is a category that negates itself. It leads nowhere. While reading, readers seemingly believe they can elicit certain insights, but in effect the allegories neither corroborate nor refute any theory whatsoever. They leave readers in a world lacking all possibilities, a world in which silence obsessively speaks for itself yet indifferently arouses dread. Kafka is perhaps the only writer who has written silence out of silence. Like the *Muselmänner* who clutches a piece of bread but knows he is no longer capable of eating it, Kafka grasps at a word but knows it has lost its meaning. He can no longer use it. If we look at Kafka's writing as a process of working through, only then does it become clear that this is an entirely different form of working through. Kafka does not create a "story" or a "narrative." He writes the impossible, using language in a way that remains loyal to absolute silence, to the trauma itself.

Kafka's life revolves around the castle. He is drawn to it as to a black hole, yet he knows he will never be able to reach it. The castle is that same empty black hole that attracts everything to itself with infinite force, exactly like the traumatic experience. Yet at the same time, the castle will always remain beyond reach. The castle is the silence within the word. It is the black hole within the world. Yet within this inability to reach the castle, a new world is created. In this impossible world silence provides an opportunity for understanding the trauma.

To return now to LaCapra, it is indeed true that the traumatic experience always involves an "excess" that cannot be conceptualized, symbolized, or represented. Without doubt, LaCapra gives a brilliant and inspirational analysis of the ways of coping with excess by means of acting out and working through. In this chapter, I have proposed distinctions with respect to dissociative attributes during the traumatic experience. I believe that these distinctions facilitate the sharpening of insights proposed by LaCapra, in particular with respect to the possibility and impossibility of coping with the condition of lack of meaning. This chapter's central claim is that there are cases that cannot be worked through. Moreover, in many cases working through is in essence a process of relinquishing the singularity of the traumatic event and turning it into a statistical incident. In such cases silence is the only option for the posttraumatic survivor, who remains faithful to the traumatic experience itself.

In this chapter I have attempted to show that Kafka writes from within nothingness and about nothingness. This statement of course has implications on the personal and cultural levels. If we return to the notion of trauma as a formative event on the national level, it seems that LaCapra's demand for "accurate memory" is impossible when it comes to extreme traumatic events. What remains are flashes of silence and representations of silence that dismantle the supposedly stable structure of culture and transform it into "seeming culture" in which nothing is certain, not even words themselves.

THE BODY AND SILENCE—TOWARD A NEW POSSIBILITY FOR COPING WITH OBSESSIVE REPETITION

Felman (2002) includes a lengthy discussion of the testimony of Holocaust survivor 135633, Ka-Tsetnik (also known as Yehiel De-Nur) at the 1961 trial of Adolf Eichmann. In the following, I outline this testimony and expand upon Felman's analysis.

The presiding judge asks Ka-Tsetnik, "What is your full name?" In turn the witness answers: "Yehiel De-Nur." At that point, the prosecutor asks: "What is the reason you took the pen name Ka-Tsetnik, Mr. De-Nur?" In reply, the witness (Ka-Tsetnik), who is not yet seated, says: "It is not a pen name." Ka-Tsetnik then sits down and continues:

> I do not regard myself as a writer who writes literature. This is a chronicle from the planet of Auschwitz. I was there for about two years. Time there was different from what it is here on earth. Every split second ran on a different cycle of time. And the inhabitants of that planet had no names. They had neither parents nor children. They did not dress as we dress here. They were not born there nor did anyone give birth. Even their breathing was regulated by the laws of another nature. They did not live, nor did they die, in accordance with the laws of this world. Their names were the numbers "K-Zetnik [Ka-Tsetnik] so and so"...They left me, they kept leaving me, left...for close to two years they left me and always left me behind...I see them, they are watching me, I see them.... (Felman 2002, p. 136)

At this point, Mr. Hausner, the prosecutor, gently interrupts Ka-Tsetnik's testimony: "Mr. De-Nur, could I perhaps put a few questions to you if you will consent?" Ka-Tsetnik ignores this request and instead continues on his own: "I see them ... I saw them standing in the line...." At this critical point, the presiding judge matter-of-factly intervened as well and says: "Mr. De-Nur, please, please listen to Mr. Hausner [the prosecutor]; wait a minute, now listen to me." In reply to these interruptions, Ka-Tsetnik stands up and without any warning collapses and seemingly faints.

Many scholars have written about this event (Arendt 1965; Caruth 2007; Felman 2002). Here I seek to clarify several insights with respect to the issue of silence and the possibilities for its expression, either through working through or through obsessive repetition. We know that Ka-Tsetnik spent his nights writing and during the day burned what he had written (Szeintuch 2003, 2009). He states that he fought over every word in an attempt to be the voice of the dead—his friends who stared at him and have not yet returned (his testimony). First, we see an attempt to testify, an attempt that could have led to a certain point. When the prosecutor and the judge each speak to him, one after the other, it seems that Ka-Tsetnik finally understands that *what he has to say cannot be said*. Perhaps *what he has to say cannot be heard*, or it can be heard but *cannot be understood*. Perhaps the worst case of all is true—*no one wants to hear what he has to say*, or he will again be asked to be quiet and do what he is told: *Now you listen to me.* When Ka-Tsetnik understands this, he chooses—whether consciously or unconsciously—to stop talking. Ka-Tsetnik then stands up and apparently faints.[1] I totally agree with Felman that we must not interpret this act as cessation of the testimony but rather the opposite. This testimony is of extraordinary importance for understanding Ka-Tsetnik's Holocaust experiences and in particular for understanding his struggle to express himself in words, the unbearable difficulty of speaking for the dead and the nullifying silence. In the following paragraphs, I explain this interpretation of Ka-Tsetnik's testimony.

Trauma is branded into the body. It does not undergo any high-level processes of working through. It remains sensory and physical. It does not undergo transcription and does not turn into something within the realms of language. Hence, it cannot be spoken. One of the only ways to represent trauma is through physical performance. This is exactly what Ka-Tsetnik does during the trial. His physical collapse is his testimony. It does not relate something else that once was but rather almost perfectly transmits the silence. While being forced to use spoken language during his testimony,

Ka-Tsetnik manages to find a loophole. Thus, like Kafka, he finds a way to transmit the silence, or more accurately, a way to enable the silence to break out. Ka-Tsetnik's means is the physical performance. The body is at the center of the discourse about trauma, for trauma is a transparent and invisible wound. Working through processes require physical work.

In the next chapter, I propose a new, feminine model. By means of the body, music, and dance, the posttraumatic figure is able to face the obsession with reenacting the traumatic moment repeatedly. By returning to the bestial body, this figure can begin the process of working through. Ka-Tsetnik understood this process but was able to implement it only partially—through obsessive repetition but not by working through the trauma. For Ka-Tsetnik, the obsessive repetition is his infinite debt to the dead, his unbearable sense of guilt that finds expression through eternal obsessive return. Hence, he repeatedly, obsessively, and uncontrolledly writes and then burns what he writes. How can this vicious cycle be broken?

NOTE

1. Here I do not discuss the issue of whether he did this deliberately or not. My intention in saying that Ka-Tsetnik "chooses" is that this is what happened. Whether Ka-Tsetnik chose to do this consciously or unconsciously is irrelevant to my argument here.

CHAPTER 9

Techno Rather than Guns

THE IMPORTANCE OF MUSIC IN OUR LIVES

Musical creation is rooted in the human body (Blacking 1990). Schopenhauer (1966a) defines music as the queen of the arts. He believes that music exists only in time. The exact nature of music as well as what it represents and what language it speaks all remains unclear (Kania 2010). According to Langer (1953) music does not resemble spoken language. Music lives beyond the sounds and certainly far beyond the imitation of sounds in nature. Schopenhauer (1966a, 1966b) also claims that the purpose of every good work of art is to capture the experience of life and to answer the primary questions of existence and that music does this in the deepest sense, for it represents the experience of desire as it truly is. Music connects between subject and object and between the outer and inner worlds. Yet music is not necessarily dependent upon the outer world, and therefore its validity is complete—precisely like the validity of mathematics. Music reveals passions, instincts, hidden secrets, and ambitions. Music is related to and even represents "the composition of melody, the disclosure in it of all the deepest secrets of human willing and feeling" (Schopenhauer 1966a, p. 260).

Music has infinite meanings. It can arouse any emotion in us, touch upon the secret strings of our souls, capture our hearts, inflame passions, and in other cases be calming. Throughout history philosophers and creators have drawn connections between the musical experience and the

© The Author(s) 2017
Y. Ataria, *The Structural Trauma of Western Culture*,
DOI 10.1007/978-3-319-53228-8_9

divine experience on the philosophical and the everyday levels (Storr 1993). Nietzsche formulates this clearly and sharply: "Without music life would be an error" (Nietzsche 2005, p. 160: Number 33 of the Maxims and Arrows section). It is difficult for people to listen to irrational music— music that shifts from one sound to another and in which the connections between the sounds generate grating disharmony—yet any attempt to relate to music as something "rational" is erroneous. That is to say, while intellectual observation of music is quite important, we will never achieve complete enjoyment of music only through this type of observation (Schopenhauer 1966a).

According to Schopenhauer (1966a) the attempt to understand harmony and melody and the ability to find the basic tone of a work help individuals understand their souls without regard for reasons or circumstances. In short, music is the language of the world, or perhaps it would be more accurate to say that music enables us to understand the world. "Music creates order out of chaos; for rhythm imposes unanimity upon the divergent, melody imposes continuity upon the disjointed, and harmony imposes compatibility upon the incongruous" (Menuhin 1972, p. 9). Further, "music is so naturally united with us that we cannot be free from it even if we so desired" (Boëthius 1989, p. 8). Music truly penetrates our very being. It is astonishing to discover how music can cause those who are ill to forget their illness, those who stutter to forget their stammering (Storr 1993). In *The Republic* (Plato 2000) Plato argues that the power of music is practically divine:

> All audible musical sound is given us for the sake of harmony, which has motions akin to the orbits in our soul, and which, as anyone who makes intelligent use of the arts knows, is not to be used, as is commonly thought, to give irrational pleasure, but as a heaven-sent ally in reducing to order and harmony any disharmony in the revolutions within us. Rhythm, again, was given us from the same heavenly source to help us in the same way; for most of us lack measure and grace. (Plato 1977, p. 65)

Music is the harmony found in contradictions, the unification of differences and the creation of agreement in nature.

Schopenhauer speaks about the difficulty in understanding causality in life. Music, he claims, helps us make peace with all causes and consequences. Music as something that is practically divine helps us rise above our everyday perspective and our permanent suffering and brings us to a broader vision and a deeper understanding. Music is an escape from life and at the same time enables us to live.

The musical composer rules us. Sometimes our expectations are reinforced and sometimes not, but with the help of music we learn to cope with disappointment, to accept it, even to enjoy it. Schopenhauer further suggests that music is linked to genuine experience and connects us, through an "underground" passage, a secret passage, directly to the "things themselves"—to the Lacanian Real. And because human beings are also the "thing itself," with the help of music they can connect to the real world in a way they cannot via any other form of art. Thus, even though music does not tell us anything about the world and does not make even one claim, it nevertheless enables us to observe ourselves from the outside, to understand our most intimate mental life, to learn something about our unconscious processes. Thus, it is possible to suggest that music has strong ties to the Platonic idea, to the Freudian unconscious, and even to the Jungian collective unconscious and to the Will of Schopenhauer. Only when we become attached to the existence of the Will, do we manage to circumvent the literal meaning and idea and arrive at the essence itself, the essence that creates the Will. In this way we can become liberated from the Will and achieve redemption. Music is directly tied to our inner life, and musical forms stem from our inner world.

Thus, not only is music the queen of all the arts. It is also the essence in that it captures and describes the ongoing and temporary existential state of human beings. Clearly, then, music should be considered within the framework of the collective unconscious that tells the real story, the one that transcends the statement of the posttraumatic subject and the posttraumatic collective. Not only does music describe a particular condition, in effect it can be, as both Kafka and Nietzsche believed, a remedy for that condition. With the help of music humans can move from slavery to freedom, be reborn, understand their true condition, speak to themselves in a language that goes far beyond the psychological/philosophical discourse—the language of the matriarchs.

TECHNO MUSIC

Among other things, the postmodernist era is characterized by techno music (Lang 1996). Techno music is anchored in rave culture. Lang claims that techno music is the strongest and most unifying cultural attribute of the younger generation. Rave culture was studied in depth by Thornton (1996). One of her conclusions is that those who engage in rave dancing to the sounds of techno music have generated a subculture of Western culture in the sense of a cultural stream that strives for unity through movement and dance. Rave symbolizes the desperate attempt to be liberated from alienation with the help of techno music, which, though not alienated from reality, would paradoxically be defined by some as the height of alienation.

Industrialized culture and techno music are very closely connected. For this reason, Thornton argues, the sounds of techno music are deliberately unnatural. Likewise, the human voice in this music is therefore always synthesized or processed. Techno music is a subculture that seeks to be political and moral, a culture of crossing borders. According to Taylor (2001) techno music emerged from admiration for technology and from a belief that technology can solve the problems of the world and of humanity. Techno music defines itself as music without roots (Thornton 1996). Techno music is an attempt to cope with the feelings of insecurity that characterize the twentieth century and it grew out of the depths of that century's Kafkaesque alienation. Techno music and rave culture have a clear purpose: to create unity with oneself and the other dancers, to escape the dimensions of time and space and *to be* time and space. Techno music is meant to return us to a pre-reflective, bestial, authentic state.

Blacking (1990) claims that music not only is a representation of the world, it is also a representation of human potential in this world. From this we can conclude that techno music symbolizes the potential (or perhaps the fantasy) of humans to live at a pulse rate of 150 beats per minute, to live in a world that is based totally upon technology. Techno music describes a reality of pure and one-dimensional captivity within a system that is meant to be enlightened. Yet industrialization has also led to industrialized death and created an impassable gap between man and nature, between heartbeats and machine guns. Techno music is the symphony of the instruments of war—tanks, airplanes, battleships, machine guns. It tells us a different story about our lives. Indeed, it tells us the real story about our lives. On the deepest level, we have become iron beasts, machines of war. One hundred years of horrifying wars have created a new reality. In this reality, there is no home. The body is no longer a living body but rather a dead body, a body-as-object that has been converted into motor oil. We are all iron men. There is a sense of infinite isolation, a deep sense of constant captivity. Captivity symbolizes the lie that goes along with us everywhere we go, the never-ending anxiety, the sense of imprisonment, the inability to describe anything in words. Techno music is a whole new chapter in the history of humankind— that of the post-human creature—for the age of humanity has ended. On the overt, surface level this music symbolizes the end of the world or at least the end of humanity, yet on the covert, below-the-surface level, precisely out of this absolute alienation, it is possible to create a new world or at least a reality that is feasible.

RUN LOLA RUN—THE MOVIE

Frame Story

Manni (acted by Moritz Bleibtreu), the boyfriend of Lola (acted by Franka Potente), heroine of *Run Lola Run*, is involved in a smuggling operation (Arndt 1998). He is charged with bringing 100,000 Deutsche Marks to his boss Ronnie. Lola is supposed to take Manni to the meeting point but her moped has been stolen. Left with no choice, the anxious Manni travels by train with the bag of money but he leaves it behind after being startled by police who by chance enter his train car. A lucky beggar who happens to be sitting next to Manni on the train takes the bag of money. Desperate, Manni phones Lola and tells her he lost the money. He cannot and does not want to run away, and he knows that if he does not bring the money to Ronnie, his boss, at 12:00 noon, in another twenty minutes, he will be killed. Lola promises Manni she will get the money and rescue him, but Manni has his own solution: robbing the supermarket in the square. Lola makes him promise to wait until noon (again we return to Nietzsche's notion of noontide) and not to do anything before that, and Manni promises to wait. It is 11:40 and the two have twenty minutes, twenty fateful minutes that mark the difference between life and death. Manni waits, while Lola sets out on her dogged, determined race against time: to obtain 100,000 Marks, to get to the meeting point exactly at the appointed time, and to prevent Manni from robbing the supermarket. Success means life and good, while failure means death.

The movie presents three scenarios, each twenty minutes long. The scenarios are separated by short scenes in which Lola and Manni talk in bed.

First Scenario

Lola sets off. She runs to the bank where her father is the manager, believing he can help her if he wants to. Her father, however, is busy with his own problems and refuses to help. He has left Lola's mother. He is not really Lola's father. He has no real interest in her fate. Lola continues on, her heart broken. She is late. Manni waits until exactly 12:00 and robs the supermarket. Lola arrives during the robbery and rescues Manni from the supermarket guard. Together they get the money but as they leave the supermarket with the money, Lola is hit by a bullet fired by a policeman and dies. End of first scenario.

Second Scenario

The opening of the second scenario is similar to that of the first scenario, though there are differences in minor details and in the atmosphere. The meeting with Lola's father is different. Lola struggles. Using the gun of a bank guard who knows her, Lola robs the bank where her father works, taking her father hostage. She gets back to Manni in time, but an ambulance speeding to the hospital runs Manni over and he dies. End of second scenario.

Third Scenario

The third scenario also has a similar opening. Yet because of being delayed on the way, Lola does not meet her father at the bank. She sees him leaving the bank, getting into a car, and driving away. Lola continues on running with her eyes closed, abandoning herself to the hands of fate. When Lola opens her eyes, she finds herself in front of a casino. She goes in and wins the needed money in a game of roulette. She arrives at the meeting point in an ambulance in which her father, who was seriously injured in an automobile accident, is being treated. In the meantime, Manni, who in the first two scenarios borrowed a telephone card from a blind woman in order to phone Lola, finishes his conversation, returns the phone card and *politely* thanks the blind woman, who suddenly points to the beggar from the train passing by on a bicycle he has purchased. The beggar is dressed in a new suit and has the money. Manni chases him, catches him and gets the money back. At exactly 12:00 Lola gets out of the ambulance at the meeting point with the money from the casino.

Manni arrives a few minutes later in the car of his boss Ronnie, who thanks him for bringing the money. Lola and Manni meet, all their problems are solved, and with the 100,000 Deutsche Marks they proceed toward their rosy future. The end.

INSIGHTS AND INTERPRETATIONS OF THE MOVIE

The Game

> The end of the game is before the game . . . the ball is round. The game lasts 90 minutes. That's a fact. Everything else is pure theory. (Arndt 1998)

Lola is allotted exactly twenty minutes to obtain 100,000 Deutsche Marks, pass the money on to her beloved Manni, and rescue him. At the end of the first round she dies. Before she sets out on another run, in an episode that connects one run to the other, she checks to see whether Manni really loves her and whether her actions will be rewarded. She plays again. At the end of the second round Manni dies. Again Lola and Manni examine their relationship and after Manni is convinced that Lola loves him and that there is a point to his life he agrees to keep on playing and Lola sets out for a third time. This time Lola wins and the game is over (Bianco 2004).

Lola, whose red hair is reminiscent of Tomb Raider from the computer game or of Margarita from Bulgakov's *The Master and Margarita,* can begin the game anew only after the result of the game is not to her benefit. Hence, the following appears written on the screen during the movie: "The end of the game is before the game" (Arndt 1998). Essentially this sentence echoes Nietzsche's doctrine of eternal return.

According to this interpretation, the movie represents the era of computer games (O'Sickey 2002). We must not forget that in such a reality the game is the real thing. In *Ender's Game,* one of the best fantasy books of the twentieth century, Ender thinks he is playing but it later becomes clear to him that everything was real (Card 1985).

It is important to note that the movie is not faithful to ordinary patterns of time. Lola can play again and again, learn from mistakes she made in the previous round, and continue until she solves the game/problem. From game to game, Lola changes from a participant in the game to the game itself. She is the decisive factor, the essence of the game. The climax comes in the third scenario, in which she controls fate, asserts her influence over the roulette wheel in the casino and saves lives with her touch (Whalen 2000). Lola passes through three stages in the game: (1) a girl who wants her "daddy to save her"; (2) still a girl but someone who begins to take responsibility; (3) a responsible adult taking charge of her life (Wilson, no date).

Cyberspace Culture

Even though the movie is set in Berlin, *Run Lola Run* represents the culture of cyberspace. The background, the cinematography, the music, and the colors of the film are related to live video/computer games (online games). The movie is a fantasy film. Hence, Lola moves easily from West Berlin to East Berlin, among other things through the fantasy of a world without borders, a world that spins at virtual speed (Mesch 2000). For example, when Lola leaves her room we are taken inside the television in her mother's room, and Lola becomes a cartoon character in an animated film. That is, the race takes place in a virtual world inside a media world based upon wireless connections and the like (Whalen 2000).

Lola—Life at a New Pace

Lola runs fast, thinks fast, decides fast. She represents a new and fast world being constructed in Berlin, the world of the techno beat (O'Sickey 2002). As noted, constant motion is an attribute of globalization and industrialization, so that the unceasing running symbolizes inner attributes of our culture (Mahler-Bungers 2003). In Lola's world, and ours as well, to stop or to stand still means to die, to lose your value in your own eyes and the eyes of those around you. Yet even running in the postmodernist world is not an internal or external harmonic movement. It is nothing more than an escape, motion out of a sense of being oppressed and pursued.

Lola is a new hero, a superhuman in the postmodernist world. She is the only possible hero, and, like Neo in *The Matrix*, the postmodernist hero attempts to escape the superficial world that is made totally of lies and to enter a new reality (Žižek 2002). When the hero understands that this world is entirely virtual he can legislate the laws according to which he lives and thus revive the old Commandant from Kafka's story "In the Penal Colony" who no longer exists. But unlike Neo and unlike Tyler Durden from *Fight Club*, Lola attempts to prevent a violent confrontation and she does so through music.

Time and the Metaphysical Problem

Mankind, probably the most mysterious species on our planet. A mystery of open questions. Who are we? Where do we come from? Where are we going? How do we know what we believe to know? Why do we believe anything at all? Innumerable questions looking for an answer, an answer which will raise the next question and the following answer will raise a following question and so on and so forth. But, in the end, isn't it always the same question and always the same answer? (Arndt 1998)

These lines are narrated in the opening scene of *Run Lola Run* in which shadowy people move frenetically across the screen. This scene is followed by a soccer official who states: "The ball is round. The game lasts ninety minutes. That's a fact. Everything else is pure theory. Here we go." He then kicks the ball high into the air. The camera zooms in from above on the letter "O" in "LOLA" as if entering the metaphysical problem of the universe—an entrance into infinite questions (Whalen 2000). The metaphysical problem is underlined at the end of Lola's telephone conversation with Manni, when for a split second the camera focuses on a turtle in order to remind us of Meno's Paradox. It does not matter how fast Lola runs—she will never catch up with the turtle. No matter how hard we try, we will never manage to deal with the metaphysical questions (Whalen 2000). The "O" and the metaphysical questions accompany us throughout the movie—not only through the photography, often 360° panoramic shots which return to the same spot, the presentation of the actors at the beginning of the film, the roulette wheel in the casino, the way in which Lola thinks, but also, and perhaps mainly, the movie's soundtrack with its rhythmic motif that runs through the movie as if returning to the same place again and again. The melody changes but the beat is fixed. In addition, the movie's director introduces a quote from T.S. Eliot's famous poem "The Waste Land" (2009): "We shall not cease from exploration, and the end of our exploring will be to arrive where we started and know the place for the first time." Once again, this notion echoes Nietzsche's doctrine of eternal return.

The Possibility of Change

"Techno" cinema disregards the past and therefore Lola can run through the streets of Berlin without any barriers and can predict a new future, one of free passages and new possibilities. The film attempts to describe how the world will look in the future and the objective of the film is to expose the (apparently) unlimited possibilities human beings have in their lives, the countless crossroads of decision, where each crossroad can lead, in a totally deterministic manner, to different results. Every change affects the entire universe. The film displays the possibilities in our lives (Whalen 2000). Life is like a game of dominoes, and the movie's producer makes sure to show us this again and again. Yet we, inside a single domino that can fall, have the chance to change things (at noontide), to leave the game and to live the game, all within the framework of the same metaphysical trap.

Fairytale Story

When we hear the poem "I Wish" (Arndt 1998) at the beginning of the movie, we cannot help but think of a fairy tale in which the viewer and the character herself desperately need a happy ending. Lola is a princess, and the guard at the bank calls her this explicitly ("the house princess"). Indeed, we are watching a modern fairy tale in which the myth of the classical hero is broken and a new hero is created. Therefore the one with the power in the movie is a woman. The father does not come across as royal, and therefore the film's producer makes sure to tell us, already in the first run, that he is not really her father. That is, he is not a king, for in the postmodernist era the image of the father has totally disintegrated.[1]

LOLA'S JOURNEY

The soundtrack of the movie *Run Lola Run* binds Lola to the viewer. The beat unites Lola's heartbeats with the heartbeats of the viewer. Lola runs into the clock, into the experience, toward the unification represented by techno music, indeed paradoxically within the alienation. Freud claims that the experience of being connected to the world (the oceanic feeling) is a connection to the world of the individual alone. Unification is with nature and not with other people—the unification of Meursault in *The Stranger* by Camus. Thus it is reasonable that the following sentence can be heard in the movie's soundtrack: "I wish I was a stranger" (Arndt 1998).

The notion of beat is already assimilated into the body when the fetus is in the womb: it is known to us from heartbeats and from sexual contact. Beat produces an internal order in our lives (Storr 1993). The music in the movie represents Lola's inner world, exactly like the music in opera, as Schopenhauer claims, represents the secret and most profound contents of our mental life. Later we will see that on the deepest level, the music and Lola represent the same process in a third posttraumatic and completely dissociated character. The philosopher Langer (1953) claims that music is what allows for the inner journey. Lola's journey should be considered in the same way. Her journey is not a journey to rescue Manni but rather a journey to rescue herself, a journey toward inner reflection whose goal is to synchronize and unite techno music with the human heartbeat. Lola's journey is tied to the Jungian principle—human beings have only one aspiration and that is to be themselves! For mental health is tied directly to a journey to become acquainted with one's own psyche.

The music in the movie *Run Lola Run* is not an unconscious representation of Lola but rather a journey into the unconscious—a journey resembling Captain Willard's journey in the movie *Apocalypse Now*. Notice, however, that Captain Willard's journey in that movie is a journey into the American unconsciousness, as we saw the jungles represent the American collective unconsciousness. Lola's desire to return to the game, to achieve the ultimate solution, can be interpreted as the journey of the self toward perfection or at least acceptance, a journey undertaken with the help of music—for music enables us to reach new realms of knowledge. Music is not simply another spoken language. Music offers us new insights into ourselves and into the world in which we live (Becker 1994). Thus, Lola does not run against the background of techno music. Rather she runs with and thus within the music. In the first stage she is driven from within the beat. When she manages to achieve unification and wholeness, she takes over the beat. The rhythm turns into her heartbeats and the melody is her inner voice. In Lola's case unification is achieved when the gap is closed between the world outside and the world within. Lola is on a personal journey. She is Kafka's villager who faces the guard in *The Trial* and dares—or at the very least tries—to enter. Thus she shatters the known systems of power, for example in the way she obtains the money in the casino or the way she cuts through the line of nuns: "No memories, no Gods" (Arndt 1998).

Lola stops ignoring what she knows. She knows she will not get money from her father. (Before she sets out it is clear that Lola knows this and we know this and yet for courtesy's sake the attempt is still made.) Therefore why should she even try? Lola becomes sober and matures. The key to this is the focus on the heartbeat, on the inner world. Her connection to the inner world finds expression in total synchronization with the music. In this situation the individual has the possibility of going outside of time, of stopping time, of making a real change in one's life. This indeed is Lola's goal.

The movie *Taxi Driver* is set in the unconscious of New York, while Lola runs through the unconscious of Berlin. Travis the "taxi driver" cannot reconcile himself to the existing social order and thus chooses a revolution. Lola is quite familiar with the social order and frustration. Her boyfriend Manni, whose name is reminiscent of the word "money," represents the new social order, the rule of money, frustration, and loneliness. Therefore Lola ultimately chooses another way. The solution is not on the outside, as Travis believes, but rather within us: "The enemy was in us," says Chris Taylor (acted by Charlie Sheen) in the movie *Platoon* (Kopelson 1986), and Camus adds: "We all carry within us our places of exile, our crimes and our ravages" (Camus 1962a, p. 265). As a historical figure, Lola has experienced the *Akeda*. She has internalized the role and the fundamental function of the woman in the postmodernist era. She understands the gap between what is gray and what is dichotomous and is aware of the passion for violence threatening to break out of the posttraumatic man. She knows she must create some sort of female alternative for men, if only to safeguard her children and to build a new set of values in a new language—a form of metalinguistic, maternal communication.

Margarita, heroine of the excellent novel *The Master and Margarita,* resembles Lola and like Lola rebels against the social order. Like Lola's journey, her journey is tied to the ability to go from one dimension to another and to move at extremely high speeds. Lola is Margarita awakening in a new world, in East Berlin, and discovering that the rigid social order still determines the truth, still generates terror. Lola emerges from the words and the pages and the hard binding to show us how it is possible to change, how it is possible to rebel without adopting the violence of *Taxi Driver*, the violence of Fanon (1968). The new social order reaches its ultimate height when Lola redefines the ontological range, that is, the range in which a human being can act and have an influence. Lola redefines what there is and what is possible, the area in which it is possible to act. Lola understands well that the only way to evade destructive forces is to stop using them. Paradoxically she does this by means of techno music, which is a totally synthetic creation. A deeper analysis shows us that the choice of techno music is not coincidental. The purpose is to highlight exactly what world we are living in and how, even in this world, it is possible to break out of the prison, of the invisible walls enclosing us. The technique is to return to the living body that is naturally immersed in the world, that is, to the pre-reflective and pre-linguistic existence.

THE SCREAM

When Lola screams, the music becomes mute. The scream silences the music. In this sense, Lola's scream resembles Ka-Tsetnik's fainting and has become a way of expressing oneself. After the scream, silence prevails. In the most basic and deepest sense, the scream symbolizes Lola's desire that things be different. The scream comes to silence the techno music and everything it represents: industrialization, Western society, capitalism, inconceivable high speeds, and intensities (Mesch 2000). Lola screams—her scream is the scream that was missing from the *Akeda* of Isaac. It is not the scream of Camus in *The Fall*. She is not seeking help from the outside. Lola turns to herself, awakening herself and the viewers to the possibility of change, to the possibility of facing up to determinism and fatalism by means of human power. Levinas (2006) claims that only human will is capable of coping with passion and only human power can avert the evil decree. The scream puts the brakes on the wild and crazy run. It is the breath after which comes thought. The scream is the beginning of the rebellion in this era, in the spirit of Camus in *The Rebel*. The scream is the opposite of the soft female voice in the movie's soundtrack. It is not sexual, it is not alluring, and to tell the truth it is distorted. According to Schopenhauer (1966b), the scream is the birth of the monster, and it seems that in order to cope with helplessness one must even connect to the monster within, as for example in the case of Captain Willard in the movie *Apocalypse Now*. Lola connects to the monster within herself in order to connect to the monster in humankind, which has already been out of control for a very long time. Maybe from the very start. At the same time, the scream is the desire to silence the pressures of the outside world, to create a moment of inner peace and contentment, of refined observation of reality (Whalen 2000). On the three occasions that Lola screams, she does so in order to stop the chaos and to set out on a new course. The scream is an intersection, a crossroads of decision-making from which point on things change totally.

According to Mahler-Bungers (2003), Lola is an authentic character on a journey toward becoming sober. This characterization reinforces the claim that Lola is a superhero in the postmodernist capitalist era, in a world without any certainty. Lola manages to connect to this world through music and through her strong connection to herself and her desires. In other words, the movie posits that by connecting to techno music and reshaping it in accordance with human experience it is possible to change reality and to cope with determinism.

At the point when Lola succeeds in connecting to the music and gaining control over it, she manages to stop it, and not only by screaming. The scream marks the extreme point. After sobering up Lola gains control over the tempo, the rhythm, and the harmony. In this sense the movie conducts a dialogue with movies like *The Matrix*, in which Neo discovers his ability to control reality because ultimately this is a virtual reality. The shift from the status of a listener controlled by the music to that of a listener-creator who really controls the music represents humans' de facto shift from being enslaved to the rhythm of life to controlling the rhythm of life and to controlling life itself, with humans indeed setting the tempo. In this shift the individual acquires the ability to stop time.

TECHNO MUSIC AS A JOURNEY OF LIBERATION

The only way to perceive the movement in the movie *Run Lola Run* is to become the movement. The only way to follow the path is to be the path itself. The only way to choose is to be the choice. And the only way to be meaningful is to give your life meaning (Bianco 2004). Authenticity is the only route to follow in a world in which the alternative to prison is an insane asylum (Foucault 1965). After mankind "killed God" (Nietzsche 1999) and after Camus in *The Fall* exposed us to the inability of the conscious individual to act, Lola is portrayed as the new superman: a superman in the post-postmodern era, the post-human era.

Nietzsche (1964) believes that music makes life possible. In the movie *Run Lola Run* the music is what leads Lola on her journey of awakening, of maturing, of becoming sober. In the post-human era, to become a human being once more, and even more to the point, to become a decent, upright, responsible and mature human being, a *mensch*, is to break the rules of the game.

The transition from a totally synthesized voice to a more human voice in the movie's soundtrack symbolizes the desire to break the rules, to become human again—to be a human being in an age marked by techni-cal-mechanical-automatic destruction. The superheroes in this age are the human beings who can look the other in the eye. The absolute other is time. Time is frozen during the traumatic experience and therefore we must shatter the clock representing what we have not managed to do and what we will not manage to do. Lola's path is a scream that skips over the signifier straight to the signified, the real, the actual thing. Yet Lola does more than scream. She is not merely talking to herself. She changes the music, the tempo of life. She struggles against the real world through a transition to a virtual life and world. More than anything she runs, sweats and, to put it simply, returns to her body. Lola engages in a close dialogue with the hero of the movie *Fight Club*. Each in his/her own way is seeking authenticity and each must cope with the capitalistic system and tempo. But in going from East to West, Lola constantly reminds us that there is a world in which one is forbidden even to think—a world administered by Joseph Stalin through Article 58, paragraph 10 of the Soviet criminal code, as in *The First Circle* by Solzhenitsyn, in which a man is accused even for the invisible intention to rebel against the regime. This is similar to what happens in our world when a person is accused if he dares not accept a credit card. The investigation according to Article 58 almost never involves clarifying the actual truth and does not deviate from the abominable. Lola's perspective is not naïve. The alternative she proposes to capitalism is no less evil. She understands that one cannot help but be part of "the system." Thus the escape to a virtual world, and thus the scream—absolute help-lessness that forces her to move constantly in a space lacking actual time. At first, time in the movie is replaced by a mechanical beat and slowly by heartbeats symbolizing humanity. On another level, Lola's passage from East to West is a passage between two inner worlds, or a passage inside the bifurcated world of the posttraumatic individual.

   On the one hand, Lola is the new Tomb Raider, yet on the other hand, and no less importantly, she is Margarita (*The Master and Margarita*) in that she represents social change from the perspective of gender. Yet the change Lola seeks to bring about is even greater. She wants to say what cannot be said. To make what is happening behind the scenes into the main event. Lola attempts to penetrate space and time, to define a world that is entirely subjective. In this sense the guardian of the gate is internal only, the world situated inside ourselves: "At the heart of the subject himself we discovered then, the presence of the world" (Merleau-Ponty 2002, p. 498).

On the one hand, Lola connects to techno music. On the other hand, she is not a slave to this deterministic music. She attempts to change it. She attempts to insert additional new elements into it. Lola breaks the dimension of time in the techno music and implements the existentialist perception to the extent that this is possible. Human beings are under a constant obligation to choose in an impossible reality. Therefore Lola has no alternative apart from the mechanical music, apart from the alienating techno. And it is precisely within this that she must live the humanity, the possibility to choose, to change, to rebel. Indeed, Lola creates the possibility for authentic life distanced from the incessant reflection and the paralyzing self-consciousness. Lola attempts to create a new model of liberation, one that does not lead us to Chigurh in the Coen Brothers movie *No Country for Old Men*.

As noted, one of the objectives of the music in the movie is to place us within the mood and atmosphere of a lively computer game. The techno tempo is the tempo of the network. The music is produced by a computer and played on a computer and it exists almost exclusively on the net (Mesch 2000). On a higher level, the music and Lola's heartbeats break the dimension of simple time. Already at the beginning of the movie Lola runs into the clock, and we hear the ticking of the clock later as well. That is, there is an external clock, but it ticks from the inside. The clock is our encounter with the world. As Lola becomes more and more sober on her journey toward awakening, the sound of the ticking clock—representing the outside world, expectations, pressures, competition, Western competition—becomes weaker. Breaking the dimension of time is a necessary condition on the journey to liberation.

Blacking (1990) claimed that dancing preceded walking. If we look at this claim from the perspective of the movie *Run Lola Run* and its soundtrack, we can think that the run resembles a more basic dance by Lola and symbolizes Lola's deeper connection to herself—the pre-reflective self: "I wish I was a hunter" (Arndt 1998).

Together with the music, running takes humans to new realms of harmony with the self and the environment. Tribal music, dance, and running help human beings solve the metaphysical problem and the problem of alienation through a more complete connection with the self and the society in which they live: "The unity of man has not yet been broken; the body has not yet been stripped of human predicates; it has not yet become a machine" (Merleau-Ponty 1965, p. 188).

A NEW INTERPRETATION OF THE MOVIE

On her first run during a conversation with her father, Lola screams. On her second run, her father slaps her. These two incidents are a sign for renewing the music. The slap and the scream awaken Lola (and the viewers as well). The scream symbolizes Lola's inner desire to change, while the slap positions Lola (and the viewers as well) in her true place in life. The dialogue here is about the authentic journey, about the inability to find the way through the virtual freedom of the Western world. In *The Fall* by Camus, the woman who fell off the bridge did not cry out but rather screamed. The scream was the feminine voice in the world of Clamence, the hero of *The Fall*. This scream could have saved him. This scream was the last call before the trains set off on their journey.

The scream and the slap—each of these motifs is found in *The Fall*—take Lola on a new journey, and each time the journey starts again, so does the music. The motifs are similar but add new information. The music symbolizes the unconscious that accompanies Lola as she becomes acquainted with reality and with herself. It should be noted that while Lola is engaged in a serious dialogue with her father, there is no music. This is reality, what Lola must now process with the help of music and of the imagination, which according to Schopenhauer is tied directly to music. Beginning a new game is nothing more than a conceptualization, a psychodrama, or any other description of dreaming about the problems of life.

In the movie, it is patently impossible to make a clear distinction between reality and dream, between game and reality, between animated characters and those that are flesh and blood, between anxieties and fantasies, between the questions and the answers, between Lola and Manni. And if it is impossible to distinguish between reality and dreams, it is possible that Lola and Manni are characters in someone else's dream and that the dialogue is between two inner characters who are dependent upon one another. Every individual contains a masculine dimension and a feminine dimension. During trauma the individual indeed feels split, and after ongoing traumas (the human condition after the twentieth century) this split becomes permanent. In this sense Lola and Manni represent the split in the posttraumatic condition and the possibility of recovery through the unification of the contrasts within the individual. The desire for unification is the aspiration of individuals to reconcile themselves to their inner conflicts, to their conscience as well as to their instincts.

If we adopt the notion that Lola and Manni are in essence a single character and that Lola is the unconscious side of that character, then the music—which is the ultimate representation of the unconscious—and Lola are in effect a single entity. When the music does not play, the living character, who is neither Lola and nor Manni, is exposed to new information. After this "realistic" information undergoes different kinds of processing, a process of digestion begins in which Lola and the music are represented as one and the same.

Manni symbolizes the immediate, rapid, and crude response to information, the anxiety, the panic, the joy and the sense of alienation in the world. Lola symbolizes the slower and more basic unconscious processes—the deeper processes. The end of the game comes when the conscious and unconscious processes meet and manage to operate in sync. It should be remembered that for the posttraumatic individual the return to the "O" described earlier is a dybbuk of sorts. The only condition for success in the game is that the conscious be "sufficiently patient" to wait for the unconscious to complete the process. For good reason, some claim that the Kafkaesque model is in essence a model of waiting. The ability to wait, to accept things as they are and set the proper priorities is a new type of redemption.

Hence, at the end of each round the director chose to display a divided photo of Lola and Manni on the screen. Therefore we hear a voice saying over and over again "wait...wait...wait." This is the voice of the unconscious asking the individual not to act before the appropriate processes have taken place, not to disregard the inner world. On another plane, the movie attempts to convey the sense of the unbearable split within the posttraumatic individual.

At the end of the first round after the supermarket robbery, we hear a new song—jazz. The words and melody of this song symbolize a sweet illusion that is disintegrating. This is the illusion of the individual who acts rashly, momentarily sees that everything is good, but because there is no harmony between the conscious and the unconscious, no unity between the beat and the heartbeats, death occurs. Jazz is an attempt to live life again at a different tempo, but as noted, in the era of the iPhone this attempt is pathetic and impossible.

If the movie symbolizes a learning game in three scenarios (within the obsessive framework of the posttraumatic individual to recreate the traumatic experience again and again), and if, as I argue, the running is equivalent to music, which is equivalent to the unconscious, which is equivalent to Lola, we must then rethink the significance of the music in each round. When the beat, the ticking of the clock, controls Lola and controls her heartbeat, Manni, who represents the conscious, acts

erroneously. He loses patience, he does not wait for Lola (the unconscious) to bring the process of digesting and coping to its end. In the first
round the beat has total control over Lola (and over her heartbeat). In the
second round Lola's influence over the music increases, but not to the
point of harmony. Only in the third round is harmony achieved between
Lola's heartbeats and the beat of the music: "a union of the heart" (Arndt
1998).

Thus, only in the third round does Lola's voice become the leading
voice, and in the background the beat and the heartbeats merge. This is
the round in which Lola finds a solution that integrates between the inner
and outer strata. The speed also leads us to think that Lola is the unconscious. Lola crosses Berlin quickly. Berlin represents humanity. It is the
entire world, containing the bad and the good, the divine and the alienated, the future and history. Thus Lola, the unconscious of Berlin, runs
through the depths of the city's soul. Every street is a memory, every
person a painful event. Every encounter represents missed opportunities.
The lack of movement is death. In this sense, running symbolizes the
desire to avoid the world itself—one of the symptoms of the posttraumatic
individual.

Blacking (1990) makes the following claim: Dance and music are
the most important tools of adaptation for human beings. They enable
humans to understand the order of things around them, help them
understand the boundaries. With the help of music, which represents
human potential, humans understand the borders of their true abilities.
From this claim and according to the interpretation I propose here, the
following conclusions can be drawn: The goal of our inner journey is
always to understand ourselves better. Hence, the rhythmic movement
through Berlin (which represents the individual in the posttraumatic
era) each time exposes more human abilities. In the third round the
definitive boundary is revealed—unity. It is more correct to say that
the boundary of human ability is the unity of multiplicity, the ability to
live in harmony with all that is inside oneself, to live in peace with the
divided world. Indeed, we can simply say that Lola and Manni represent two poles of the posttraumatic individual and the movie is a
journey to *recovery*.

In this case, Berlin symbolizes the individual in the posttraumatic era.
There is some logic to this because Berlin, perhaps more than any other
city, symbolizes the huge shock that befell the world when the city served
as the focus of the evil that brought about World War II, a shock from

which we have not yet liberated ourselves—and perhaps we cannot and should not liberate ourselves from it. Berlin symbolizes the German nation coping with its past over the last sixty years. Thus, if there is a place where it is possible to talk about the posttraumatic era, that place is Berlin, and if there is a people affected by posttrauma, it is the German people. Divided Berlin, Berlin after the fall of the Wall, Berlin that contains two worlds, two prisons—all these have come together. In my view the role of the characters can be defined as follows:

- Lola is the music. She is the experience of the will and she is the unconscious of another character—the character that is Berlin.
- Manni represents the conscious side of humanity (Berlin).
- The different characters symbolize multiple aspects of the human psyche.
- The relations between Lola and Manni symbolize the relations between the unconscious and the conscious.
- The relations among the characters symbolize the complex relations among the various aspects of human beings.
- The music is the unconscious. It is the soul of humanity (Berlin). The music exposes individuals to their true condition, whether they are helpless or whether they have achieved harmony and unity.

Lola—A Turning Point in Western (Posttraumatic) Culture

Lola returns to her body but from a totally different place—not from the desire to destroy the other that is the self, but rather from a place of accepting oneself, accepting Germany, accepting the guilt as is. To accept the responsibility for her life without committing herself to that eternal sense of guilt—that is the feminine version of the superman proposed by Nietzsche. To accept the body, which over the course of 2,000 years Christianity totally rejected. Not only is Lola's journey authentic. It is also a journey that redefines the condition of the white man—a man in need of immediate rescue, in need of a home, a man who cannot take even one step without everything slipping through his fingertips, a sick individual who is still recuperating. As noted, the movie *Run Lola Run* begins with a desperate phone call from Manni, Lola's lover. This is reminiscent of Nick (*The Deer*

Hunter) phoning his lover Linda from Vietnam and then being unable to talk to her. Manni represents masculinity that has collapsed, as we have seen throughout the book. The male model and the male discourse have come to an end. The model of male liberation is Chigurh (*No Country for Old Men*). Hence the male dimension must undergo a radical change, and this change is possible only with the help of a renewed feminine discourse (not one that itself attempts to be masculine). We can thus say that while Chigurh or Captain Kurtz represents the masculine version of the superman, Lola represents a feminine alternative to Nietzsche's superman.

In that same Germany a few years earlier, Hans from Thomas Mann's *The Magic Mountain* set out to that cursed war, World War I, and now he has no choice. He must return to be rehabilitated. He needs treatment. He went crazy. All the blood drove him crazy. The music, that synthetic music, the techno music that lacks all human warmth, is the only solution for him, simply because the only language he understands is the language of weapons and rifles and bombs and blood—and from there the beating of the heart. The posttraumatic hero no longer believes in words, does not believe in men, does not believe in himself. He is a man divided within himself, taken apart, violent, obsessive, and automatic. Certainly he does not believe in love. Indeed, in essence he is totally incapable of feeling. The feminine character is the last chance for the posttraumatic hero to find salvation. Yet he is incapable of exchanging a word with this character. This is true for Kurtz from *Apocalypse Now*, for Nick and Michael from *Deer Hunter* and also for Travis from *Taxi Driver*.

Women must understand, as Lola understands, that there is nothing left in the world except for one's fellow man, the breath and the heartbeat of the other. Thus, with the help of the connection between the electronic beat and the beating heart, Lola manages to instill humanity, and not just authenticity, into her crazy run. With the help of the heartbeats, she attempts to begin at the beginning, from a place of compassion, from a place where words truly lack all meaning. This is the place of music. This humanity is the only chance for men, who only know how to destroy, who no longer know how to speak, who are incapable of making a reasonable decision—individuals who are managed totally by trauma.

And so, no matter where we turn we see labor camps, prison camps, camps where people die of hunger. Camps in which words have no meaning—for only the music in our heads can give meaning to the words and provide salvation. For music is an action that is rooted in the body. It is prelingual and pre-reflective. Music enhances the experience and imbues a new dimension in which to live. Music does not make any claims and does not represent any theory whatsoever. With all its heart, music is tied to emotions. Music is the source of the sense of solidarity and of tribal belonging. It constitutes a baby's first contact with the world and its mother. Moreover, music is closely tied to motion, to dance. Music provides a home in the tumult of everyday life. It enables us to revive our bodies, not however through violence and murder but rather through dance and by entering a profound rave—a rave that totally encompasses heartbeats, dance, and the desire to live yet remain human.

The broken posttraumatic hero can no longer use words. Hence the only means remaining to connect to the world, and thus in effect to be saved, is on the one hand music, which enables him to set out on an internal journey through the depths of the unconscious and even to achieve a certain sense of unity. On the other hand is the feminine character that is tied to the man through the womb and through nursing and that is capable of engaging the man in dialogue that skips over the signifying words and proceeds directly to actual reality. Music and the feminine character enable the posttraumatic individual to move from a condition of either–or to one of both this and that and thus to save himself from himself—from the mechanism of self-destruction that erupts all around.

I believe that by returning to the body and by creating a new language that respects and emerges from the silence, Lola succeeds in creating a new model that can cope, at least partially, with the three destructive cycles: the *Akeda,* eternal and obsessive return, and guilt.

Yet I cannot conclude this book without considering another issue: the transition from individual to social trauma. Throughout the book, I have discussed the posttraumatic subject and posttraumatic society as if the transition between them is natural and obvious, but this is not the case. Therefore, in the concluding chapter I discuss this transition from individual to social trauma in detail. The objective of the chapter is to examine posttraumatic society, albeit with caution, and to raise a number of limitations to the insights emerging from this book.

NOTE

1. It is important to note that in the movie it becomes clear that the father has a mistress who is pregnant, apparently by him. At this point the father has the option of reproducing the abandonment Lola experienced with her real father or fixing it. The movie appears to create an infinite number of repetitive games that reproduce mistakes and the possibility of fixing them. In this sense this is an expression of Freud's theory regarding the repetition obsession of the traumatized individual.

CHAPTER 10

Culture-Trauma: Some Critical Remarks

TRAUMA AND CULTURE: THE MAIN PROBLEMS

Trauma is a life-altering event for an individual—about this, there is no disagreement. To borrow a term from the field of consciousness studies, the "hard problem" (Chalmers 1995) is the shift from the psyche of the individual to the "spiritual life of a people" (Freud 1939, p. 87). Freud goes on to say that in this regard "we find ourselves in a domain of mass psychology where we do not feel at home" (p. 87), due among other things to the difficulty in understanding how a particular people, community, or group has been influenced by its forgotten and hidden past. The question then becomes whether trauma can take place on a level that is not that of the individual. This also raises another question: Is it possible to make reference to "national/collective memory," "collective trauma," and similar concepts?

Despite these difficulties, which Freud was undoubtedly aware of, he nevertheless maintained that the individual and the masses can be compared. "I hold that the concordance between the individual and the mass is in this point almost complete. The masses, too, retain an impression of the past in unconscious memory traces" (p. 151). Freud and other major thinkers and scholars such as LaCapra (2001), Felman (1992), and others cannot refrain from taking the leap from individual psychology to mass psychology, a leap that according to Freud (1939) is "bold, but inevitable" (p. 161).

© The Author(s) 2017
Y. Ataria, *The Structural Trauma of Western Culture*,
DOI 10.1007/978-3-319-53228-8_10

Indeed, this appears to be a working assumption among those who naturally link trauma and culture, despite the real difficulty in corroborating this assumption. As a result, contemporary discourse on trauma almost always begins on the second floor—it lacks foundations. Hence the question that needs to be posed is the following: What is there in the nature of the traumatic experience that enables it to be transformed from an individual experience to one that shapes an entire nation, as has been claimed over and over again? In this chapter, I attempt to examine what it is about the traumatic experience that turns it into something that shapes not only the life of the individual (survivor) but also the very structure of culture.

A MAP WITHOUT ITS TERRITORY

The difficulty in understanding and defining the traumatic experience can already be seen in its definition as an "invisible wound." Ordinarily when an individual has been injured, the signs are apparent externally: lacerations, bleeding, cuts, fractures, burns, and the like. In this sense we can say that in at least most cases a physical injury can be identified, diagnosed, and treated, even if not immediately. Emotional trauma, on the other hand, is not necessarily connected to any physical injury. Indeed, Freud claimed that physical injury on the battlefield does not involve trauma. We can also say that the locus of the trauma is invisible. On a deeper level, the question then becomes whether it is even possible to talk about the "locus of the trauma" in terms of time and place and to what extent trauma is an "event" that does or does not occur. To take this to the extreme, we can even speculate whether trauma is an "event" at all.

"What actually happened to you?" Difficulty in answering this ostensibly simple question constitutes the core of the problem for trauma victims, among other reasons because they often believe that the trauma took place in an entirely different dimension. This is what Ka-Tsetnik (Yehiel De-Nur) meant when he described Auschwitz as being another planet. The victim has difficulty describing what happened, and where and when the event occurred.

Historians are concerned, and rightly so from their perspective, with what they see as a gap between the "narrative story" and the "facts." Traumatic memory lacks any coordinates to facilitate cross-checking it with the "cold facts" and is devoid of either map or territory.

Hence, much of the evidence is deeply split between a description of the subjective experience on the one hand and a factual description on the other. Even when both the narrative and the factual descriptions are given by the same person, it is difficult to find the point at which they meet. This seems to be an attribute of trauma—it cannot be positioned or fixed.

Most references to trauma are formulated in terms of frozen time, as elucidated below. I believe that the matter of geographic "place" is to some extent missing in the literature. What comes to mind in this context is the remarkable action taken by Bergson[1] at the end of his life and the way he refers to time in terms of space: "It is enough for us to have shown that, from the moment when you attribute the least homogeneity to duration, you surreptitiously introduce space" (Bergson 1950, p. 104). In this sense, time cannot be separated from space and trauma that distorts time distorts space as well. Space is broken down into its elementary particles, and the ability to assemble a unified picture dissipates. After the trauma, the individual is left in a space that has lost its unity. The trauma takes place in *no place*, or nowhere, thus revoking the very notion of a place. Yet in actuality, during trauma space returns to what it always has been—empty, disassembled, and disintegrated, devoid of humanity and devoid of unity. Hence trauma can be defined as an event that dismantles all cognitive constructions.

Trauma, then, can be characterized as an injury that at its core revokes the notion of a locus in time and place. Because the traumatic event cannot be positioned or fixed, the trauma is able to take place in the here and now, at least from the victim's perspective. For this reason, victims carry the trauma within their bodies at every given moment (an agent of trauma) and make its presence known in the public arena.

TRAUMA IN THE SPIRAL-REGRESSIVE DIMENSION OF TIME

Trauma has difficulty fitting into a narrative. It refuses to become a "story" with a beginning, middle, and end that is positioned at a particular time and place. Clearly the invisible wound of the trauma continues to bleed, and the trauma does not come to an end. This inability to position trauma has led postmodern humanity, through processes of acting out, to reconstruct the traumatic moment in an attempt to fix the traumatic event in time and in space (Freud 1939).

At the moment of trauma, time freezes and splits. On one level the individual continues to progress along the ordinary chronological time line. On another level he remains in the traumatic moment, and a new chronological time line emerges for him, one that is nonlinear, spiral, and infinitely regressive. The gap between the linear time line representing an individual who continues forward, an apparently normal individual, and the spiral time line representing an individual frozen in time widens to the point of becoming unbearable.

The fissure created between these two dimensions of time finds expression in different types of outbursts: flashbacks in which the subject feels the trauma is happening "here and now"; violent penetrations of the spiral-regressive dimension (which has no beginning and no end) into the linear time line; clashes between the spiral-regressive dimension and the linear time line, leaving the survivor unable to position himself, not in one dimension and not in the other. Sometimes the survivor is uncontrollably thrown from one dimension to the other, resulting in the emergence of dissociative symptoms. In more severe cases, the survivor is "stuck" in between the two dimensions—not in the past and not in the present, cut off from the dimension of time. An interesting example of this can be found in the character of K. in Kafka's *The Castle*, who lives in the twilight zone of time. The same is true of Clamence in *The Fall* by Camus. These cases describe a climate in which the individual is immersed in a state of *no time*—the state of mind of an individual who is totally exposed, wandering, and homeless.

The spiral timeline, drawn into the empty traumatic moment, constantly penetrates and biases the linear timeline. In a distorted manner the trauma victim "deals with" this problem by creating a renewed moment of trauma in the future. In this state the posttraumatic survivor returns to being what Heidegger refers to as "Being-ahead-of-itself" (1996). Indeed, "Being-ahead-of-itself" enables the subject to act in the world since the futural dimension is inherent in one's being. Yet due to the endless regression in time back to the moment of trauma, this horizon is colored in the apocalyptic tones of the initial trauma, which continues to pursue him, or more accurately, to draw him in by means of uncontrollable obsessive-compulsive forces. The result is that the agent of the trauma violently inserts the trauma into the public sphere of time. The victim's need to insert the trauma into the sphere of time on the one hand and his inability to integrate the trauma into the time line of the "past" (as part of the narrative) on the other lead to a situation in which the victim attempts to integrate the trauma into the present or future time line as an apocalyptic possibility that creates a new horizon. This finds expression in the violent insertion of the trauma into the public sphere by the creation of additional cycles of trauma involving persecutors and victims.

TRAUMA BRANDED INTO THE BODY: WIDTHWISE AND DEPTHWISE RAMIFICATIONS

Trauma does not undergo high-level processing (Ehlers and Clark 2000), nor does it turn into a symbol, but rather remains sensory and somatic. Hence the title of Van Der Kolk's (1994) well-known article, "The Body Keeps the Score." Consequently, trauma does not turn into explicit memory but rather remains implicit.

Because the trauma is "preserved" and fixed on the physical level, every movement, every posture, indeed the very presence of the body in the world elicits the traumatic experience again (Ataria 2016b) Post-traumatic stress disorder: A theory of perception. The body is a direct mediator of the traumatic experience. The body is the source of the trauma. Stimuli we are unaware of, such as odors and sounds, arouse the physical level of the trauma and by means of classical conditioning mechanisms project the victim into the traumatic moment (Ehlers et al. 2004). This is a vicious cycle that brings about a sense of constant threat. It is very difficult, we can conclude, to break out of this vicious cycle (Rothschild 2000).

If the source of the trauma is within the body, victims will always feel they are in a strange, threatening, and dangerous world, for their own body, the body that defines them and through which they exert their presence in the world, has become the source of their suffering. Under such conditions, victims are often uncontrollably pushed to harming or destroying their own bodies as the source of pain and suffering (Van Der Kolk et al. 1991). Because the trauma has been branded in the body and because we perceive the world through our bodies and have no way to "circumvent" them (Husserl 1989; Merleau-Ponty 2002; Noë 2004), trauma victims perceive the world through the filter of the trauma, through the traumatic body. Therefore, in an attempt to be-in-the-world that does not go through the traumatic body, the trauma victim can choose to destroy the body itself (Ataria 2016a, 2016b, 2016c; Ataria and Gallagher 2015). In this sense the trauma "nurtures" a passion for self-destruction.

The movie *Taxi Driver* teaches us a great deal about the widthwise and depthwise ramifications of the passion for self-destruction. The story of Travis is in no way unique and represents a well-known situation in which soldiers suffering from posttrauma are motivated by self-destructive mechanisms (and by mechanisms of spiral time, as demonstrated in the previous section) to injure themselves and/or their surroundings, thus expanding the circles of the trauma. In addition, the movie itself has had broad repercussions on audiences across the globe, and through the movie the trauma permeates the consciousness of the viewers. Of course a movie in itself cannot generate trauma in its viewers, but after a critical mass has accumulated the viewers become witnesses to the trauma and even partners to the initial traumatic exposure, even if at a lesser intensity. In this regard, the movie *Fight Club* serves as an echo of the generation comprising the children of those who fought in the Vietnam War. In this movie we encounter the passion to injure the body in order to revive it. The goal is to bring a body back to life which as a result of the trauma has become robotic and lifeless. In this sense, the movie *Fight Club* represents an attempt to insert the real into the symbolic order, or perhaps more accurately, to dismantle the symbolic order completely in order to reconstruct it anew. In essence, *Fight Club* is a reverberation of *Taxi Driver*, which demonstrates the extent to which physical trauma has pervaded the culture wars of America.

On another level the notion that trauma is branded into the body appears to form the basis for the view that a new language must be invented or found to describe trauma. The way in which trauma is branded into the body prevents the traumatic event from turning into a narrative. The memory remains physical and nonverbal. The inability to describe the trauma in words, to transform it into part of the narrative, is affixed precisely to this attribute of trauma—that it is physical in its very essence. Yet this notion can be understood on an even deeper level. If we adopt the approach that language itself is rooted in—and constructed by—the body (Lakoff and Johnson 1999; Merleau-Ponty 2002; Varela et al. 1991), we must rethink the very notion of language, and particularly the metaphors, used by survivors. The trauma is branded into their bodies and creates a new reality, yet language itself is incapable of catching up to the radical changes that have taken place in their bodies and thus continues to represent the old reality, the "old body" prior to the trauma. A large and immediate gap is thus created between the familiar language representing the previous systems of power and the new language that is affixed deeply within the encounter between what is real and the trauma. Thus it seems that the posttraumatic survivor has no way of expressing the trauma and must find new forms of expression.

These forms of expression are essential for the so-called Freudian leap, the transition from individual to society. When trauma is expressed by means of an unknown language, it inserts new structures into "cultured" language. This is a language within a language, a state within the state, a type of explosive positioned at the heart of the cultural structure, for language and culture are intimately related. In other words, this new language, even if it uses the exact same words, brings with it new physical representations, traumatic representations that by their very nature operate by means of absence, void, and dissociation, thus inserting "nothingness" into the "somethingness" of spoken language. When the language of trauma that is fixed in the traumatic body takes control of the discourse, the very structure of language begins to collapse.

A WORLD WITHOUT (BODILY) PERSPECTIVE

In everyday life our perspective on the world derives from our bodies. This is the initial condition for being-in-the-world (Sartre 1956). According to Zahavi (2006), this is the first and most basic condition for any minimal sense of self. A physical perspective is a condition for subjective experience. The body is our zero-point or point of reference with respect to the world (Husserl 1989). During trauma, the individual is liable to lose the sense of a central and unifying force. The victim ceases to experience the event "within his or her body." Hence, trauma is often accompanied by a sense of dissociation, including out-of-body experiences (Herman 1992). During trauma, individuals in effect find themselves outside of themselves. This occurs for the most part when they find themselves unable to use the fight or flight response. With no other choice, they enter into a psychotic state, adopting a strategy of emotional coping (Folkman and Lazarus 1980). As a type of defense mechanism in such a situation, the individual "escapes" to an alternative reality (Cannon 1929). Such defense mechanisms appear to be dissociative. But even though this defense mechanism is essential for the organism to survive in the short term, it also has far-reaching symptomatic implications for the long term (Ataria 2014a, 2015). Indeed, traumatic dissociation is considered to be the number-one risk factor for the development of posttraumatic symptoms (Breh and Seidler 2007; Ozer et al. 2003).

On the one hand, during traumatic experiences subjects are characterized as being "outside of their bodies"—lacking a physical (bodily, ego-centric, and first-person) perspective on the world. On the other hand, as we have seen, the victims of trauma are present in the world, indeed are thrown into the world by the traumatized body. Victims of posttrauma are torn between two worlds in a state of either—or, two individuals within a single body. One is completely dissociated from the traumatic experience, unable to acknowledge the trauma and cut off from the body. The other is connected to the physical dimension and senses the trauma in the here and now without being able to retreat or to avoid collapsing inwardly into the trauma itself.

This duality is intolerable. The two identities cannot live together in the same *body*, and the victim must unwillingly cope with this inner rift. In this regard trauma can be thought of as an internal enemy. It is an abyss between two identities in which each (1) denies the reality of the other, (2) desires the other, and (3) seeks to destroy the other. The consequence of this impossible conflict is the victim's recurring attempt to destroy one of these personality aspects. This can be seen, for example, in the final scene of the film *The Deer Hunter* when Mike and Nick are playing Russian roulette, or in *Apocalypse Now* when Captain Willard (Sheen) murders Captain Kurtz (Brando). Indeed, unable to bridge between these inner personalities, the traumatic subject chooses a radical solution that does not leave anyone indifferent.

As I will subsequently explain, the loss of the body sends the trauma victim into what Kierkegaard refers to as a religious circle (Kierkegaard 1985), but this circle lacks a deity. In Kierkegaardian terms, we can say that the traumatic individual cannot continue to exist within an ethical circle controlled by the principles of obligation on the one hand and those of free will on the other. Often trauma victims feel that society "allowed this to happen," that society did nothing less than betray and sacrifice them. This is a unique climate for it enables and practically forces the trauma victims to dive into the religious circle and totally commit themselves to God, because during the trauma the subject understands that the ethical circle is fraudulent and cannot stand up to the test of reality. It is important to note, however, that victims cannot return to the "aesthetic circle" that was based on sensual pleasures and on physical experiences. For these victims the body is the source of suffering, and therefore they are shoved into the religious circle. Yet the main notion is that this religious circle lacks a deity, even—or maybe especially—because God was silent during the trauma, or even worse, was an active partner to the crime. This godless religious circle produces traumatic figures that reify the trauma in the public sphere. A classic example of this can be seen in *Taxi Driver* when Travis operates out of a sense of "divine mission" in a godless world. Indeed, this appears to be an *Akeda*, a binding and sacrifice, which obsessively recycles itself over and over again.

Thus, out of a sense of loyalty to the trauma, and on occasion loyalty to the perpetrator of the trauma, the trauma victim generates a new religious circle situated beyond good and evil. I believe that this forced transition to a godless religious circle occurs because during the trauma the subject loses a sense of physical (bodily, egocentric, and first-person) perspective. The body ceases to be the subject's point of reference in the world and is no longer the basis for any sort of subjective experience. To lose one's perspective means to lose one's interpersonal connections, to lose the human dimension. Without perspective we are incapable of seeing the other, nor is the other capable of seeing us, so that in the eyes of the other we are no longer subjects, indeed we cease to be human (Levinas 2006; Sartre 1956).

During the trench warfare of World War I, soldiers often found themselves in dead-end situations without any possibility of fight or flight. In such a situation, the only option is to come to a standstill, to freeze. The individual is dissociated and loses the physical perspective on the world. The climate created during World War I was of a world devoid of a subjective-physical point of view. In general terms we can also say that lack of a subjective-physical point of view is one of the major characteristics of the Nazi machinery of destruction (Felman and Laub 1992). In this sense, the initial experience of losing the subjective-physical point of view as part of the dissociative defense mechanism prevalent during World War I (Myers 1940; War Office Committee 1922) can also be linked to the establishment of the first extermination camps twenty-five years later. In the deepest sense possible, the concentration camps deprived individuals of the possibility of looking, of observing, of being human. The camps were established by people who had grown up experiencing a lack of perspective (as soldiers during World War I) or who were educated by fathers who had returned from the war in the trenches without a bodily, egocentric, and first-person point of view. In this sense these fathers are present in the world without any point of view, cut off, dulled. This is a form of binding, of sacrifice, where fathers bind their sons by raising them without any bodily point of view and thus pass on the trauma. This trauma leads to the loss of that bodily point of view, to the collapse of the subjective experience, and therefore the world is perceived as nowhere and indeed becomes *nowhere*.

I believe that the loss of perspective during radically traumatic events has major implications that extend beyond the boundaries of the individual. The victims are sent back into a world devoid of perspective, where they exist like robots. Trauma of the magnitude of the Holocaust, Hiroshima, and the like has many circles of influence. The first circle comprises the family of the victim, whose loved one (son or daughter, father or mother, husband or wife) now observes life from the outside, lives adjacent to but not within life. After the immediate family, broader circles are also affected. When a group within society undergoes extreme trauma and as a result loses its physical perspective on the world, the ramifications are far-reaching. In this regard, Felman and Laub (1992) are correct in defining World War II as an historical watershed line. In this war, mass numbers of people experienced extreme states of trauma and consequently lost their subjective perspective, their physical point of view, on the world. This critical mass went on to educate subsequent generations, continued to produce, continued to talk (and to be silent), continued to be part of the community, and thus produced a critical change in the society to which it belonged. In Israel, for example, the numbers tattooed on the arms of many Holocaust survivors made their trauma present in the public sphere, even when they tried to hide it. The focus of the trauma converged on that number. More than anything else, the numbers on the arm symbolize the loss of identity, the loss of perspective. Yet at the same time that number on the arm has the ability to generate a new identity, and not only for the individual. Indeed, the very notion of a number tattooed on someone's arm instead of a name is enough to rock the very foundations not only of the person who bears the number but also of anyone who comes into contact with it: with the number, with the person bearing the number, with the person who is the number, and with the number that is the person. As a symbol, the number on the arm is the most radical and virulent mark of Cain present in the public sphere, exactly like the distorted bodies of the victims of Hiroshima (who are known as Hibakusha). As such, it changes the individual. It is a black hole, an absence that is present in and shapes the public sphere, turning it into a space lacking perspective, lacking subjective experience and, ultimately, lacking the notion of subject as well.

LANGUAGE, STORY, AND TRAUMA

The traumatic experience transcends words. This issue has been discussed in depth with respect to various circumstances and contexts (Janet 1889, 1925; Van Der Hart et al. 2000; Van Der Kolk and Fisler 1995). When examining this issue in depth, two important and fascinating factors emerge:

- The events taking place at the time of the trauma are encoded in a way that is "inaccessible" to language. The trauma is encoded on the physical level, and its factors do not undergo high-level processing, leaving them outside the realm of speech.
- It is language itself that is traumatized, so that the trauma takes place on the level of language. As Hiroko put it: "What words can we now use, and to what ends? Even: what are words?" (quoted in Treat 1995, p. 27). Hence the traumatic subject is unable to continue using "old" and "familiar" words, for these words have become foreign, leaving the subject forced to invent an entirely new language.

As a result of this "foreignness" of and within the language, indeed the very nature of the language as foreign, the traumatic event often remains outside the boundaries of the individual's narrative, outside the autobiographical self. Even when victims "speak the trauma," their story remains foreign to them, not only because of its content but also, indeed mainly, because the words themselves have become a strange entity to survivors.

Hence Elie Wiesel's description (1979) of concentration camp language: "Rather than a link, it became a wall" (p. 202). He then goes on to explain: "All I know is that Treblinka and Auschwitz cannot be told. And yet I have tried. God knows I have tried" (p. 203). The narrative is the story that defines us. Yet without language to tell, to touch, and to expose the trauma, it cannot be reduced to a story and hence remains completely cut off from the autobiographical sense of self. Moreover, the fact that language has become strange and devoid of meaning may explain why a large portion of the writers of Holocaust journals felt they were failing in their verbal description of the experience they were undergoing, even though from a factual perspective they often seemed to be describing the situation quite accurately.

By its very nature, then, trauma shakes the foundations of language so deeply that posttraumatic survivors must wonder whether they can use language as a means of communication. This feeling forces survivors to find other means, because the trauma is first and foremost silence (Laub 1995). In this context, speech too comes from, and is rooted within, silence. And this silence is analogous to the omnipresent scream in the public discourse, a scream that changes this discourse, sometimes even radically. This is the experience of many who have grown up with silent-traumatic parents, whose silence cries out the most important event of their lives and dominates a discourse that is nothing other than silence. This is a discourse in which people talk a great deal and say nothing—and what is important is what is not said. It is a discourse of empty spaces.

Indeed, there are two survivors who experience the trauma together: the individual with the language and the language that is the individual. In 1958 Paul Celan wrote the following on the occasion of receiving the Bremen Literature Prize:

> Only one thing remained reachable, close and secure amid all losses: language. Yes, language. In spite of everything, it remained secure against loss. But it had to go through its own lack of answers, through terrifying silence, through the thousand darknesses of murderous speech. It went through. It gave me no words for what was happening, but went through it. Went through and could resurface, "enriched" by it all. (Celan 1986, p. 34)

Clearly, then, in the posttraumatic era it is necessary to find new forms of expression that will enable the victims to express their experiences in a way that will touch the experience itself yet will not cover it up.

The crisis of language in trauma has major implications on the very relationship between testimony and words, between spoken language and "facts." The crisis of language in trauma describes an impossible rift between the subjective experience of trauma and the objective description of the traumatic event. Felman and Laub (1992) describes trauma in terms of inaccessible truth. Yet this seems to be a somewhat naïve approach, originating in Freud's (1939) discussion of a concealed basic truth. Indeed, according to Caruth (1995), "its truth is bound up with its crisis of truth" (p. 8). In this sense the problem is not merely one of "inaccessibility." Thus, diverse studies have shown that in some cases the traumatic event itself was not encoded (McNally 2003). Such cases leave us no option other than to say that the traumatic event is missing and that the testimony indeed lacks roots. The event is missing from a memory in which there is clearly no "truth" whatsoever. In such cases the testimony lacks any anchor. It is nothing more than a story lacking a grip on reality. The atom bomb is a good example of this.

LITTLE BOY

On August 6, 1945 at 8:15 am Hiroshima time, the atom bomb code-named Little Boy was dropped from a Boeing B-29 bomber on the center of Hiroshima. This event was well defined in time and in space, with agreed-upon objective coordinates sketched upon the borders of historical discourse. And yet do these facts mean anything? Is this objective documentation sufficient? Do these documents say anything about:

> "What happened there really"
> "What happened there? Really?"
> "What happened ... there? Really?"
> "What happened—there?"
> "What happened?"
> "What?"
> "Really?"
> "?"
> " "

The bombing of Hiroshima on X date at Y time is a fact that cannot be disputed. Yet there is no way to apply any concept of truth to what the residents of Hiroshima went through, to what those who were there experienced. In addition to material objects, traumatic events seem to turn concepts, perspectives, ideas, and dreams into vapor as well (Lifton 1967). The atom bomb vaporized the very concept of truth. A traumatic event is a situation in which the truth and the facts are cut off from each other: "a non-coincidence between facts and truth" (Agamben 1999, p. 12). In this context it is interesting to examine the testimony of Jorge Semprún,[2] a prisoner at Buchenwald:

> Even if an absolutely accurate testimony existed, totally objective in all its details—something that is in and of itself impossible based on the definition of individual testimony—even in such a case what is essential would be missed. For what is essential is not concealed in the cumulative horror, whose details can be clarified ad infinitum. It is possible to tell about each day, from the time of awakening at four in the morning until the hour of the curfew: the exhausting work, the ongoing starvation, the constant lack of

sleep, the abuse of the kapos, cleaning the nauseating latrines, the sense of exhaustion and powerlessness, the death of friends—and still not touch upon the essence. (Semprun 1998, p. 84)

Indeed, if we insist on hearing the survivor's "truth" we will hear shocking responses such as "I have ceased to be human, all my humanity was burned to ashes." Such responses find expression in the collapse of the language that also represents the subject's culture.

Asking a trauma survivor "what happened there" can be considered a form of mockery. Elie Wiesel believes that when a person writes about the Holocaust "words become obstacles rather than vehicles; he writes not with words but against words. For there are no words to describe what the victims felt when death was the norm and life a miracle" (Wiesel 2005, p. vi). When Ka-Tsetnik was asked at the Eichmann trial what really happened there, he fainted. He had no other option, for he had sworn to tell the truth, the whole truth, and nothing but the truth. To put this even more accurately, even if the survivor has the option to tell, we have no chance of understanding. No option remains but to say that this inability to function through and in language represents a deep metaphysical breakdown in which the very concept of truth has dissolved. Yet this process does not end on the level of the individual. Rather it penetrates the structure of language itself. After life-altering traumatic events, the concept of "truth" must be written in inverted commas, for it is totally unclear what this "truth" is referring to. Other basic concepts such as "human beings" must be written in inverted commas as well, totally changing the way in which we read and interpret texts. These inverted commas cause us to cast doubt upon what is "obvious" and "goes without saying." Ultimately they cast doubt on the very existence of humanity.

REJECTING THE VERY NOTION OF HUMANITY

McNally (2003) defines posttrauma as a memory disorder. Whether this is a problem of encoding information at the time of the trauma, a problem of memory retrieval after the trauma, or both of these possibilities at the same time (Spiegel 1997), clearly it is impossible to separate the traumatic experience itself from the lacking/missing/absent/destroyed memory of it. Consequently, it is also clear that testimony regarding trauma is a sensitive matter in the context of investigating trauma (as well as in other contexts, for example the legal context), for under certain circumstances trauma is a witnessless event.

In this regard, LaCapra (2001) expresses concern about the point at which trauma ceases to be an event that can be positioned in time and space and can therefore be defined as a trans-historical event. Yet we must distinguish between the need to document, catalog, and establish a traumatic event as an event on the human axis of history and the experience of a single individual under extreme circumstances. The fact that in certain cases trauma victims are able to recite their stories to provide factual documentation does not mean that this is anything beyond a collection of facts devoid of people. In the extremism marking traumatic events we find an almost desperate attempt to create a "documentary historical document." Hence more than one journal has been uncovered that describes everything except the subjective experience of the writer—everything except testimony. In other words, factual documentation cannot be considered something that exists from the subjective perspective—as testimony. On the contrary, this very something conceals the nothing, the lack of subjective experience of the traumatic event. In this context we should again recall Ka-Tsetnik, who asked the pupils of his eyes to film the sights. Yet in doing so he admits that he did not see, did not look, did not observe, but rather filmed, totally rejecting the human-subjective point of view in favor of an objective-factual description. Indeed, Ka-Tsetnik ultimately did not testify at the Eichmann trial. He was unable to endure it.

Trauma, so it seems, conceals the information that concerns it. Those who have been truly exposed to trauma lose their ability to testify about it (Agamben 1999; Levi 1993). Thus we are exposed to two types of testimony: factual testimony lacking any subjective-personal dimension, and subjective description lacking any links to real coordinates. This subjective description is also marked by two types, two maps, but it is impossible to place one slide on top of the other to attain a complete and accurate picture, for each slide/map describes a different world entirely. Not only are these worlds not engaged in dialogue with each other, they actually reject one another.

Even those observing from the sidelines cannot look at the trauma, for in doing so they are immediately flooded by it and drawn into it. They cannot preserve the witness (onlooker trauma) within themselves, and they become victims or full partners to the experience (Douglass and Vogler 2003). In other words, in the case of trauma there are no observers from the sidelines, indeed there cannot be. Observing from the sidelines requires denying one's humanity, ceasing to be human. In this regard, in order to be an "objective" observer of trauma an individual must give up on being human. Thus, a side effect of trauma is the rejection of humanity altogether.

BIPOLAR WORLD: DENIAL VERSUS MYSTIFICATION

Trauma does not accommodate knowing. To understand this statement better, let us consider the well-known black-hole information paradox. According to this paradox, the information contained in material that enters a black hole is liable to disappear due to the evaporation process of black holes (Greene 2005). This description is precisely appropriate for describing the processes of the traumatic experience. The traumatic story only encircles the black hole and always remains at a safe distance from it, because if the story gets too close it will evaporate. The story of the witness can describe the cold facts, completely dissociated from the subjective experience. Alternatively, the story can describe the subjective experience but remain completely disconnected from the "cold facts."

Laub (1995) is not disturbed by the fact that the testimony does not necessarily go along with the "cold facts" for he sees a greater danger in silence, in obsessive avoidance of the story of the event. In his view, secrecy perpetuates the trauma and turns it into an omnipotent dictator. This is indeed an acute problem. Yet if we allow ourselves to renounce the facts, a dual risk arises, of denial on the one hand and mystification on the other. It would not be an exaggeration to say that this is an attribute of life-altering traumatic events: Holocaust denial vs. Holocaust mystification, mystification of the trauma of Vietnam War veterans vs. denial of the My Lai Massacre.

Thus, because the trauma insists on being unrepresented and noninstitutionalized, the various institutions of documentation move along a continuum ranging from denial to mystification. Perhaps the best example of this is the response of the Jewish settlement of Palestine (Yishuv), in the context of the Holocaust—indeed the height of hypocrisy. On the one hand, the years of destruction were marked by silence, disregard, and obsessive clinging to arguments such as "there was nothing we could do." Indeed, until the end of the war many Jews in prestate Israel did not believe that such a thing was possible, and they denied the existence of the Holocaust. Yet subsequently, and particularly after the Eichmann trial (1961), the Holocaust underwent a mystification process and became a myth à la the Ten Plagues and the Exodus from Egypt in a somewhat different guise—that of a legend that had never really happened.

I argue that this is a representative case. The polar structure of denial/mystification is not a marginal effect but rather an almost unavoidable consequence of the traumatic experience itself, which does not allow for a middle ground and leaves us fluctuating between denial and mystification. The lack of dialogue between the "narrative story" and the "facts" is the cause of this.

When the narrative story is in essence nothing but an empty void, form without content, a situation emerges in which the traumatic experience becomes truly an experience of mystic sanctification—ecstatic yet victimized heights that are yearned for as a basis for joint and organized existence in the image of the trauma. The moment of mystification is the moment at which we as researchers/interviewers/listeners understand that we will never be able to understand because understanding is, by definition, impossible. At the same time we are also flooded with an infinite sense of guilt for our indifference in real time. Thus we allow ourselves, perhaps out of an uncontrolled and exaggerated sense of identification with the victim as well as out of an inability to contain this feeling of guilt, to generate the "story" of what happened. Our inability to live with the "no story" leads us to write our own story. Yet in creating this story we again and unavoidably become part of the trauma itself (secondary victimhood). We transform ourselves into trauma victims and trauma agents and thus resolve our sense of unbearable guilt.

It appears, then, that with respect to describing and exposing the traumatic experience, the role of the listener, the observer from the sidelines, the researcher, is beyond all understanding. Because trauma is so nullifying, it has the ability to transfer and project onto a single listener and onto listeners as a group and turn them into its agents. Indeed the power of trauma lies in its absence, its nonexistence. A listener or a group of listeners are drawn by mighty forces to fill the void. This is what happened with Felman when she and her class reached a serious and even radical state of crisis (Felman and Laub 1992). Because the testimony is so hollow, those listening in the surroundings have enormous power. This problem is intensified though a model in which responsibility (and responsibility is always accompanied by guilt) for "relieving" the trauma is transferred to the listener/interviewer. This can find expression in the adoption of the victim's experiences and (missing) voice to the point of genuine mystic appropriation of the trauma, so that empathy for the victim turns into identity. The activism on the part of the listeners draws them all the more forcefully into the trauma—into the black hole.

Trauma as a Black Hole

There appears to be no better way to describe the traumatic experience than as a "black hole." A black hole is a place in space whose gravitational field is so strong that nothing, including light, can escape it. The same is true of trauma. For trauma victims, the traumatic event turns into an axis around which their entire world revolves. The intensity of the traumatic memory, even if it is dismantled, perforated, and lacking in details, only becomes stronger. The event is not only a life-altering Event with a capital E. It becomes the only event in the victim's life. Indeed, the lives of victims revolve around the traumatic event as if having been led there. In other cases the traumatic event becomes a secret, a form without content. In such cases the victims do not say anything, and the secret becomes the center of their lives and in turn intensifies even more (Laub 1995).

In referring to the "secret" we should again return to the definition of the black hole. The outer boundary of the black hole is known as the event horizon. An external observer can neither see nor influence what takes place inside the boundary of the black hole. No object or radiation that crosses the observer's event horizon will ever be seen again. Ultimately, these will accumulate at a particular point in time-space. At the moment a particle passes the horizon, its progress toward the center of the hole is inevitable. Trauma operates in exactly the same way. Trauma is an invisible boundary to which things are attracted, and at the moment they enter the black hole they become invisible and inaccessible. The larger the mass that is attracted to the black hole, the stronger the hole becomes. There is no nuclear truth at the center of the black hole, however—only total nothingness. In the case of trauma, the more events that are added to the traumatic event, the greater the power of the life-altering event becomes (Ataria 2014b). The secret intensifies and the very essence of the narrative itself becomes concealed and mysterious.

Touching a black hole is impossible, for it is absolute nothingness. So, too, is trauma. Trauma is not a wound. Indeed it is more correct to talk about trauma in terms of forces in space, and even more accurate in terms of distorted forces of time-space. Just like a black hole, the traumatic individual creates a traumatic space, a climate in which the trauma shapes the way in which we think, experience, and act in the world.

I believe that this is the attribute that turns trauma into a life-altering event, not only on the individual level but also on the social level. A traumatic individual turns into a black hole that distorts the social dimension (trauma agent), and national traumas such as the Holocaust and the Hiroshima bombings distort the time-space in the deepest sense, among other things because of the critical mass of victims. This is even truer when the trauma is passed institutionally from one generation to another. Indeed, by its very nature the traumatic experience generates negative magnetic forces at the core of the structures of society. Hence, it unintentionally strives to dismantle and smash the existing structures, yet—and this is a critical point—without offering any "positive" alternative whatsoever.

To conclude this chapter, the working assumption that social trauma can be discussed in the same terms as individual trauma is extremely difficult to corroborate. Even though Freud dared to make this conceptual leap, as did many other investigators in his wake, we must take proper caution in considering this transition. I believe that what transforms trauma from an individual to a collective event is precisely the absence that characterizes trauma—the excess branded into the body that defies representation.

NOTES

1. I would like to thank Koji Yamashiro for this insight.
2. I would like to thank Amos Goldberg for this reference (and to be honest, for many others as well).

BIBLIOGRAPHY

Agamben, G. (1998). *Homo sacer: Sovereign power and bare life*. Stanford: Stanford University Press.

Agamben, G. (1999). *Remnants of Auschwitz*. (D. Heller-Roazen, Trans.). New York: Zone Books.

Applebaum, A. (2004). *Gulag: A history*. New York: Anchor Books edition.

Arendt, H. (1965). *Eichmann in Jerusalem: A report on the banality of evil*. New York: Penguin.

Arendt, H. (1973). *The origins of totalitarianism*. New York: Harcourt, Brace and World, 1973.

Arndt, S. (Producer), Tykwer, T. (Writer), & Tykwer, T. (Director). (1998). *Run Lola run* ([Motion Picture]). Sony Pictures Classics.

Ataria, Y. (2010). Consciousness-body-time: How do people think lacking their body? MA Thesis. The Hebrew University of Jerusalem.

Ataria, Y. (2014a). Acute peritraumatic dissociation: In favor of a phenomenological inquiry. *Journal of Trauma & Dissociation, 15*(3), 332–347. doi:10.1080/15299732.2013.853722.

Ataria, Y. (2014b). Traumatic memories as black holes: A qualitative-phenomenological approach. *Qualitative Psychology, 1*(2), 123–140. doi:10.1037/qup0000009.

Ataria, Y. (2015). Sense of ownership and sense of agency during trauma. *Phenomenology and the Cognitive Sciences, 14*(1), 199–212. doi:10.1007/s11097-013-9334-y.

© The Author(s) 2017
Y. Ataria, *The Structural Trauma of Western Culture*,
DOI 10.1007/978-3-319-53228-8

Ataria, Y. (2016a). I am not my body, this is not my body. *Human Studies, 39*(2), 217–229. doi:10.1007/s10746-015-9366-0.

Ataria, Y. (2016b). Post-traumatic stress disorder: A theory of perception. *Body, Movement and Dance in Psychotherapy, 11*(1), 19–30. doi:10.1080/17432979.2015.1064828.

Ataria, Y. (2016c). When the Body Becomes the Enemy: Disownership toward the Body. *Philosophy, Psychiatry & Psychology, 23*(1), 1–15. doi:10.1353/ppp.2016.0002

Ataria, Y. (2016). The Crisis of Manhood. In Y. Ataria, D. Gurevitz, H. Pedaya, & Y. Neria (Eds.), Interdisciplinary Handbook of Trauma and Culture (pp. 267–278). Springe

Ataria, Y., & Gallagher, S. (2015). Somatic apathy: Body disownership in the context of torture. *Journal of Phenomenological Psychology, 46*(1), 105–122. doi:10.1163/15691624-12341286.

Ataria, Y., & Neria, Y. (2013). Consciousness-body-time: How do people think lacking their body? *Humans Studies, 36*(2), 159–178. doi:10.1007/s10746-013-9263-3.

Barri, Shoshana (1997). "The Question of Kastner's Testimonies on Behalf of Nazi War Criminals," *The Journal of Israeli History*, Vol. 18, No. 2–3, pp. 139–165.

Becker, J. (1994). Music and trance. *Leonardo Music Journal, 4*, 41–51.

Benyamini, I. (2016). *A Critical Theology of Genesis.* New York: Palgrave Macmillan US.

Bergson, H. (1950). *Time and free will: An essay on the immediate data of consciousness.* New York: Macmillan.

Bianco, J. (2004). Comparative literature studies. *Techno - cinema, 4*(3), 377–410.

Bilsky, Leora (2001). "Judging Evil in the Trial of Kastner", *Law and History Review*, Vol. 19, No. 1, Spring.

Blacking, J. (1990). *A commonsense view of all music.* Cambridge: Cambridge University Press.

Boell, H. (1976). *Group portrait with lady.* (L. Vennewitz, Trans.). Harmondsworth: Penguin Books.

Boëthius, A. M. (1989). *Fundamentals of music.* (C. Palisca, Ed. & C. Bower, Trans.). New Haven: Yale University Press.

Breh, D. C., & Seidler, G. H. (2007). Is peritraumatic dissociation a risk factor for PTSD? *Journal of Trauma & Dissociation, 8*(1), 53–69.

Bulgakov, M. (1997). *The master and Margarita.* (R. Pevear & L. Volokhonsky, Trans.). London: Penguin Books.

Camus, A. (1954). *The rebel.* (A. Bower, Trans.). New York: Vintage Books.

Camus, A. (1955). *The myth of Sisyphus and other essays.* (J. O'Brien, Trans.). New York: Random House.

Camus, A. (1962a). *The rebel.* (A. Bower, Trans.). Harmondsworth: Penguin Books.

Camus, A. (1962b). *The stranger*. (S. Gilbert, Trans.). New York: Vintage Books.

Camus, A. (1975). *The myth of Sisyphus*. (J. O'Brien, Trans.). London: Penguin.

Camus, A. (1984). *The fall*. (J. O'Brien, Trans.). New York: Vintage International.

Camus, A. (1995). *The first man*. (D. Hapgood, Trans.). New York: Vintage Books.

Camus, A. (2000). *The fall*. (J. O'Brien, Trans.). London: Penguin.

Canetti, E. (1974). *Kafka's Other Trial: the Letters to Felice*. New York: Schocken Books.

Cannon, W. B. (1929). *Bodily changes in pain, hunger, fear, and rage*. New York: Appleton-Century-Crofts.

Card, O. S. (1985). *Ender's game*. New York: Tor Books.

Caruth, C. (Ed.). (1995). *Trauma: Explorations in memory*. Baltimore, MD: Johns Hopkins University Press.

Caruth, C. (2007). Trauma, justice and the political unconscious: Arendt and Felman's journey to Jerusalem. In E. Sun, E. Peretz, & U. Baer (Eds.), *The claims of literature: A Shoshana Felman reader*. New York: Fordham University Press.

Celan, P. (1986). Speech on the occasion of receiving the literature prize of the free Hanseatic City of Bremen. In R. Waldrop (Trans.), *Celan's collected prose* (p. 34). Riverdale-on-Hudson. New York: The Sheep Meadow Press.

Chalmers, D. (1995). Facing up to the problem of consciousness. *Journal of Consciousness Studies*, 2(3), 200–219.

Cimino, M. (Director). (1978). *The deer hunter*. [Motion Picture].

Coen, J., & Coen, E. (Directors). (2007). *No country for old men* [Motion Picture]. Miramax Films, Paramount Vantage.

Coen, J., Coen, E. (Producers), Coen, J., Coen, E. (Writers), Coen, J., & Coen, E. (Directors). (2009). *A serious man* [Motion Picture].

Conrad, J. (1990). *Heart of darkness*. New York: Dover Publications.

Coppola, F. F. (Producer), Conrad, J. (Writer), & Coppola, F. F. (Director). (1979). *Apocalypse now* [Motion Picture].

Cohen, L. (2016) "You Want It Darker." (Producer Leonard Cohen, Adam Cohen, Patrick Leonard) Recorded April 2015–July 2016. Length 36:07. Label Columbia. Released 21 October 2016. Los Angeles: Studio Leonard Cohen's house in Wilshire.

De Saint-Exupery, A. (1971). *The little prince*. (K. Woods, Trans.). Harmondsworth, MX: Penguin Books.

Deleuze, G., & Guattari, F. (1986). *Kafka: toward a minor literature*. (D. Polan, Trans.) Minneapol and London: University of Minnesota Press.

Descartes, R. (1637/1996). *Discourse on the method: Meditations of first philosophy*. (D. Weissman, Ed.). New Haven, CT: Yale University Press.

Dostoyevsky, F. (1992). *The brothers Karamazov*. (W. J. Leatherbarrow, Trans.). Cambridge: Cambridge University Press.

Douglass, A., & Vogler, T. A. (2003). Introduction. In A. Douglass & T. A. Vogler (Eds.), *Witness and memory: The discourse of trauma* (pp. 1–53). New York: Routledge.

Ehlers, A., & Clark, D. (2000). A cognitive model of posttraumatic stress disorder. *Behaviour Research and Therapy, 38,* 319–345.

Ehlers, A., Hackmann, A., & Michael, T. (2004). Intrusive re-experiencing in post-traumatic stress disorder: Phenomenology, theory, and therapy. *Memory, 12*(4), 403–415.

Eliot, T. S. (2009). *Collected poems 1909–1962.* London: Harcourt Brace.

Evans, D. (1996). *An introductory dictionary of Lacanian psychoanalysis.* New York: Routledge.

Fanon, F. (1968). *The wretched of the earth.* (C. Farrington, Trans.). New York: Grove Press.

Farrell, K. (1998). *Post-traumatic culture.* Baltimore, MD: Johns Hopkins University Press.

Felman, S. (2002). *The juridical unconscious.* Cambridge, MA: Harvard University Press.

Felman, S., & Laub, D. (1992). *Testimony: Crises of witnessing in literature, psychoanalysis, and history.* Florence, KY: Taylor & Francis/Routledge.

Fletcher, A. (1964). *Allegory: The theory of a symbolic mode.* Ithaca, NY: Cornell.

Floyd, P. (1973). *Us and them. The dark side of the moon.* P. Floyd. Producer Pink Floyd. London, UK: Abbey Road Studios.

Floyd, P. (1979). *Run like hell. The wall.* P. Floyd. Studio: Britannia Row, Super Bear Studio, Studio Miraval (France); CBS 30th Street Studio (New York); Producers Workshop (Los Angeles).

Folkman, S., & Lazarus, R. (1980). An analysis of coping in a middle-aged community sample. *American Sociological Association, 21,* 219–239.

Foucault, M. (1965). *Madness and civilization.* New York: Pantheon Books.

Freud, S. (1939). *Moses and monotheism.* (K. Jones, Trans.). New York: Vintage Books.

Freud, S. (1950). *Totem and taboo.* (J. Strachey, Trans.). London: Routledge & K. Paul.

Freud, S. (1959). *The uncanny* (Vol. 4). (A. Strachey, Trans.). New York: Basic Books.

Friedländer, S. (2007). *The years of extermination: Nazi Germany and the Jews, 1939–1945.* New York, NY: Harper Collins.

Goyer, D., Nolan, C. (Writers), & Nolan, C. (Director). (2008). *The Dark Knight* [Motion Picture].

Greene, B. (2005). *The fabric of the cosmos.* New York: Alfred A. Knopf.

Grotstein, J. S. (1990a). Nothingness, meaninglessness, chaos, and the "Black Hole" I: The importance of nothingness, meaninglessness, and chaos in psychoanalysis. *Contemporary Psychoanalysis, 26*(2), 257–290.

Grotstein, J. S. (1990b). Nothingness, meaninglessness, chaos, and the "Black Hole" II. *Contemporary Psychoanalysis, 26*(3), 377–407.

Hegel, G. W. (1948). *Early theological writings.* (T. M. Knox, Trans.). Chicago: University of Chicago Press.

Heidegger, M. (1996). *Being and time.* (J. Stambaugh, Trans.) Albany, NY: New York Press.

Heller, J. (1961). *Catch-22.* New York: Simon & Schuster.

Herman, J. L. (1992). *Trauma and recovery.* New York: Basic Books.

Houellebecq, M. (2000). *The elementary particles.* (F. Wynne, Trans.). New York: Knopf.

Houellebecq, M. (2002). *Platform.* (F. Wynne, Trans.). London: Heinemann.

Houellebecq, M. (2006). *The possibility of an island.* (G. Bowd, Trans.). New York: Alfred A. Knopf.

Houellebecq, M. (2012). *The map and the territory.* (G. Bowd, Trans.). New York: Alfred A. Knopf.

Husserl, E. (1970). *The crisis of European sciences and transcendental phenomenology.* (D. Carr, Trans.). Evanston IL: Northwestern University Press.

Husserl, E. (1989). *Ideas pertaining to a pure phenomenology and to a phenomenological philosophy—Second book: Studies in the phenomenology of constitution.* (R. Rojcewicz & A. Schuwer, Trans.). Dordrecht: Kluwer.

Irwin, W. (Ed.) (2002). *The Matrix and philosophy.* Chicago: Open Court.

James, W. (1902). *The Varieties of Religious Experience.* New York: Collier Books.

Janet, P. (1889). *L'automatisme psychologique.* Paris: Alcan.

Janet, P. (1925). *Psychological healing; A historical and clinical study.* (E. Paul & C. Paul, Trans.). New York: Macmillan.

Jaspers, K. (2001). *The question of German guilt.* (E. B. Ashton, Trans.). New York: Fordham University Press.

Jarrard, R. (Writer) (1967). Somebody to love. [Recorded by Jefferson Airplane]. *Surrealistic Pillow* [Record]. Studio: RCA Victor's Music Center, Hollywood, California.

Kafka, F. (1948). *The diaries of Franz Kafka, 1910–1923.* (M. Brod & J. Kresh Trans.). London: Secker and Warburg.

Kafka, F. (1949). *The diaries of Franz Kafka* (Vol. 1). (M. Brod & J. Kresh Trans.). New York: Schocken Books.

Kafka, F. (1952). Josephine the Singer, or the Mouse Folk. In W. Muir & E. Muir (Trans.), *Selected short stories of Franz Kafka.* New York: The Modern Library.

Kafka, F. (1953). *Letters to lena.* (T. Stern & J. Stern, Trans.) New York: Schocken Books.

Kafka, F. (1971a). *Letter to his father.* (E. Kaiser & E. Wilkins, Trans.) New York: Schocken Books.

Kafka, F. (1971b). The judgment. In W. Muir & E. Muir, (Trans.), *The complete stories by Franz Kafka* (pp. 101–113). New York: Schocken Books.

Kafka, F. (1974). *Letters to Felice.* (E. Heller, J. Born, J. Stern, & E. Duckworth Trans.). London: Secker & Warburg.

Kafka, F. (1976). *Diaries 1910–1913.* (J. Kresh, Trans.). New York: Schocken Books.

Kafka, F. (1996). A hunger artist. In D. Freed (Trans.), *The metamorphosis and other stories.* New York: Barnes & Noble.

Kafka, F. (1998). *The castle.* (M. Harman, Trans.). New York: Schocken Books.

Kafka, F. (2002). *The metamorphosis.* (D. Wyllie, Trans.). The Project Gutenberg. https://www.gutenberg.org/files/5200/5200-h/5200-h.htm

Kafka, F. (2006). *The trial.* (D. Wyllie, Trans.). Teddington: Echo Library.

Kafka, F. (2007). In the penal colony. In S. Corngold (Trans.), *Kafka's selected stories, Norton critical edition* (pp. 35–59). New York: Norton.

Kafka, F. (2009). *The castle.* (A. Bell, Trans.). Oxford: Oxford University Press.

Kania, A. (2010). *The Philosophy of Music.* (E. N. Zalta, Ed.) Retrieved from The Stanford Encyclopedia of Philosophy: http://plato.stanford.edu/archives/fall2010/entries/music/

Kierkegaard, S. (1985). *Fear and trembling.* (A. Hannay, Trans.). Harmondsworth, UK: Penguin.

Kindta, M., Van Den Hout, M., & Buck, N. (2005). Dissociation related to subjective memory fragmentation and intrusions but not to objective memory disturbances. *Journal of Behavior Therapy and Experimental Psychiatry, 36,* 43–59.

Kranzler, David (2000). *The Man Who Stopped the Trains to Auschwitz.* Syracuse, NY: Syracuse University Press.

Kopelson, A. (Producer), Stone, O. (Writer), & Stone, O. (Director). (1986). *Platoon* [Motion Picture].

Kubrick, S., Harlan, J. (Producers), & Kubrick, S. (Director). (1987). *Full Metal Jacket* [Motion Picture].

Lang, M. (1996). *Futuresound: Techno Music and Mediatio.* Retrieved June 10, 2009, from http://music.hyperreal.org/library/fewerchur.txt

LaCapra, D. (1994). *Representing the Holocaust: History, theory, trauma.* Ithaca, NY: Cornell University Press.

LaCapra, D. (1998, June 9). "Acting-out" and "Working-through" trauma. (A. Goldberg, Interviewer).

LaCapra, D. (2001). *Writing history, writing trauma.* Baltimore, MD: Johns Hopkins University Press.

Lakoff, G., & Johnson, M. (1999). *Philosophy in the flesh: The embodied mind and its challenge to Western thought.* New York: Basic Books.

Langer, S. (1953). *Feeling and form: A theory of art. Developed from philosophy in a new key.* New York: C. Scribner's Sons.

Laub, D. (1995). Truth and testimony: The process and the struggle. In C. Caruth (Ed.), *Trauma: Explorations in memory* (pp. 61–45). Baltimore, MD: Johns Hopkins University Press.

Levi, P. (1959). *If this is a man.* (S. Woolf, IL Trans.). New York: The Orion Press.

Levi, P. (1993). *The drowned and the saved.* (R. Rosenthal, Trans.). London: Abacus.

Levinas, E. (2006). *Humanism of the other.* (N. Poller, Trans.). Urbana; Chicago: University of Illinois Press.

Leys, R. (2000). *Trauma: A genealogy.* Chicago and London: University of Chicago Press.

Lifton, R. (1967). *Death in life: Survivors of Hiroshima.* New York: Random House.

Linson, A., Chaffin, C., Bell, R. G. (Producers), & Fincher, D. (Director). (1999). *Fight club* [Motion Picture]).

Luckhurst, R. (2008). *The trauma question.* London: Routledge.

Mahler-Bungers, A. (2003). A post-postmodern walkyrie: Psychoanalytic considerations on Tom Tykwer's *Run, Lola, Run* (1998). In A. Sabbadini (Ed.), *The couch and the silver screen: Psychoanalytic reflections on European cinema* (Vol. 44, pp. 82–92). London: Routledge, Psychology Press.

Mann, T. (1980). *Death in Venice.* (H. T. Lowe-Porter, Trans.). Harmondsworth: Penguin Books.

Mann, T. (1929). *The magic mountain.* (H. T. Lowe-Porter, Trans.). London: Secker.

Marcuse, H. (1964). *One-dimensional man.* Boston, MA: Beacon Press.

McNally, R. J. (2003). *Remembering trauma.* Cambridge, MA: Belknap Press of Harvard University Press.

Menuhin, Y. (1972). *Theme and variations.* New York: Stein and Day.

Merleau-Ponty, M. (1965). *The structure of behaviour.* (A. Fisher, Trans.). London: Methuen.

Merleau-Ponty, M. (2002). *Phenomenology of perception.* (C. Smith, Trans.). London: Routledge and Kegan Paul.

Mesch, C. (2000). *Racing Berlin: The games of Run Lola Run.* Retrieved May 11, 2014, from M/C: *A Journal of Media and Culture*: http://www.api-network. com/mc/0006/speed.php

Morag, R. (2009). *Defeated masculinity: Post-traumatic cinema in the aftermath of war.* New York: P.I.E. Peter Lang.

Murray, N. (2004). *Kafka: A biography.* New York: Little, Brown; New Haven, CT: Yale University Press.

Myers, C. (1940). *Shell shock in France 1914–18.* Cambridge: Cambridge University Press.

Nietzsche, F. (1956). *The birth of tragedy from the spirit of music.* (F. Golffing, Trans.). Garden City, NY: Doubleday.

Nietzsche, F. (1964). *The dawn of day.* (J. M. Kennedy, Trans.). New York: Russell & Russell.

Nietzsche, F. (1994). *On the genealogy of morality.* (C. Diethe, Trans.). Cambridge: Cambridge University Press.

Nietzsche, F. (1999). *Thus Spoke Zarathustra.* (T. Common, Trans.). Mineola, NY: Dover Thrift Editions.

Nietzsche, F. (2001). *The gay science.* (J. Nauckhoff, Trans.). Cambridge, UK; New York: Cambridge University Press.

Nietzsche, F. (2002). *Beyond good and evil: Prelude to a philosophy of the future.* (J. Norman, Trans.). Cambridge: Cambridge University Press.

Nietzsche, F. (2005). *Nietzsche: The Anti-Christ, Ecce homo, twilight of the idols.* (J. Norman, Trans.). Cambridge: Cambridge University Press.

Nijenhuis, E., Van Der Hart, O., & Steele, K. (2010). Trauma-related structural dissociation of the personality. *Activitas Nervosa Superior, 52*(1), 1–23.

Noë, A. (2004). *Action in perception.* Cambridge, MA: The MIT Press.

O'Sickey, I. (2002). Whatever Lola wants, Lola gets (or does she?): Time and desire in Tom Tykwer's *Run Lola Run. Quarterly Review of Film & Video, 19*(2), 123–131.

Ozer, E. J., Best, S. R., Lipsey, T. L., & Weiss, D. S. (2003). Predictors of posttraumatic stress disorder and symptoms in adults: A meta-analysis. *Psychological Trauma: Theory, Research, Practice, and Policy, 129*(1), 52–73.

Pawel, E. (1984). *The nightmare of reason: A life of Franz Kafka.* New York: Farrar, Straus, Giroux.

Perec, G. (2003). *W, or, the memory of childhood.* (D. Bellos, Trans.). Boston, MA: David R. Godine.

Perlman, M. (1988). *Imaginal memory and the place of Hiroshima.* Albany, NY: State University of New York Press.

Pitman, R. K., & Orr, S. P. (1990). The black hole of trauma. *Biological Psychiatry, 27*(5), 469–471.

Plato (1977). *Timaeus and Critias.* (L. Desmond, Trans). London: Penguin.

Plato (2000). *The republic.* (T. Griffith, Trans). Cambridge, UK: Cambridge University Press.

Quintilianus, M. F. (1953). *Institutes of oratory.* Cambridge, MA: Harvard University Press.

Rothschild, B. (2000). *The body remembers.* New York: Norton.

Sartre, J.-P. (1956). *Being and nothingness.* (H. Barnes, Trans.). New York: Philosophical Library.

Schopenhauer, A. (1966a). *The world as will and representation.* (Vol. 1). (E. F. Payne, Trans.). New York: Dover Publications.

Schopenhauer, A. (1966b). *The world as will and representation* (Vol. 2). (E. F. Payne, Trans.). New York: Dover Publications.

Schrader, P. (Writer), & M. Scorsese (Director). (1976). *Taxi driver* [Motion Picture].

Seltzer, M. (1997). Wound culture: Trauma in the pathological public sphere. *October, 80,* 3–26.

Semprun, J. (1998). *Literature or life.* (L. Coverdale, Trans.). New York: Penguin Books.

Simeon, D., & Abugel, J. (2006). *Feeling unreal: Depersonalization disorder and the loss of the self.* Oxford, USA: Oxford University Press.

Solzhenitsyn, A. (1968). *The first circle.* (T. P. Whitney, Trans.). New York: Harper & Row.

Spiegel, D. (1997). Trauma, dissociation, and memory. *Psychobiology of Posttraumatic Stress Disorder, 821,* 225–237.

Storr, A. (1993). *Music and the mind.* New York: Ballantine.

Sutherland, K., & Bryant, R. A. (2008). Autobiographical memory and the self-memory system in posttraumatic stress disorder. *Journal of Anxiety Disorders, 22,* 555–560.

Szeintuch, Y. (2003). *Katzetnik 135633: A series of dialogues with Yechiel De-Nur [Hebrew].* Jerusalem: Ghetto Fighters House & Dov Sadan Institute.

Szeintuch, Y. (2009). *Salamandra: Myth and history in the writings of Katzetnik [Hebrew].* Jerusalem: Dov Sadan Project, Hebrew University & Carmel Publishing House.

Tal, K. (1996). *Worlds of hurt.* Cambridge: Cambridge University Press.

Taylor, T. (2001). *Strange sounds: Music, technology and culture.* New York: Routledge.

Terr, L. (1984). Time and trauma. *Psychoanalytic Study of the Child, 39,* 633–665.

Thacker, A. (2003). *Moving through modernity: Space and geography in modernism.* Oxford: Manchester University Press.

Thompson, E. (2007). *Mind in life.* Cambridge and London: Harvard University Press.

Thornton, S. (1996). *Club cultures: Music, media, and subcultural capital.* Hanover: University Press of New England.

Treat, J. W. (1995). *Writing ground zero: Japanese literature and the atomic bomb.* Chicago: University of Chicago Press.

Trumbo, D. (1997). *Johnny got his gone.* New York: Citadel Press: Kensington Publishing Corp.

Van Der Hart, O., Nijenhuis, E., Steele, K., & Brown, D. (2004). Trauma-related dissociation: Conceptual clarity lost and found. *Australian and New Zealand Journal of Psychiatry, 38,* 906–914.

Van Der Hart, O., Van Dijke, A., Van Son, M., & Steele, K. (2000). Somatoform dissociation in traumatized World War I combat soldiers: A neglected clinical heritage. *Journal of Trauma and Dissociation, 1*(4), 33–66.

Van Der Kolk, B. A. (1987). *Psychological trauma.* Washington: Amrican Psychiatric Press.

Van Der Kolk, B. A. (1994). The body keeps the score: Memory and the evolving psychobiology of posttraumatic stress. *Harvard Review of Psychiatry, 1*(5), 253–265.

Van Der Kolk, B. A., & Fisler, R. (1995). *Dissociation and the fragmentary nature of traumatic memories: Overview and exploratory study.* Retrieved January 11, 2011, from David Baldwin's Trauma Pages: http://www.trauma-pages.com/a/vanderk2.php.

Van Der Kolk, B. A., & McFarlane, A. C. (Eds.). (1996). *Traumatic stress: The effects of overwhelming experience on mind, body, and society.* New York: Guilford Press.

Van Der Kolk, B. A., & Van Der Hart, O. (1989). Pierre Janet and the breakdown of adaptation in psychological trauma. *American Journal of Psychiatry, 146* (12), 1530–1540.

Van Der Kolk, B. A., Pelcovitz, D., Roth, S., & Mandel, F. S. (1996). Dissociation, somatization, and affect dysregulation: The complexity of adaption to trauma. *The American Journal of Psychiatry, 53*(Suppl), 83–93.

Van Der Kolk, B. A., Perry, C. J., & Herman, J. L. (1991). Childhood origins of self-destructive behavior. *American Journal of Psychiatry, 148*(12), 1665–1671.

Varela, F., Thompson, E., & Rosch, E. (1991). *The embodied mind: Cognitive science and human experience.* Cambridge, MA: MIT Press.

Wachowski, A., Wachowski, L. (Writers), Wachowski, A., & Wachowski, L. (Directors). (1999). *The matrix* [Motion Picture].

War Office Committee. (1922). *Report of the War Office Committee of Enquiry into "Shell-shock".* London: His Majesty's Stationary Office.

Whalen, T. (2000). Run Lola Run. *Film Quarterly, 53*(3), 33–40.

Wiesel, E. (1979). Why I write. In A. H. Rosenfeld, I. Greenber, & B. Gree (Eds.), *Confronting the Holocaust* (pp. 202–203). Bloomington, IN: Indiana University Press.

Wiesel, E. (2005). *One generation after.* New York: Schocken.

Wilson, B. (no date). *What's it about?* Retrieved June 10, 2010, from Barrie Wilson: http://www.barriewilson.com/pdf/Run-Lola-Run-Reflections-Barrie-Wilson.pdf.

Wilson, J. P. (2006). The posttraumatic self. In J. P. Wilson (Ed.), *The posttraumatic self* (pp. 9–68). New York: Routledge.

Yovell, Y., Bannett, Y., & Shalev, A. (2003). Amnesia for traumatic events among recent survivors: A pilot study. *CNS Spectrums, 9*, 676–680.

Zahavi, D. (2006). *Subjectivity and selfhood.* Cambridge, MA: The MIT Press.

Žižek, S. (1991). *Looking awry: An introduction to Jacques Lacan through popular culture.* Cambridge, MA: MIT Press.

Žižek, S. (2002). *Welcome to the desert of the real!.* London; New York: Verso.

Žižek, S. (2006). *Interrogating the real.* (R. Butler & S. Stephens, Eds.). London; New York: Continuum.

INDEX

© The Author(s) 2017
Y. Ataria, *The Structural Trauma of Western Culture*,
DOI 10.1007/978-3-319-53228-8

Printed by Printforce, the Netherlands